Warriors, Merchants, and Slaves

Warriors, Merchants, and Slaves

The State and the Economy in the Middle Niger Valley, 1700-1914

RICHARD L. ROBERTS

Stanford University Press, Stanford, California
1987

Stanford University Press
Stanford, California

Printed in the United States of America

CIP data appear at the end of the book

Preface

THE RELATIONSHIPS between warriors, merchants, and slaves took many forms in precolonial Africa, but almost always those relationships were central to the regional political economy and the structure and performance of the economy. This is a study of warriors, merchants, and slaves in three successive states in the Middle Niger valley of what is now the Republic of Mali: the Segu Bambara state, the Umarian state, and the French colonial state. Although this study does not claim to exhaust the range of possible variations in the relationships between the groups as they vied for power, accumulation, and autonomy, it does seek to identify the significant trends and explain how the changing relationships affected the structure of the successive states and the performance of the economy over a span of two hundred years.

The initial research for this study was conducted for a dissertation presented to the University of Toronto in 1978. My original study, although critical of conventions in the field of West African economic history, was nonetheless shaped by them: it was primarily a cross-sectional study of the economy of the Middle Niger valley, focussing on a community of long-distance traders. My uneasiness about presenting the economy as a more or less autonomous sphere of the past was reflected in a long, but separate, historical introduction to that study. Since then, my thinking on the nature of West African precolonial economic history has made me increasingly aware of the need to view the structure and performance of the economy as an integral part of the political economy that shaped it and was also shaped by it. During subsequent research in Mali in 1981 and 1984, and in France in

1984, I gathered additional data and recast my study to demonstrate this relationship in the history of the Middle Niger valley.

I wish to acknowledge support from the Canada Council for research in Mali, Senegal, and France in 1976–77, from the Social Science Research Council for research in Mali during the summer of 1981, and from the National Endowment for the Humanities and from the Pew Foundation for research in Mali and France in 1983–84. The Killam Foundation of Dalhousie University provided a postdoctoral fellowship early in the process of rethinking the data I had originally collected. Further assistance from the Hewlett Fund and from the Center for Research in International Studies at Stanford University contributed to data collection and to the publication of this manuscript.

Anyone who has undertaken historical research realizes the immense collaborative effort it entails. Our ability to reconstruct the past is dependent upon the men and women who lived it and those who recorded it. This dependence is perhaps nowhere more obvious than in Africa, where historians must rely, often by necessity but also by avocation, on the traditions and histories retained by living men and women. I was and continue to be deeply appreciative of my informants' willingness to share their past with me. I also thank my two research assistants, Mulaye Ismaila Dembele, who accompanied me in my research throughout the Beledugu region in 1981, and especially Aliou Kone of Segu. I have worked with Aliou Kone during each of my three research trips to Mali, and each time I have been increasingly grateful for his understanding of Bambara society and history and for his assistance in the pursuit of history.

Throughout my research in Mali, I was graciously received by Alpha Konare and Kleena Sanogo, the directors of the Institut des Sciences Humaines, Bamako, who expedited and facilitated my research. The archivists at the National Archives of Mali, Senegal, and France have responded with good cheer to my nearly insatiable requests for files.

Where my own ideas begin and where they derive from views held by others is no longer clearly discernible. Scholarship is not only dependent upon the goodwill of collectors and custodians past and present, but it is also the product of sustained intellectual exchange. I would like to thank Fred Cooper, Soumaila Diakite, Jim Lance, Paul Lovejoy, Pat Manning, David Robinson, and Tom Reefe for reading all or parts of this manuscript. I would also like to thank Jean-Loup Amselle, Jean Bazin, David Cohen, Philip Curtin, Kennell Jackson, Ann McDougall, Claude Meillassoux, Marie Perinbam, and Yves Person for responding to parts of my argument as it appeared in various forms. My greatest intellectual debt has been and continues to be to Martin Klein, who has participated in this study from its inception as a graduate student research project to its present form.

I would also like to thank Norris Pope and John Feneron of Stanford University Press for their encouragement and advice. And, although I have said it many times to them personally, I appreciate Amy, Sam, and Sophie's patience during the long months of neglect. While researching and writing, I often felt like a bigamist, having two competing families, each with its own obligations and rewards.

R.L.R.

Contents

Maps

A Note on Orthography

Despite efforts to normalize and to phoneticize Bambara and Malinke, there has been little agreement about the systematization of Malinke languages. Since most Malian languages were until recently oral, the spelling has usually been filtered through French. For historians, this poses particular problems in the spelling of surnames and place names. In this study I have been concerned with consistency. The voiced palatal affricates expressed by the French *dj*, *dy*, or *di* are presented as the English *j*, as in the Bambara term for trader, *juula*. I have made several exceptions to this practice, especially in dealing with place names, when I have thought that changing the spelling would confuse the reader. Thus, the *di* is retained in *Bandiagara*. The long *u* sound presented in French as *ou* (as in *Segou*) is presented here as *u* (thus, *Segu*). I have only retained the *ou* spelling when it appears as the first vowel sound of a place name, as in the French *Bougouni*, which appears as *Bouguni* in this study. I have done so to ensure recognition. An exception is my translation of *Soudan*, which refers to the interior of French West Africa generally and to the colony so designated in 1920, as "Western Sudan" in order to clearly differentiate it from the Democratic Republic of Sudan (formerly the Anglo-Egyptian Condominium) in northeastern Africa. I have distinguished Bambara plurals with the suffix *w* unless the singular form of the word in question adequately conveys both singular and plural (e.g., *juula*, *sofa*). And finally, I have not used the French acute accents on Malian surnames or place names, nor have I used the Arabic ʿain (ʿ), as it would appear in ʿUmar.

I have translated all the French quotations used in this study, and with Aliou Kone and Soumaila Diakite I have translated the Bambara. In doing so, I have standardized personal and place names even if this meant changing a peculiar orthography in the original. For readers unaccustomed to histories involving multiple ethnicities and unfamiliar places, African history is sufficiently complex unencumbered by variant orthographies.

Warriors, Merchants, and Slaves

ONE

Introduction

DURING his visit to the Western Sudan in 1848, the French explorer Anne Raffenel observed that the incessant wars between the neighboring states of Masina and Segu did not disrupt trade. "I have noted this circumstance, which forms the inverse to our commercial principle: the flag follows the merchandise. In effect, it is the merchandise that follows the flag along the [Niger River] and serves as safe conduct for the inhabitants to continue their reciprocal [commercial] relations during the war."[1] Nineteen years earlier, René Caillié, another Frenchman, traveled through the eastern parts of the same region and came to a different conclusion:

> Cheiku Amadu, chief of the land of Jenne, constantly carries on an active war with the Bambara of Segu, whom he wants to convert. But these Bambara are belligerent and resist. This war has severely damaged Jenne's commerce, because it prevents all trade and contact with Nyamina, Sinsani, Bamako, and Buré, where the gold is procured. Today, the city of Jenne cannot be considered the central point of commerce; it is Nyamina, Sinsani, and Bamako that are the real entrepôts: the Moors from all over the desert and the blacks from the Western Sudan all the way to Kong, Galam, Bendu, and the Futa Jallon go there to trade. . . . The merchants and wholesalers of Jenne have suffered from that war, but they are afraid to complain openly.[2]

Neither Raffenel's nor Caillié's observations were wrong; nor were they fully correct. For Caillié, the relationship of war to commerce was clearly functional. War interrupted commerce, but Caillié also noted that commerce shifted to areas that offered conditions more attractive to merchants. Raffenel was struck by the protected sphere of commerce even during active warfare, and indeed, many precolonial states protected traders. Asante attracted merchants to its entrepôts with gifts and favorable terms of trade. Segu Bambara adjudicated conflicts in favor of merchants and against the interests of local chiefs. Samori compensated merchants for the value of horses that had died en route to his markets. Raffenel and Caillié had, in fact, seen only parts of what was a very complex relationship. The interaction between warfare and the economy was not reducible to a simple causality.

This study examines the resilience and fragility of the economy and social relations of production in the Middle Niger valley over the course of two centuries, from about 1712 to 1914. During this period, the region was dominated by three successive states: the pagan Segu Bambara state, the Islamic Umarian state, and the French colonial state. In each of these states, warriors were the rulers and not surprisingly warfare was the primary expression of state power. The survival of each state depended on its ability to reproduce its capacity to make war. In order to do so, the warrior state intervened in the economy. In each of these states, the interrelationship of warfare, the state, and the economy produced different results. How the state actually intervened in the economy and how this intervention influenced the structure and performance of the economy is central to the argument presented here.

When I began to study the economy of the Middle Niger valley, I was troubled by the way the market perspective, widely used by economic historians, indelibly imprinted an apparent stasis on the precolonial economy. Although the trade-and-market approach could identify the contours of the economy, it was less able to account for changes. Certainly long-term global changes could be explained by exogenous variables such as international trade, and local changes could be understood as responses to periodic climatic disasters. But because it focused primarily on the circulation of goods, the market approach proved unable to account for periods of marked economic growth or decline within regions and for changing social relations of production.

My research on the Middle Niger valley had to confront the thirty-year period of economic decline that coincided with the Umarian conquest and subsequent rule. It also coincided with the gradual disappearance of the transatlantic slave trade and the expansion of French colonial conquests. During the same period, however, other regions in Africa witnessed dramatic increases in slavery, an expansion of commerce, and the emergence and consolidation of states. External variables were undoubtedly important, but they alone cannot explain the history of the Umarian period. Climatic conditions were actually quite favorable for the most part. Moreover, once the French conquered the Umarian state, the region again experienced considerable expansion in trade and production. Obviously, something about the Umarian period contributed to the performance of the economy.

My inability to explain economic performance from a market standpoint demanded that I integrate the economy as a facet of political economy. The Umarians were seemingly never able to establish the safeguards on trade and production that had existed under the Bambara. This failure suggested that the state had an active role in economic history. Moreover, the fact that the Segu Bambara, Umarian, and French colonial states were dominated by warriors provided me with an obvious comparison and a means of examining the patterns and conditions under which the state intervened in the economy.

I shall argue that the state played an important role in determining the structure and performance of the economy, and that the state's particular role must be understood as a process of social reproduction of the power and social structure of the ruling group. I do not, however, wish to portray the economy merely as an amorphous terrain in which the state materializes its presence. The regional economy of the Middle Niger valley had distinct characteristics that had nothing to do with political factors. Even the most powerful states had little success directing production and controlling social change. Some patterns of trade and production proved resilient, despite fundamental changes in the conditions in which the economy operated and in the forms of labor.

The Setting

The Middle Niger valley of what is now the Republic of Mali is close to the geographical center of continental West Africa. The region is characterized by the classic Sudan savanna of dry un-

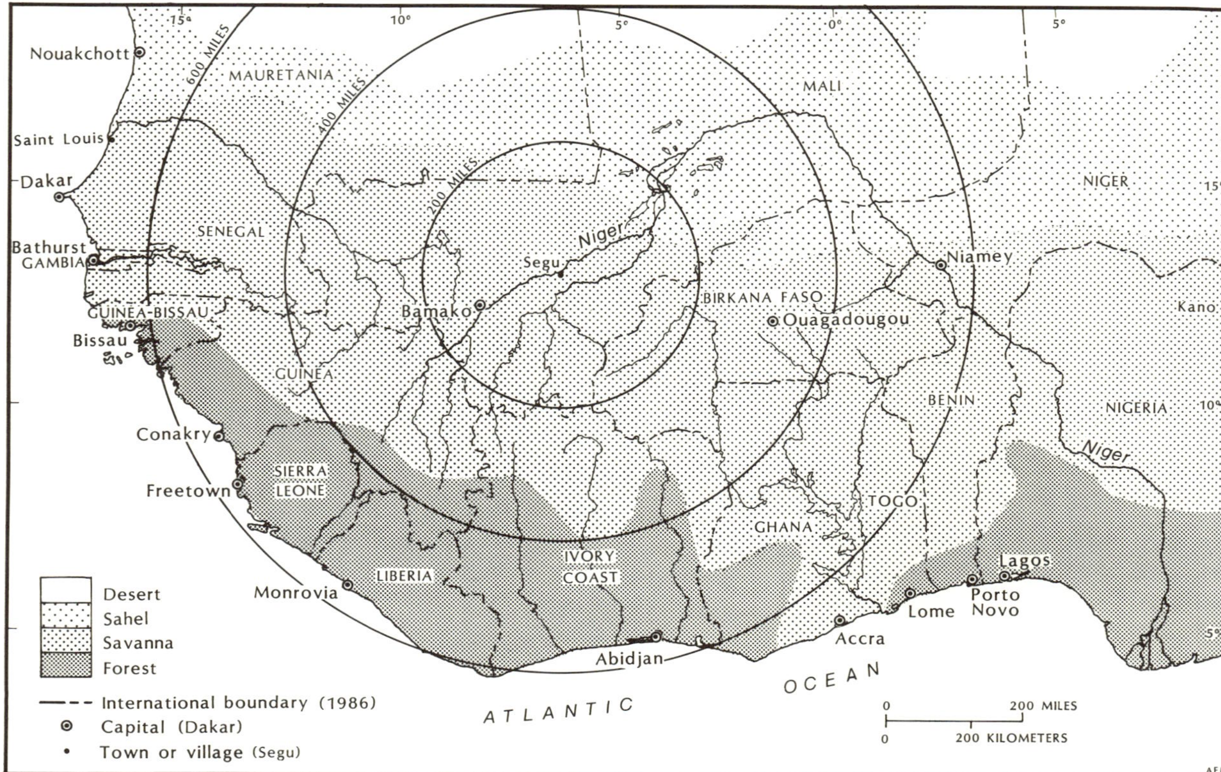

Map 1. The Major Ecological Zones of West Africa

dulating plains. The more wooded Guinean savanna prevails at the southern and southeastern extremes of the region. Both savanna regions are characterized by distinct and alternating wet and dry seasons. Annual rainfall, between May and November, ranges from 500 to 1,000 mm a year, and decreases as one moves north. The wettest months are June to September. The soils on the right bank of the Niger tend to be heavy, hydromorphic clays that require considerable labor, but they return dividends to those who manage to understand their limitations and seasonal imperatives. On the left bank, the soils tend toward eroded ferruginous types. There are notable exceptions, especially in the Beledugu escarpment, where the soils are richer and the land better suited to raising livestock.

Within these savanna plains, the dominant ecological feature is the Niger River. In the Middle Niger valley, the river annually swells from a shallow stream in the river basin during April and May to a flood nearly two kilometers wide at high water in October. Fish abound in its waters, and for much of its span the Niger facilitates long-distance trade. In its upper reaches above Siguiri, the Niger passes through mountainous terrain, where it is relatively narrow and swift. When the Milo River joins the Niger below Siguiri, the river becomes navigable for small shallow-draft canoes. Downstream from Bamako (see Map 2), as the Niger spills over the Sotuba rapids, it enters the Middle Niger valley and becomes wide, graceful, and slow moving. Here the river can support larger craft. As the river moves northward from Mopti, it meets the Bani and enters the massive interior delta, where it forms an ecological mosaic.[3] Only after the river departs from the lakes region of the interior delta does it resume its graceful unitary character before it arrives at Timbuktu. At this point, the Niger traces a deep arc into the desert before it begins its long southward flow to the ocean.

Most of the inhabitants of the Middle Niger valley are Bambara, and Bambara is the main language of the region. Bambara is part of the Mande or Malinke language family, which is spoken from the headwaters of the Gambia River in the west to the Volta River in the east. Together with the Malinke spoken on the Upper Niger, Bambara forms the core of the Mande language family.[4] Soninke, the original language of the Maraka, is a northern vari-

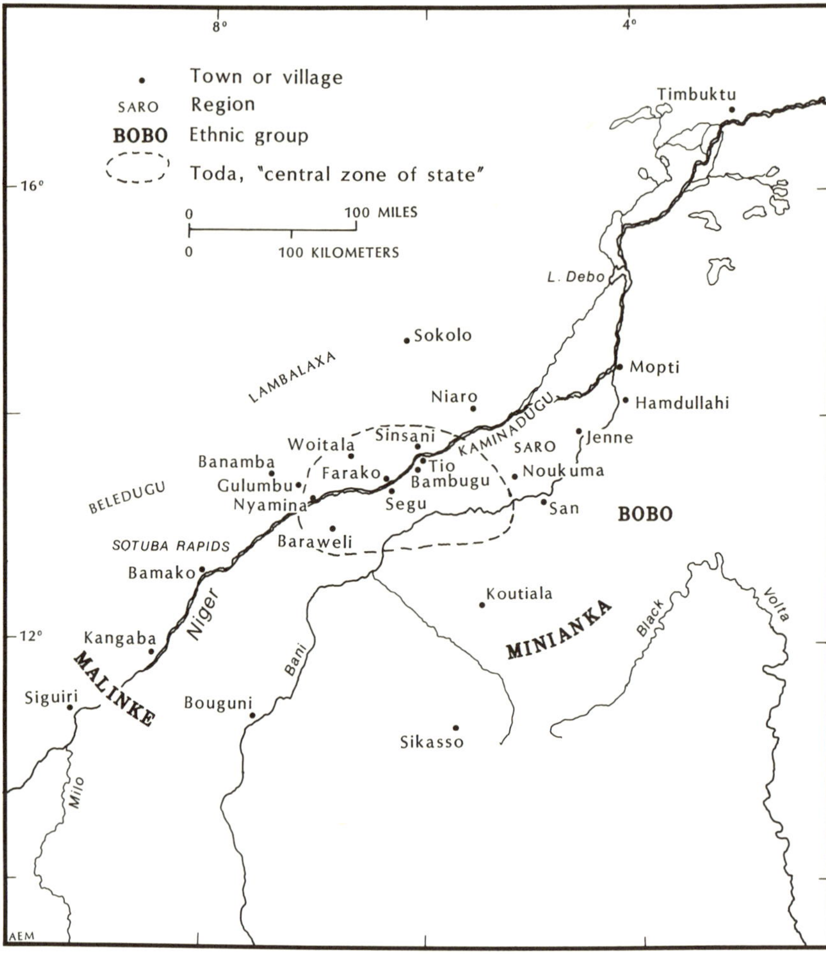

Map 2. The Middle Niger Valley, 1712–1861

ant of Malinke. Pular, the language of the FulBe, is not related to Mandekan, and the FulBe presence is the result of that people's thousand-year migration across the semi-arid western sahel. Although the Maraka retain a sense of their Soninke origins, they speak Bambara.

Ethnicity in the region was defined by ecology, production techniques, religion, and historical traditions, especially those glorifying and sustaining distinctiveness. For instance, the FulBe, Moors, and Tuareg are all herders, but their pastoral techniques, their ecological niches, and their view of their place in history differ. Both the Bozo and the Somono fish, but they fish differently. Ethnic boundaries were fluid, however, and it was not uncommon for FulBe to become Bozo, Bozo to become Somono, and Bobo animist farmers to become Maraka Muslim traders. Although the variations may be limitless, historical circumstances favored certain changes. During the rise of the Segu Bambara warrior state in the eighteenth century, Bambara identity was ascendant. In the process of reproducing the state, members of many different ethnic communities were forged into the Bambara warrior group. Thus the production and reproduction of the social formation often determined the direction of ethnic change.[5]

The central actors in this study are the Bambara, the Maraka, the Umarians, and the French. Bambara traditions often speak of mythical origins and migrations, and many are contradictory. In the absence of refined historical linguistic studies, the most we can say is that Bambara and Malinke are mutually intelligible, that they share common sociocultural attributes, and that the Bambara migration to the Middle Niger valley was fairly recent. In the eighteenth century, most Bambara were polytheists who recognized a common core of clan and territorial cults and spirits. They were farmers and they tended to live in close-knit corporate villages that relied primarily on a rainfed millet and sorghum agriculture.[6]

The Maraka, in contrast, were urban, cosmopolitan Muslims. The Maraka did not, however, form a unified ethnic or linguistic group. Some consider themselves *Maraka je* (white Maraka) and claim origin from the Soninke. Some white Maraka claim to be descended from original migrants from the kingdom of Wagadu (ancient Ghana); others were nineteenth-century migrants from the Upper Senegal. Still others are considered to be *Maraka fin* (black Maraka) or *Maraka jalon* (the term means dyed or colored Maraka and has come to refer to recently converted Muslims).

Most of the Maraka who settled in the Maraka towns in the Middle Niger valley and in the cluster of Maraka towns in Beledugu claim to be white Maraka.[7]

The history of the Bambara and the Maraka in the Middle Niger valley before the eighteenth century remains vague. The Malian empire maintained a presence there, although the decline of Mali and the rise of Songhay in the fifteenth century made the Middle Niger a contested buffer between the two empires. The decline of Songhay in the late sixteenth century, the expansion of the transatlantic slave trade, and the growth of militant Islamic revivalism unleashed tremendous political, economic, and intellectual ferment throughout the West African interior. In about 1712, during this period of increased commercial and political activity surrounding competition for control over economic resources, political power, and labor, the Segu Bambara state emerged.[8]

The third group of actors is the Umarians. The classification is historical rather than ethnic, although the core members of al hajj Umar's movement were Futanke from the Futa Toro belt of the Middle Senegal River and from the Futanke migrants to the Upper Senegal region. Historically, the Umarians were the followers of Umar in the jihad and the conquest of the Middle Niger valley in 1859–61. The Umarians had little long-term influence on the ethnic character of the region. They perceived themselves as conquerers and many thought of returning home after realizing the fruits of their conquest.

Nonetheless, the Umarian experience was important in the Islamization of the region, for the period of Umarian conquest reinforced the marked anti-Muslim character of Bambara identity and served as a means of rallying and sustaining resistance. Following the collapse of the Umarian state between 1890 and 1893, the virulent anti-Islamic component to Bambara identity gradually disappeared and the boundaries between the Bambara and the Maraka blurred.

The final group of actors, the French, were first represented by the military officers in the vanguard of colonial conquest who arrived in Bamako in 1883. In contrast to the Umarians, the French made a lasting impact on the economy and society of the

Middle Niger valley, but not always as they might have anticipated. For the first 25 years of their rule, they assimilated and supported many precolonial institutions. These officers were aware of their limited power and the need to form alliances with indigenous elites, ruling classes, and local military auxiliaries. The crisis for the colonial state came in 1905, when the slaves of the Maraka plantations around Banamba began a massive and spontaneous exodus that spread throughout the Western Sudan over the next six years. The events of 1905 marked the end of an era in the history of the Middle Niger valley.

The State

During the 200 years under study, the regional economy of the Middle Niger valley expanded and contracted in response to the state's capacity to provide conditions favorable to commercial development, capital accumulation, and investment. But the economy was not merely an extension of the state. The deep structures of the regional economy were generated by particular and complementary ecological endowments shared by broad horizontal zones that traversed West Africa. The degree to which local producers were willing and able to harness their resources to the larger intercommunicating economy of continental West Africa depended on whether the state contributed to the expanded capacity to produce commodities for exchange. Within the Middle Niger valley the state must be seen as a participant in the complex relationships that determined the course of historical and social change.

With few exceptions, African precolonial states were not very powerful. Their ability to transform societies and social reality were limited. Analogies to European state forms are not very helpful. African states commanded neither people nor territory on the same scale as their European counterparts. They lacked the ability to sustain state-sponsored projects that was characteristic of the hydraulic societies in Asia and pre-Columbian America. There appears to be a direct correlation between meager development of the forces of production and weak state power.[9] Warfare, which often involved important investment in what Jack Goody called the "means of destruction" and in support services, was the significant exception to this generalization. Warfare, however, had very contradictory effects on the economy and society in the Middle Niger valley.

Warrior states of precolonial West Africa developed a peculiar spatial character. There was often a core comprising the social and economic heartland. The heartland was composed of either a homogeneous population, as in Asante and Kenedugu (Sikasso), or a fairly stable articulation of different ethnic groups, as in Segu and the Sokoto Caliphate. The central core was encircled by a tributary zone with fluctuating boundaries. This zone of incomplete submission required periodic reconquest, reinforcing the military expression of state power.[10]

Despite their small size and the restricted development of effective state institutions, these were states. They had more or less clearly defined boundaries, more or less paramount control within those boundaries, and greater or lesser legitimacy in imposing their decisions on the population residing there. Most states had some form of superimposed judicial authority that reserved the power of life or death to the ruler, and most had the foundations of fiscal administration. Most states developed a coercive capacity that took the forms of legitimated violence, waging war, and preparing defense.[11]

These institutions, however, were the manifestation of a much more complex phenomenon: the state was never merely the sum of its parts. In John Lonsdale's words, "the state, if not to be a redundant synonym for government, implies something wider, more inclusive, more confusing."[12] The state's ability to influence societies, even if it cannot control them, is much wider than the effective reach of its actual institutions. As so conceived, the state is also much more difficult to identify and to study. This was especially true of African states.

Because of the complexity of the social formation of which they were a part, precolonial African states were necessarily more ambiguous in their relationship to the development of forces of production than advanced capitalist states. More often than not, the social formation consisted of several overlapping modes of production, each with a set of real or potential class conflicts. Sometimes the state form preceded the relations of production to which it most closely corresponded. When this occurred, the state acted as a means for transforming social reality.[13] The French colonial state played such a role. It preceded the emergence of capitalist relations of production in the Western Sudan, but helped bring about their development. If the state was capable of encouraging the development of new forms of production, it was also capable of eroding those already in existence. Such was the case of the Umarian state in the Middle Niger valley.

The state, therefore, should be considered a factor in the constitution and reproduction of the relations of production.[14] The state became so deeply entangled in the processes of production that it was no longer possible to reproduce them without the intervention of the state. The emergence of the state gave coherence to the social formation in the Middle Niger valley, home to groups as diverse as simple cultivators, professional fishermen, specialized herdsmen, and slaveowners. The state provided the conditions for the reproduction of each group not as an individual community but as a set of interpenetrated units. This interpenetration of communities and their forms of reproduction was especially important in the precolonial Middle Niger valley, where the social character of production resulted from restricted access to economic resources and where specialized occupations constituted part of ethnic boundaries.

The state was not always able to provide these conditions. Because African states were essentially fragile, they constantly faced the crisis of their own dissolution through their failures to reestablish the conditions for the reproduction of social relations of production. These failures provide historians with moments of visible historical crisis and the elements to reconstruct the past.[15]

Such failures also suggest that the reproduction of society, of the form and content of relations of production, was not automatic and could not be taken for granted. For societies to persist, the biological reproduction of the members of the community and the reproduction of the social relations of production must be a continuously renewed activity. In this study I use the concept of social reproduction as a political act that reveals the set of alliances between and among members of a community or social formation. This point is crucial to Marx's analysis: "Whatever the form of the process of production in a society, it must be a continuous process, must continue to go periodically through the same phases. A society can no more cease to produce than it can cease to consume. When viewed, therefore, as a connected whole, and as flowing on with incessant renewal, every social process of production is, at the same time, a process of reproduction."[16] The precolonial state in the Middle Niger valley struggled constantly to reproduce its capacity to exert its dominance within a given historical situation. When it succeeded, it contributed to the expanded scale of both social reproduction and commercial activity. When it failed, the integrity of social formation weakened, the locus of social reproduction returned to the individual communities, and regional trade and occupational specialization declined.

Crisis in state power could also result from events external to the state, such as the long drought during the mid eighteenth century, which led to the disintegration of the first Segu Bambara state. The Umarian conquest led to the collapse of the second Segu Bambara state. External events were especially decisive when state power was weakly structured. In both the Segu Bambara and the Umarian state, the rulers' claim to obedience from their warriors was not assured. Their ability to rule required constant attention. The state, however, was a principal accumulator in the Middle Niger valley, and those who controlled the state were in a position to benefit directly from the operation of state activities. As long as the state was able to organize large military campaigns, participation in the state provided warriors with material and social rewards. The fluctuating relationship between rulers and warriors was central to the internal dynamic of warrior states at Segu.

The consequences of the state's presence within the social formation were uneven. Some forms of production were more dependent on the state's presence than others. The form that warfare took depended directly on the degree of state involvement. The Maraka system of slavery, which was harsh by African standards, also depended on the state. The state both supplied new recruits to the Maraka plantations and supported the power of the master over his slaves. The Somono, who trace their origin to a direct relationship to the state, were a group of fishermen in the Middle Niger valley. They controlled a privileged niche in the regional economy in exchange for supplying goods and services that helped the state organize and wage war. The Somono fared differently under the Umarians and under the French. Together, the Maraka and the Somono exemplify the process of articulation between the state and the economy in the Middle Niger valley.

The state, therefore, should be understood as a "field of force," which shaped both deep structures of the society and economy (including patterns of production and trade) and social relations (including ways of organizing work, relations of production and reproduction, and patterns of consumption). The state became a means, certainly not the only one, for intensifying relationships between members of the same and different ethnic groups. Although this is the most difficult part of the state's influences to trace during the precolonial period, it seems clear that relations within the household between men and women and between elders and cadets shifted in response to the intervention of the state and the prevailing conditions within the social formation.[17] Despite its relative weakness, the precolonial state was a component of the reproduction of social relations of production. It thus contributed to the calculus of economic decision making on the part of producers and traders alike.

The Economy

The interrelationship between the state, warfare, and the economy provides a historically sensitive means for understanding the forces that shaped the precapitalist economy of the Middle Niger valley. Only by including the state as an actor in the structure and performance of the economy can we begin to explain short-term fluctuations in market conditions, long-term economic growth and decline, and changing social relations. The warrior state was obviously better able to cause decline than to stimulate growth, but the state did influence market conditions and producer strategies. While the economic fortunes of regions might rise and fall, the deeper continent-wide currents of the economy persisted well into the twentieth century. This is important. No matter what the state did or did not do, people produced, traded, and consumed. What needs to be explained, however, is the particular form the economy took at given historical periods, and how the economy changed.

The underlying dynamic of the West African continental market was ecological specialization. The economics of ecological specialization form the basis of an insightful commentary by a French colonial official in 1903.

> There exist in the Western Sudan very rich zones of production, but very distinct and based on monoproduction. This results in the economic situation that in each of these zones the large majority of merchandise produced has a low value and creates conditions for a favorable market for buying. Transported by the Juula [African traders] to another unique production region, where these goods are totally absent, they acquire a very high value when exchanged for local products. For the same reason, the latter products, which exist in abundance in one area, are transported to another, where they do not grow spontaneously and sell for a profitable price.[18]

When viewed from the perspective of market demand, long-distance trade catered primarily to the mass of consumers with little purchasing power. Consumers need not be wealthy to participate in these types of transactions. Few could have bought a full load of 3,000 kola nuts, although many could buy a few nuts.[19]

Ecological specialization profoundly influenced the spatial character of long-distance trade. All precapitalist merchants needed to resolve certain technical problems, such as rapid turnaround of perishable produce, access to reliable market information, and consistent adjudication of conflicts. Merchants employed considerable innovation and ingenuity to meet changing markets and supplies. Islam and ethnic diasporas provided mechanisms to resolve many of these problems. Diasporas often emerged to facilitate long-distance trade, and local brokers mediated between foreign traders and local merchants.[20]

Although merchants avoided politically troubled areas and changed directions in response to market information, African traders concentrated their efforts along established routes and usually dealt in specific commodities. Most of the major commercial routes of the savanna and sahel regions followed broad east-west corridors that took advantage of the suitability of different forms of overland carriage to environmental conditions. Camels performed best in the desert and sahel regions; oxen were most efficient along the sahel and in the relatively flat savanna plains; and donkeys carried lighter loads, but were more agile in dense bush and over rugged terrain. Camels, oxen, and donkeys did not survive well in the forest zones, where human porterage predominated. Transporting goods by canoes, however, was the most efficient form of long-distance carriage.

The nature of market demand in West Africa fostered trade across ecological zones, and thus when caravans traversed these zones, merchants expected losses to their animals and losses due to the carriers' inefficiency. Hausa kola merchants, for example, began their trade by acquiring natron in Borno. They then returned through Hausaland and added textiles and dried onions for their voyage to Salaga in Asante, where they exchanged their imports for kola. Maraka traders in the Middle Niger received desert salt in exchange for cloth and grain, and then set out for the kola forest armed with salt and an assortment of commodities acquired locally, including cloth and fish.[21]

My discussion thus far has focused on the broad patterns of exchange. But the economy was more than the sum of commercial transactions, the geographical determinants of trade, and the social composition of buyers and sellers.[22] The economy was composed of the social and spatial linkages that integrated producers and consumers from different regions and directed their production. At the base of the economy was the social organization of production, which determined the quantities and the form of goods and services both on the market and hidden from it. Economic life might seem to revolve around colorful periodic markets, but the economy was not reducible to what occurred at the marketplace.

We should regard the economy as a web of relations that transcended ecological regions and ethnic boundaries. During periods of expanded commodity production, webs linking producers were tightly drawn; during periods of economic decline, the webs were weakened and the forces directing production were local household and intracommunity ones. The notion of a regional economy, which I employ here, is conceived spatially and socially, and its boundaries remained flexible.

Market forces within regional economies had little power to transform producers' strategies and their social relations of production directly. Merchant capital, which derived from the movement of goods across zones of different natural endowments, did not necessarily result in the transformation of relations of production. Peasant producers could retreat from the exchange circuits and survive as subsistence agriculturalists. The valorization of surplus labor through sustained incorporation within exchange networks, which eventually dissolved precapitalist forms of production, occurred unevenly and sporadically in precolonial West Africa. For most producers, exchange value was coincidental to production.[23]

There were some partial exceptions. Commodities like salt, kola, and gold were produced for exchange, although even in these cases producers were not wholly subordinated to merchant capital.[24] These producers were like artisans, who provided for their own subsistence and worked at their crafts only during the dry season when the opportunity cost of their labor was low. In periods of economic downturn, these producers too could forgo exchange without threatening their survival. This was not the case when the combination of market forces and state intervention led to changes in social relations of production. Such changes occurred most dramatically among the Maraka, whose investment in significant numbers of slaves led to changes in the organization of production and in household social relations. Relations of production were also transformed among the Somono.

When the state assured the necessary conditions for investment in productive and commercial capital, producers specialized and expanded their commodity production. As a result, a complex social division of labor developed in the Middle Niger valley. Members of ethnic groups and craftsmen's castes produced goods for both the continental market and the local market. Each major ethnic group included an economic resource in the definition of its social boundaries. Bambara farmers produced surplus grain. Bambara slave warriors produced slaves and booty. The Maraka produced white and indigo-dyed cloth and surplus grain. The FulBe tended livestock and controlled the milk supply. The Somono fished and planted tobacco on the river banks. Ethnicity and occupation were closely linked and ethnic groups often monopolized economic resources.[25]

The boundaries were not rigid, but in order to acquire the protected resources on a regular basis, producers needed to conform to the dominant social characteristics associated with the ethnic group that controlled those resources. When the webs of relationships were tightly drawn, exchange rested on restricted access to economic resources, which further tied separate communities to the social formation. Only through their interaction with other specialized producers, most often through the market, could those who controlled resources realize the product of their labor. The state thus provided conditions for both the articulation of ethnic identity and the interpenetration of producers' strategies.

Warfare

Warfare was an inseparable component of the political economy of the Middle Niger valley. Capturing slaves and conquering territory were its clearest expressions. Mungo Park, who traveled to the Middle Niger region at the end of the eighteenth century, understood the relationship between war and enslavement. "War is, of all others, the most productive source [of slaves]. . . . It is a known fact that prisoners of war in Africa are the slaves of the conquerors."[26] The relationship between warfare and enslavement was more complex than this simple assessment indicates. Warfare netted slaves, but it also contributed to the foundations of state power at Segu and influenced the forms of state intervention in the economy and thus the economy's performance.

No historian of Africa disagrees that long-term demand for slaves in the New World, North Africa, and the Middle East was felt throughout the continent. But there is little agreement among historians on how the demand for slaves influenced African institutions and societies.[27] The emergence of the Segu Bambara state at the beginning of the eighteenth century coincided with the era of increased slave exports. Curtin estimated that 80 percent of the total slave exports to the New World were transported between 1710 and 1850, or roughly during the entire era of the Segu Bambara state. Slaves from Segu destined for the Atlantic trade were probably sent to Senegambia and Sierra

Leone. Slaves from these two regions accounted for only 10–15 percent of the total slave exports from 1701 to 1867 and Bambara slaves constituted only a fraction of this total.[28]

All the slaves produced by the Bambara were unlikely to be exported overseas. The Segu state, unlike its coastal counterparts, managed to avoid dependence on one primary market. Slaves captured by Segu warriors were sent to the Atlantic, the desert, and interior markets. Some were retained locally. The numbers of slaves exported in any one direction were not as important as the social, political, and economic consequences of enslavement. In the course of supplying slaves, warfare and enslavement became foundations for state power.

For the professional warriors of Segu, slaves were a commodity produced in order to be exchanged. Warriors often exchanged slaves for their means of production (weapons), their means of subsistence (food and drink), and luxuries. Even when a ruler decided to wage war for political motives, warriors fought in the hope of economic gain.[29] In the Middle Niger valley, I can identify two broad categories of warriors. Some were conscripts who fought occasionally, but who farmed, fished, or herded for most of the year. The rest were professional warriors, most of them slaves themselves. In contrast to conscripts, professional warriors earned their livelihoods primarily from making war.[30] Among the Bambara, warriors earned their livelihood from a specific action: capturing booty.

Warriors were like artisans; they transformed a raw material into something else. The act of enslavement was a physical and often violent enactment of a symbolic transformation: the person's free status was transformed into unfree status. This transformation, although existing only in a symbolic form, was nonetheless crucial to the subsequent stages of sale, purchase, shipment across the Atlantic or the desert, or reinsertion into another society in Africa.[31] Mungo Park captured the sense of this process: "When the weak or unsuccessful warrior begs for mercy beneath the uplifted spear of his opponent, he gives up at the same time his claim to liberty; and purchases his life at the expense of his freedom."[32]

Certainly warriors did not produce slaves the way farmers produce grain or weavers cloth. But the change in raw material was no less significant. Enslavement as the transformation of status was a necessary aspect of making people into commodities that could then be bought and sold. The moment we conceive of warfare and enslavement as work, as productive activity, the political economy of warfare and enslavement becomes explicable. The study of the political economy of warfare is especially appropriate where warriors dominated the state, as they did in Segu and in many other regions of West Africa. Moreover, the political economic analysis examines not only the interrelationship between warfare and the economy, but the way warfare became an expression of the internal cohesion of the state. Warfare was one of the elements of societal construction as well as destruction.

This argument also applies to the Umarian state at Segu. As in the Bambara state, warfare reflected the complex interplay of state power and economic performance, but it contributed to a different political economy. Warfare remained the principal expression of state power and remained the primary form of enterprise for the conquerors. But Umarian conquest and subsequent forms of warfare and state intervention in the economy led to economic collapse in the riverine districts of the Middle Niger valley. Instead of acting as an engine of economic growth as it had under the Bambara, warfare now led to economic decline.

For the French, warfare was the foundation of the colonial empire in the Western Sudan. Even in its colonial guise, warfare contributed to the persistence of the precolonial character of the colonial state. Over the first quarter century of colonial rule, different ideologies of state and society pushed and pulled policies and structures of the colonial state. With the capture of Samori and the conquest of Sikasso in 1898, the precolonial relationship between warfare, enslavement, and the state was finally altered. As a consequence, the colonial state gradually loosened its support for the precolonial institutions of the economy. The 1905 exodus of the slaves marked the demise of the precolonial political economy.

Warfare was thus much more than the tactics and matériel of war. It was a social process that produced asymmetrical consequences on several levels. Warfare was part of the dynamic in secondary state formation in the era of the slave trade. It was also an expression of state power. Armies marched. Sometimes they conquered and sometimes they were defeated. The success of a military venture, whether as a slave raid, an Islamic holy war, or colonial conquest, had deep ramifications within the structure of the state itself. Too few successes cast doubt on the legitimacy of state power in its present form. Too many successes expanded the state beyond the limits effectively controlled by existing forms of rule and institutions of state. Finally, warfare was an expression of state involvement in the larger social formation. To make war successfully, and thus to fulfill the expectations of the warriors and the groups involved in support services, required conscious intervention in the economy in order to replenish the material conditions for making war. The viability of the military state ultimately depended on how it provided for the reproduction of its ability to make war successfully. Failure to do so threatened the cohesiveness of the state in its current form.

Warfare had profoundly contradictory effects on the economy. Warfare could provide a tremendous stimulus to the economy, but it could also skew the organization of productive forces. Warfare provided the occasion for states to intervene more forcefully in the economy by mobilizing resources, controlling markets and prices, and engaging directly in production. At the same time, the form of the economy and the development of productive forces set clear limits on both the forms of state intervention in the economy and the forms of military activity.[33] In the following chapters, I shall examine the interrelationship of the state, warfare, and the economy of three successive states over two hundred years.

TWO

The Segu Bambara State and the Economy, 1712-1861

THE NIGER RIVER, broad and smooth-flowing at Segu, was the dominant feature of the otherwise open and gently rolling plain of the Middle Niger valley. The river was at once a continuous stream of water and a means of communication, tracing an arc into the desert steppe before heading to its ocean outlet on the Bight of Biafra. The Niger river had long been used by fishermen, herders, traders, and cultivators. The annual flood gave those who controlled the river banks an extra harvest and more pasture.

Millet and sorghum formed the base of the agrarian order. Grain provided both subsistence and the means to expand the economy through exchanges across ecological zones. Savanna agriculture could yield considerable surplus, often two to three times in excess of the producers' needs. How much of the harvest ultimately entered the larger commercial system depended on the development cycle of the domestic farming group, the degree to which the farming group invested in labor, and climatic conditions. A prudent farmer, at least in Bambara terms, would store enough to get through one season without recourse to the current crop.

More than anything else, climate determined the seasonal round of livelihood and the viability of commerce in an area where rainfed agriculture was basic to the economy as a whole. Droughts and epidemics, which came with grinding regularity during the middle of the eighteenth century, led to marked contractions of the commercial horizon and to political instability.[1]

They weakened the webs of relationships radiating out from the Middle Niger valley, and disrupted the ecological specialization that fed the continental commerce of West Africa. Economic recovery, accomplished by tightening social and spatial linkages of production, depended on replenishing herds and stores of grain. It could take a decade to restore production and commerce to their former levels.[2] Droughts, therefore, revealed just how fragile a motor agriculture was for economic growth in the Middle Niger valley.

All the elements of an articulated regional economy, in which specialized producers serviced other specialists through the mediation of the market, antedated the establishment of the Segu Bambara state at the beginning of the eighteenth century. The state established the means to transform these elements into an expanding regional economy that grew significantly although unevenly over the next 150 years. In the process, the state drove economic growth.

At the beginning of the eighteenth century, the Bambara established a warrior state in Segu. The peculiar structure and dynamic of the warrior state required that the state intervene in the economy. The reproduction of state institutions and state power was indistinguishable from state intervention in the economy. Waging war successfully presupposed a developed and articulated commercial infrastructure. By the early nineteenth century, the Middle Niger valley had become a center of production and exchange in Western Sudan.

Systemic warfare practiced by the Bambara of the Middle Niger region had profoundly paradoxical effects on the regional economy. Warfare led to insecurity, death, and destruction. It tore able-bodied men, women, and children from their homes and enslaved them. Groups that were raided, especially those along the Bani, in Kaarta, and on the border between Segu and the interior delta, lived a precarious existence antithetical to productive capital investment. Defense required significant investment of labor and capital to construct town walls and defenses.[3] This investment was a limited form of insurance, for it rarely covered fields, crops, and livestock. Endemic warfare encouraged investments in quickly disposable goods such as jewelry and gold. In such circumstances, capital was rarely returned to production. Warfare also raised trading costs as merchants changed routes to avoid unsettled areas, hired protection, and armed themselves.

Warfare also stimulated the economy, however, or rather certain sectors of the economy. When state power was firmly established, warfare stimulated production within the central heartland of the state. By guaranteeing security within the realm, the state encouraged investment in trade and production. The state actively solicited trade by establishing institutions that favored commerce. For example, Segu had market police to protect merchants against fraud in weights and measures. The state also adjudicated commercial conflicts between traders and local officials and thus ensured that traders were not unduly relieved of their goods.[4] Strangers could enter the region with relative impunity.

Above all, the warrior state encouraged trade and production because warfare yielded a commodity—slaves—that was in great demand. Slaves from Segu's military campaigns fed the expanding market for manpower in the New World, North Africa, and pockets scattered across West Africa. Some were also retained in the region by groups that relied on slave labor to expand the scale of their production—the Maraka, for instance, who developed a distinctive plantation sector, and the Somono, who expanded the scale of their transport services and fishing. Fresh fish became a staple in local diets and dried fish constituted an important component of the assortment of goods exported over long distances to the lands of kola.

Warfare in the eighteenth and nineteenth centuries also led to changes in trade routes. The major north-south commercial axis, from Jenne to the kola and gold fields of the Volta basin, followed the Bani River and skirted the Middle Niger valley. Segu's wars along Jenne's southern periphery and into the Baninko region disrupted this route and made the Niger corridor more attractive to merchants. Moreover, the expansion of the Somono during this period led to the development of the riverine transportation system, a rapid and cost-efficient means of moving bulky goods over long distances. This commercial reorientation encouraged economic growth and specialization in the Middle Niger valley.

State intervention and commercial reorientation altered the

conditions under which the regional economy operated. Some changes were minor, merely tugging at the established axes of commerce and bringing more trade to the commercial centers of the region. Others were more profound, altering the basic forms of investment and the conditions under which production was organized. Most sensitive to the consequences of state intervention were producers whose occupations lent themselves more fully to commoditization, especially traders and fishermen.

Merchants within West Africa's regional economies shared certain characteristics. First, the merchant communities tended to be residential, since merchants working within their own regions enjoyed considerable advantages over those who were only irregular visitors. Second, most merchants consistently followed the same routes, dominating trade along those routes even if they did not monopolize it.[5] Third, most merchants were also farmers who returned to their homes each rainy season. Occasionally they were stranded far from their homes when the rains made travel difficult, and they tried to minimize the costs of this delay by farming in foreign communities. Some merchants departed from their homes with the intention of returning only after they had made their fortunes, perhaps some five or six years later, but these were the exceptions.[6] The case of the Maraka was different again. The center of their commercial strategy rested on producing commodities for the desert-side trade, and out of this specialized exchange they accumulated the means to engage in long-distance trade. The Maraka were successful long-distance traders, but they were primarily managers of complex production and commercial enterprises.

Merchants were ready to take considerable risks in their search for profitable avenues for capital accumulation. This basic rationality, however, should not disguise the fact that merchants were often at the mercy of conditions in their homelands. If, for example, the Moors did not arrive because of adverse political or climatic conditions along the desert-edge or within the Niger valley, the fabric of Maraka long-distance commerce began to crumble. The fortunes of merchant groups and commercial centers rose and fell as a direct result of changes in the political and natural environments.

Despite the importance of trade, the economy of the Middle

Niger valley remained essentially agrarian. From the standpoint of both the gross domestic product and the deep structures of everyday life, cereal production was probably the region's most important economic activity. Precolonial farmers in the Middle Niger valley have left very few records of their production strategies, forms of investment, and productivity, so that the common measures of the growth and performance of the economy cannot be applied. We must look instead to the broader patterns of the economy, identifying how they were organized and how they changed in response to market opportunities and institutional changes.[7] In particular, two ethnic groups in the Middle Niger valley, the Maraka as commercial producers and traders and the Somono as fishermen and transporters, had distinctive roles in the economy, roles that were sensitive to economic and political change. In good times, both were more likely to fully engage in market activities; in bad, they retracted. The Maraka and the Somono therefore provide "windows" onto the economy.[8] They also reveal different patterns and consequences of the Segu state's intervention in the economy.

But besides the Maraka and the Somono, three other occupational groups had distinctive roles in the regional economy, their members sharing a central core of traits. First, the Bambara constituted close-knit corporate farming communities. For the Bambara who predominated in the heartland of the state (and for the Malinke, Bobo, and Minianka on the fringes of the state), the production of an adequate cereal crop was part of the reproduction of social form. Cooperative labor provided by young unmarried men was a central feature of Bambara villages. During the eighteenth and nineteenth centuries, when the Segu armies recruited heavily among young Bambara, the elders probably needed to redouble their efforts to control their youth. Their efforts were successful, and the distinctive Bambara farming community survives to this day. Maraka also farmed, but their production strategies differed from those of the other farming groups. The black Maraka between the Niger and the Bani rivers, who were more accumulative than their Bambara neighbors, farmed primarily as independent families.[9] The cosmopolitan white Maraka of the left bank of the Niger preferred to rely on farm slaves.

The second occupational group was composed of the FulBe, who were primarily herders. The FulBe (singular, Pullo) were part of a much wider group of Fulfulde-speaking peoples found throughout the savanna and sahel from the Senegal River in the west to Borno in the east. The FulBe preferred tending cattle to farming, but cattle are a precarious resource and a Pullo could find himself farming to survive. Under ideal conditions, which the FulBe of Masina achieved to some degree, they tended their herds and relegated the mundane concerns of farming to their slaves. The best pastures lay within the complex ecology of the interior delta, where different grasses supplied adequate forage for most of the year. Leading the herds on a regular transhumance from pasture to pasture facilitated trade with farmers. It was easy to acquire grain in return for the products of the herd. Under less-than-ideal conditions, some FulBe herded the livestock belonging to Bambara or Maraka farmers in return for one or two days of the milk supply and a share of the offspring.[10]

The Segu state intervened dramatically in the organization of the FulBe by raiding their herds and settling captured FulBe and livestock within the central zone of the state. The state occasionally had huge herds, and the *forabafula*, the state's FulBe slaves, thus provided a crucial service to the state. The state encouraged livestock and herding in the Segu heartland, which probably had not had extensive herds before.

The final occupational category consisted of the *nyamakala*, or members of the major endogamous artisan groups. West African artisans formed groups that have been labeled "castes," and they resembled, at least superficially, the hierarchy of social classes found in Hindu culture. In both West Africa and India, castes combined occupation and status within a social hierarchy. In both areas, religious prohibitions limited social mobility and social contact. Members of castes were feared as well as respected. Their profession brought them into direct contact with fearsome powers, whether earth spirits or those associated with specialized knowledge. In both areas, the maintenance of fairly rigid social boundaries also protected important economic resources.[11]

In the Middle Niger valley, the most important castes were the *numu*, or ironworkers, the *garanke*, or leatherworkers, and the *jeli*, or bards. Of the three, male and female ironworkers controlled the most important economic resources and the most powerful spirits, those of fire and earth. Male ironworkers mined ore, prepared charcoal, smelted, and worked the iron. They thus controlled the supply of agricultural tools. Working in wood, they made wooden tools and handles, doors, and many religious articles. Male ironworkers also dug wells. Female ironworkers dug clay, threw pots, and fired them. Both male and female *numu* controlled the symbolic right of passage into adulthood when they performed male and female circumcision.[12]

Before the formation of the Segu state, the social landscape of the Middle Niger consisted of webs of social and commercial relations linking the Maraka, the Bambara, the FulBe, and the nyamakala together. The Somono came later; they trace their origins directly to the rise of the Segu state. The emergence of the state led to profound changes in the sets of interactions between these groups and in their relationships to the regional economy. These changes are evident in the Bambara traditions of the origin of the state.

The formation of the Segu state at the beginning of the eighteenth century rested on a profound rupture in the structure and social organization of Bambara society in the Middle Niger valley. Neither Bambara farming communities nor their ideology of corporate community disappeared with the emergence of a warrior state. Instead, the new state and the new structures of power were legitimated through the retention of the ideology of the bachelors' association. Sustaining political unity on the scale of the Segu state after about 1712, however, required much more than the marriage of the old ideology to the new institutionalized violence on which the new order rested. The state's longevity depended, paradoxically, on the maintenance of a constant war economy. As long as the Bambara waged war successfully, the state persisted. When military campaigns were unsuccessful, centrifugal forces within the structure of the state led to marked crises of state power.

The Making of the Segu State, ca. 1712

The legend of the origins of the Segu state tells of the rise of Mamari Kulubali, also called Biton. Whereas legends often begin with mythical origins, states are the result of complex historical processes.[13] The Kulubali legend has two dimensions, a magico-mythical element and a historical-structural blueprint. They are presented as linked pairs of opposites: farmer/hunter, protector of agriculture/neglecter of agriculture, member of the age set/outsider, and hunter of animals/hunter of men. These paired opposites center on the character of Mamari Kulubali and they reveal the structural tensions inherent in his actions. Among the Bambara, oral tradition rarely follows a rigid form. Instead, the Mande *jeli* (Malinke: bard, griot) has a considerable license to amplify this or that point, to educate, to instill a proper sense of awe and respect, or merely to amuse. The main episodes of the Kulubali legend are found in most of the recorded versions of the tradition.[14] In assembling the following version, I have neglected the rich artistic and literary character of the individual traditions that are so important for the public presentations of the legend.[15] I am interested in the clues the tale provides for understanding the historical context and form of the Bambara state in the Middle Niger valley.

A hunter who came from the east had a son born at Bendugu-Nyamana, near the Bani. His name was Mamari Kulubali. One day the son wounded an animal near Bendugu and the animal fled across the Bani toward the Niger. He went to his mother, Masunu Sako, and told her that he was giving chase. He followed the animal to Sekoro, a village of spirits on the banks of the Niger. While he was resting, he overheard an old vulture chatting with a hyena. The animals prophesied that a hunter would someday rule the region.

Shortly thereafter, Mamari convinced his mother to move to the banks of the Niger, where she planted a field of eggplant, a favorite delicacy of the water spirits. One such water spirit devoured the crop. Mamari's mother reprimanded Mamari, since a son must protect the ripening crops. Mamari caught the thieving spirit, who invited him to come into the river to meet his parents. Mamari met the water spirit's parents, who offered him an exchange for their child: Mamari could have one hundred horses, one hundred slaves, one hundred virgins, one hundred uncircumcised boys, one hundred thousand cowries, or one hundred of each. But Mamari had been forewarned by the captured spirit not to accept anything but some grain, so he declined all offers. Exasperated, the water spirits asked Mamari what he wanted. He responded by requesting some fonio seeds to plant, which he received. He also received clear instructions: he was to plant the seeds, and weed and care for them, but once the grain ripened he was to let the birds eat the crop without stopping them. The birds in turn would carry the seeds of the harvest far and wide. These areas would know Mamari's power. Mamari prepared a field near Sekoro and cultivated the fonio, and when the birds came he did nothing to stop them.

About this time, the young bachelors of the area were in the process of selecting by mutual consent the leader of the age society. Everyone in the community could belong: nobles, nyamakala, and even strangers. But a stranger could never be its chief. The majority eventually decided on Mamari, even though he was a stranger. Mamari was a strong and able leader, but the bachelors of noble origin resented Mamari's prestige and power. Mamari's power also worried the elders, who feared that they might lose the respect of their cadets. A struggle for leadership began between Mamari and Kassoum Bware, son of the chief of Doua. The elders sided with Kassoum, since he was of a well-established family. Because of the rivalry, the bachelors' association divided into two factions, one led by Kassoum and the other led by Mamari. Competition between them resulted in even more serious conflicts. The elders attempted a reconciliation, but it failed and Mamari was expelled from the community.

Mamari asked his followers to help him build a house at Segu-Sekoro. His followers eventually joined him there, where they began to cultivate and live independently. Mamari's mother came and made millet beer for them. Kassoum's followers continued to harass the new community, and on one occasion a member of Kassoum's association was accidentally killed. The elders again tried to reconcile the two groups, but this effort failed too. Mamari and his followers were no longer subject to the judicial sanctions of Bambara society.

The life of Mamari's followers appealed to others who sought to escape their restrictive roles in the Bambara society. An old slave sought admission to the association and became its first slave. Others followed. Mamari also paid fines for debtors and criminals, who also joined the association as its slaves. Mamari led his followers on raids on nearby communities and returned with booty. With each success, more people sought to join the group. Mamari and his followers eventually forced Kassoum and his followers to Kirango, and Mamari became the leader of a much-enlarged association, an association that now depended as much on successful raids as it did on successful cultivation.

The Mamari Kulubali legend contains elements describing and justifying the new political system. Yet there are structural paradoxes contained within it. Mamari was clearly the agent of change, but he was both a hunter and a stranger, roles marginal to the logic of Bambara social reproduction and social control.

Mamari's alleged double status has led several students of Bambara history to suggest that the nucleus of the Segu state and its warrior tradition lay in the hunters' association. In Bambara society, the hunters' association was parallel to the age-grade system and peripheral to the generational patterns of social reproduction. Hunters were feared and respected, but they did not have an organization or an ideology that could have motivated the structure and ideology of the Segu state by itself.[16]

That Mamari was a stranger, however, helps explain some of his actions, especially those that shocked the agrarian sensibilities of the Bambara. To permit the birds to steal the grain crop was a fundamental insult to farmers for whom grain was the source of their subsistence. One of the important tasks of the Bambara age association was to protect the crop from animal predators just before harvest. For Mamari to consent to the theft of the crop represented a profound degradation of agricultural work, which was subsequently embedded in the ideology of state power at Segu. Hence, Mamari's election as leader of the association, although contested, represents the beginning of the symbolic break with traditional society.

Of all the elements in the Mamari legend, the retention of the age association [Bambara: *ton*] terminology in both the tradition and the organization of the Segu state is clearly the most significant. Charles Monteil, author of the first major history of the Bambara, made this point in his discussion of the origins of the Segu kingdom and developed it into a major argument concerning the indigenous dynamic in African societies: "It is very interesting, in effect, to see how an empire developed step by step out of a *flanton* [age association]: this change in a strictly native form of association is most instructive. It shows in detail how one of these Sudanese empires, and certainly not the least, was organized. It is essential to know this if one is to penetrate the secret and to understand the political history of the land."[17] Claude Meillassoux's concept of the "domestic community" provides a key to decoding the legend of Mamari Kulubali.

Central to Meillassoux's argument is the tension between elders and cadets. Meillassoux's model seems to have the greatest applicability to small-scale cereal-cultivating societies in which the very cycle of sowing, weeding, harvesting, and storing provides the material conditions that favor the elders' power. Stocks must be maintained and rationed until the new harvest is ready. Once harvested, even the new crop must be rationed, so that the cycle can be renewed once again. Elders' power thus rested on their management functions, through which they organized and limited access to food (and by implication seeds for the renewal of the cycle), to wives (and therefore to the means to establish one's own family), and to knowledge of both practical concerns such as when, where, and how to plant, and esoteric concerns, including the means to influence and tame the spiritual world.

Although elders exercised control over their cadets with varying degrees of harshness and effectiveness, the cadets seemed to accept the ideology of gerontocratic domination. They did so because they understood that at some distant date they would be elders with power over their own cadets. Social reproduction of the society was therefore assured through appropriation and distribution of surplus, access to the means of production, and general acceptance of the ideology of generational succession.[18]

The Bambara lived in corporate farming communities that generally followed patrilineal descent and virilocal residence within a collateral inheritance pattern. Cereal agriculture determined the routine of daily life. Occasional fishing and hunting supplemented the food supply. Within an age-specific status system two cross-cutting institutions, the hunters' association and the age sets, established countervailing subsystems of authority and structure. Hunters were respected and feared, but they were largely on the periphery of power, which actually rested with the elders and their manipulation of the agrarian cycle. Age was therefore the fundamental principle of organization, respect, and inheritance. Eldest brothers succeeded one another, but they also fought each other and rivalries between brothers often led to fission within Bambara domestic groups.[19]

When viewed over several generations, age sets were the primary vehicle for socialization and, in Monteil's terms, for the "cultivation of discipline." Bambara society had five age sets: boys up to six years; boys from six to ten; boys from ten to fifteen;

bachelors; and married adults. Girls had parallel age sets, but they did not seem to have the same political and ideological significance as the male groupings.[20] Membership in these age associations was open to all members of the community regardless of lineage, class, and usually ethnic origin. Such was the ideology. Practice was undoubtedly different, and subtle distinctions were often made between those of free (Bambara: *horon*) origin, those of slave or caste origins, and outsiders. We can glimpse these distinctions in the traditions surrounding both Mamari Kulubali and Ngolo Jara, the founder of Segu's second dynasty.

Of all the pre-elder age sets, the bachelors were certainly the most important. They provided most of the labor for social production and defense. But they had little control over the product of their labor. Because elders controlled the pool of potential wives and goods available as bridewealth, they controlled the timing of marriage among their cadets. Bachelors were probably those most conscious of restrictions on access to elderhood.

Meillassoux's model of generational reproduction would anticipate that this group was most likely to manifest discontent with the system and provide a spark for change. There were, however, powerful countervailing pressures. First, young men had no viable alternatives to remaining in their natal villages. Although a young man could go off and found a homestead on his own, this was impossible in practice. Without the protection of a lineage or a patron, the task of facing both physical and spiritual forces alone was a daunting one. And seeking a new patron in another village meant replacing one repressive agrarian community with another. Second, the young men's association had a sophisticated internal organization and a distinctive ethos, which may have deflected some of the tensions generated by the generational system. It probably wasn't so bad to eat, drink, and make merry with one's peers before the responsibility of marriage and family.

The bachelors' association also organized labor for widows, the sick, and other households with insufficient manpower. In return, the association usually received grain and small livestock. The association also collected regular dues of labor and money from its members, and thus built a stock of mutual funds. To a large extent the bachelors' association constituted a democratic community in which rank and status were achieved. Officials were elected by mutual consent. Officers included the leader (Bambara: *tontigi*), his assistant, and a treasurer who assembled and distributed the mutual holdings. Finally, the group had its own bard, who was drawn from among the jeli caste. All members were considered "children of the association" (Bambara: *tondenw*), which suggested a generational subservience to the association as a whole. The officers were empowered to levy and collect fines from among their members and to enforce discipline. The uses to which the association put its mutual funds were a sharp contrast to the sober and rationed consumption of the community as a whole.

The "children of the association" were committed to drinking millet beer and eating in the company of their fellows as often as possible. In eating together, the young men who were denied access to the product of the labor they performed for their elders found an alternative to the established household structure. In the process, the bachelors made an important statement about the limits of *faya*, power based on the gerontocratic model. Monteil's description of the bachelors' association captures the tensions in Bambara society:

> Among the flanton, the most conspicuous is the one having the largest number of young bachelors, known as *kamalenw.* Being much given to idleness, the kamalenw are troublemakers and rebels who seek all material pleasure and devote their talents to opposing the *fa*, the *bina* (Bambara: elders), and those who as masters of the community impose on young people the whole weight of an authority that is often absolute and often niggling.[21]

The bachelors' organization thus combined two prerequisites to the building of a new social order: they had a well-established administrative structure and an ideology that motivated the group as a whole. In the legend, Mamari Kulubali provides the catalyst for change. Despite strong opposition, Mamari was elected leader and led his followers through a series of skirmishes first with a rival age faction composed of noble cadets, and then with the elders themselves. After admonishing him with no result, the elders finally ostracized Mamari from the community.[22]

This ultimate sanction, the deprivation of social ties, misfired when Mamari Kulubali rallied his followers and established a separate home at Segu-Sekoro. From this point on, Mamari's association was the nucleus of a new social group, radically altering the traditional patterns of authority and social reproduction in Bambara society. Combining the original noble members and the new slave members recruited from among the criminals, adventurers, and flotsam of agrarian society, Mamari and his followers raided the surrounding countryside. By such actions, Mamari transformed the bachelors' association from a pacific agricultural age set into an offensive and militarized unit capable of reproducing itself constantly by creating new dependents.[23] Instead of reproducing biologically, as the Bambara agricultural society did, the new social unit reproduced laterally, by incorporating young men taken as captives into the ranks of the *ton* itself.

As warfare increased, the new recruits, mostly slaves, outnumbered the original "children of the association." This new development consisted of two countervailing tendencies: first, as slaves, violently removed from their previous social matrix, they were inserted into a new role wholly dependent on their masters (in this case, Mamari Kulubali as *tontigi*); second, as warriors, they controlled sufficient power to depose their master.[24]

With the expansion of warfare, the leader of the association became *faama* (Bambara: war chief, ruler), but his role was ultimately dependent on a "social contract" with the slave warriors of the association to organize successful military campaigns. When the faama failed to bring his followers military successes, the warriors, who controlled their own means of production, engaged in uncoordinated and uncontrolled predation. The result was a rapid decomposition of state power and the king's authority. I use the notion of a social contract to underline the essentially fragile nature of state power in the Segu warrior state. The faama was powerful only as long as he was able to organize state institutions and direct them specifically toward launching campaigns. The Segu faama was by no means a ritual or sacred king, although both the Kulubali and the successor Ngolossi rulers sought to control the ritual life of the association. Making war successfully and redistributing the booty judiciously were the primary means by which the ruler maintained state power.

The Segu kings also maintained their power through personal

loyalty. The Kulubali kings (ca. 1712–56) nominated slave warrior chiefs as leaders of regiments and as administrators of conquered territories. The Ngolossi kings (1766–1861) did the same, although Ngolo Jara and his son Monzon appointed their sons to the provincial administration. Neither the Kulubali nor the Ngolossi fully controlled the power of the slave warriors. Slave warriors became kingmakers, which in part explains the inability of the Kulubalis to secure dynastic succession after the death of the founder of the state.

Under both the Kulubali and the Ngolossi, the Segu state was based on warfare. Slave warriors produced little if any food; instead, they produced slaves. Their subsistence derived from a variety of sources: from the labor of their wives, many of whom were slaves retained after successful military campaigns, from neighboring villages obliged to provide food for the garrisons, from the king's redistribution of food and booty, from exchanges of booty with visiting merchants, and from participation in the continuous cycles of hospitality that characterized warriors' relations with each other. Slave warriors of Segu did not farm.

The slave warriors' aversion to farming indicates a profound change within Bambara society. Before the emergence of the warrior state under Mamari Kulubali, agriculture was the basic element of Bambara social organization. For the warrior slaves of Segu to farm would have reduced them to the level of ordinary farm slaves. For them to trade would have made them equal to the accumulating Maraka. The progressive degradation of agricultural work in the ideology of Segu's warriors only underlines how far and how rapidly a warrior class had differentiated itself from its agrarian roots. Making war not only gave slave warriors their specialized occupation; it gave them the means to renew their tools of production. Warriors needed a constant supply of weapons, including lances, horses, and, after the mid eighteenth century, steady supplies of firearms, flints, lead shot, sulfur, and gunpowder.[25]

Warfare was also a means of accumulation. Warriors, however, found it difficult to hoard wealth. They drank hard and fought hard, and they developed an ideology that equated honor with redistribution. This ideology of unrestrained consumption had its roots in the bachelors' age set from which the warrior state emerged. And this ideology persisted despite political upheavals. When Ngolo Jara seized power around 1766, he is supposed to have told the assembled warriors, "I have no doubts about the future; we will live from pillage."[26]

However, warfare was a distinctive form of accumulation. Warfare externalized accumulation at the expense of the social production of neighboring communities. To some extent, commerce operated in the same way, but there were limits to what could be extracted by trade. As a form of accumulation, warfare reflected the inherent weakness of the domestic community as a provider of sustained and significant surpluses. Efforts to exploit one's cadets, as the Bambara did, or to exploit one's slaves, as the Maraka did, could only go so far. Going beyond the limits led to social conflict. The externalization of accumulation, an ethos that stressed consumption and disparaged hoarding, the constant need to renew the means of production, and the distribution of booty—all were basic to the political economy of warfare at Segu.

The degree of state involvement determined both the three kinds of military operations common among Segu warriors and the principles of dividing the booty. *Kele* was the official military campaign usually staged during the dry season and directed toward an objective that promised significant returns.[27] Kele was the most productive form of warfare because it brought to bear the full weight of the state and the state's capacity to organize support services and logistics. The oral literature of Da Monzon (1808–26), the Ngolossi ruler at the height of Segu Bambara state power, recounted how he fielded 100,000 soldiers. More realistically, Tauxier suggests that the Segu army contained no more than 20,000. At the decisive battle of Noukuma, which marked the founding of the theocratic state of Masina around 1816, Segu fielded 15,000 troops. For other campaigns, the army's size often reflected the military objective. Monzon fielded 9,000 warriors for his march against Kaarta in 1796, and Ali had 15,000 for his defense of Woitala against al hajj Umar in 1860. The basic military unit of the Segu army was the *kelebugu*, a division of 300 to 600 warriors. Cavalry units were considerably smaller.[28]

The second form of warfare was the *soboli* (Bambara: *so*, horse, and *boli*, to gallop). The word denotes a cavalry troop of about forty warriors, most of them *sofa* (Bambara: father of the horse). They raided zones not completely subjected to the state. Whereas the full army campaign was a dry-season endeavor, the soboli could be mounted at any time. The warriors, usually sent out on the king's orders, were thus agents of his power, and the king accordingly claimed a share of the booty. During periods when state power waned, soboli was indistinguishable from brigandage.[29]

The third form of warfare was *jado*, or brigandage. It was commonly undertaken by a band of ten to twenty warriors, but occasionally by a lone warrior. Brigandage was conducted without formal organization and without the king's consent. It was strictly clandestine. Brigandage was considered a capital offense because it weakened the legitimacy of the king and created disorder within the state.[30] It was thus the most telling form of warfare because it reflected the structural tensions within the state and the complex dynamic behind warfare. Curtin's otherwise brilliant assessment of price elasticity of supply and his discussion of political and economic motivations for enslavement misses this point. Warriors were not simply reacting to market demand. They were responding to the dialectic of state power.

The frequency of brigandage was related inversely to the strength of the social contract between warriors and king. If the king fulfilled his obligations to launch successful raids, then the warriors were relatively content. As soon as the king was unable to meet these obligations, warriors no longer felt bound by their agreement with the king, and they raided indiscriminately. The resulting crisis led to a further deterioration of state power. Throughout the eighteenth and nineteenth centuries, the Segu state constantly struggled to maintain state power through external conquest lest it perish from internal brigandage.

The Segu king tried to control the centrifugal tendencies among warriors by monopolizing resources and institutions for warfare and by rewarding warriors with booty. Booty was divided according to the form of warfare and the degree of state involvement. In both the formal military campaign and the cavalry raid, the king claimed one-half to two-thirds of the booty, distributing the remainder among the warriors. Anything captured could be divided this way: livestock, grain, tools, and people. Two kinds of slaves were produced: *jonba* (Bambara: big slaves), who were not marketable, and *jonfin* (Bambara: black slaves), who were marketable. If several warriors captured one slave, the king claimed the slave and reimbursed the warriors with a cash equivalent, which they divided among themselves. The social contract between the warriors and the king obliged the king to redistribute a large portion of his own share, especially among the warrior chiefs. Bards also benefited from this generosity, since they contributed to the king's prestige.

Slaves captured through brigandage were handled differently. When captured in an illegal form of warrior violence, slaves had to be sold rapidly and for a fraction of their market value. The transactions between brigands and merchants were usually disguised and took place either in the warrior's home or in the merchant's home, a procedure that favored local merchants, who would be both known to the warrior and available at all times. Certainly the brigand can be studied from the standpoint of the entrepreneur, according to which the costs and benefits were clearly anticipated. But such a perspective neglects the social context of enslavement and its place within the structure and ideology of state power.

With his share of human booty, the king tried to contain the dissolution of the state. Whereas the warriors' slaves were all marketable, the king's were both jonba and jonfin. Big slaves, as they were called, were inserted into the apparatus of the state. Some, especially boys too young to remember much about their previous homes, were recruited into the elite guard and cavalry troops. Young men were recruited as slave warriors, whose ranks were decimated regularly by warfare. Only rarely did slave warriors' progeny become second-generation warriors. Instead, the state system needed to replenish its supply of slave warriors constantly.

The agricultural slaves who worked the state's fields around Segu were also taken from the king's share of the non-marketable booty. These *forabajonw* (Bambara: slaves of the big field) provided food for the court and for the standing army. Captured herdsmen were often retained as *forabafula* to tend the state's herds. The final portion of the king's share of non-marketable slaves became the Somono, the Segu fishermen. They provided military and troop transport and a steady stream of fresh fish to the court, and made gunpowder from the saltpeter scraped from the walls of the mud-sided buildings. Captured ironworkers made and repaired weapons and shot.[31]

Slaves who were not inserted into the state's institutions were sold. Usually they were sold to local Maraka merchants of Nyamina and Sinsani, but sometimes they were sent directly to Kangaba for the southern and western trade or to Jenne for the desert-side and trans-Saharan markets. In exchange for the marketable slaves, the king received horses, firearms and other weaponry, and luxury consumer goods.[32]

The king accumulated, and in large quantities, but he was also obligated to redistribute his holdings to ensure the loyalty of his followers. To be considered unwilling to share wealth, like Amadu Shehu during the 1860's, was to threaten the state. But the king did not redistribute his holdings equitably. Firearms, for example, were ostensibly a state monopoly, even if restrictions on weapons sales were probably not very effective. Warriors needed an independent source of firearms, and as a result, an active but hidden trade in firearms went on between warriors and Maraka merchants, which undermined the king's efforts to monopolize this technology of warfare.[33]

This cycle of centralization and decomposition was an organic factor in the organization of the warrior state. Since enslavement was only permitted on the fringes of the state, the cycle created flexible boundaries. During periods of expanding state power, when borders were pushed ever farther afield, the costs and logistics of launching full-scale campaigns over long distances must have been formidable. During periods of decomposing state power, when frontier regions fell from the state, the proximity of enslavement zones to the heartland of Segu indirectly lowered the costs of military activity. Less elaborate and therefore less costly military campaigns probably raised the returns available to both warriors and the king, prompting a renewal of state power. During Monzon's reign (1794–1808), an administrative innovation created a permanent justification for raiding within the borders of the state. Areas beyond the central zone were administered by the king's chosen representative. If he failed to deliver taxes or tribute on a set date, which was probably a common occurrence in an era when communications were difficult at best, the area was considered rebellious and a punitive expedition was dispatched.[34]

Although accumulation through predation was certainly swifter and offered greater yields than most other pre-industrial activities available to farmers, artisans, and merchants, the state's finances were not derived solely from its share of the booty. The state also instituted a system of taxation.[35] Tax collection played a prominent part in the legend of state foundation. Mamari Kulubali required that each member of the association provide a small amount of cash, which he then gave to his mother to make millet beer. Most variants of the legend contain a simple but logical escalation of the *djisongo* (Bambara: the price of millet beer, hydromiel) from a voluntary contribution made by a small community of equals into a political system based on violence. For those with political power—the slave warriors, their chiefs, and the king—the old community based on volition persisted. For those upon whom the social formation ultimately rested—farmers, fishermen, merchants, and common slaves—the notion of community was illusory.

In the region of Bouguni, well outside the central zone, the inhabitants did not pay djisongo. They paid *nisongo* (Bambara: head price, *ni* meaning soul). This shift suggests the changing character of the state: conquered areas were obliged to contribute to the well-being of the association. The shift is captured in Baba Kale's version of the traditions: "At the interviews and the assemblies of the people [the slave warriors] ate until everything was gone. In so doing, they were almost reduced to pillage. The people were thus advised that each family must give five cowries to be assembled by the village chief, who then handed it over to the chief of the association."[36] The payment of five cowries was not in itself burdensome, but the combined revenue from the thousands of hamlets and towns that eventually formed the Segu state was considerable. Certain groups paid higher taxes, notably the Maraka towns of the Middle Niger valley. Even the Maraka of Banamba, on the western frontier of the Segu state, paid taxes regularly—to demonstrate their good faith and guarantee their access to state markets and routes. Zones outside the heartland and under nominal rule from Segu sent tribute, usually consisting of the specialized produce of the area. Masina, for example, sent livestock. All conquered lands sent slaves.[37]

The economic and political consequences of the Segu state system differed between the central zone and the outlying conquest regions. The heartland of the Segu state, known as *toda* (Bambara: pot of gruel), extended from Koulikoro to Sinsani along the Niger and from the left bank of the Niger to the right bank of the Bani. It was an area about 150 kilometers long by 50 kilometers wide, and the power of the slave warriors there was uncontested. The social composition of the region reflected the tripartite character of the new social order. At the base of the society were agricultural communities that predated the Segu state. They included the original Bambara villages, which supported Mamari and his companions during their establishment. These communities retained their original agrarian and generational character. Their allegiance was measured in terms of their annual tax and their contribution of military recruits, who returned to their agricultural pursuits once the fighting ended. The second form consisted of new communities of farmers, fishermen, herders, and artisans, communities founded and nurtured by the state. Typically, they were villages that had initially resisted Bambara conquest, but they had surrendered before their military defeat and had been relocated in another corner of the state. The Bozo of Banankoro were settled in the Segu heartland, under the watchful eye of the head of the local garrison. The old riverine Maraka towns were also included in this central zone, although Sinsani, which was to become the most important Maraka city in the first half of the nineteenth century, appears to have been incorporated only by the end of Mamari's reign.[38]

The central zone thus constituted a mixed yet overlapping series of communities whose particular composition reflected both the needs of the state and its capacity for integration. The king's involvement in organizing agricultural and artisanal production changed Segu's social landscape and helped transform the structure and performance of the regional economy.

The Segu state did not assert its hegemony over the central zone until about the time of Mamari's death in 1754 or 1755. It took nearly 25 years for Mamari to destroy the Bware, who had established themselves at Kirango, a mere 50 kilometers from

Segu. The Bware, as the traditions recount, were the noble leaders of the anti-Mamari coalition before the rupture in Bambara society. In 1753–54, the revolts of Tio and Tayo in the northwest corner of the central zone seriously challenged the state's position. The Maraka of Sinsani joined the revolt, which suggests that they did not yet regard the state as integral to their social and economic organization. At about the same time, Mamari crossed the Niger and conquered the region of Lambalaxe, ruled by a rival Bambara lineage. The conquered people were employed as mercenaries in the west, and within a decade they organized a new Kulubali state in Kaarta, which replicated in significant ways the ideology and political structure of the Segu state. To the northeast, Jenne recognized Segu's power through tribute, but never had a formal Seguvian administration. Timbuktu was conquered by Segu's armies, but the city was probably never ruled directly by the king's representative. At no time in its history did Segu exert effective territorial administration beyond Lake Debo, some 200 kilometers downstream from the central zone.[39]

Mamari Kulubali's death resulted in a rapid decomposition of state power. Neither of his two sons, Bakari and Jekoro, was able to hold power. Moreover, the failure of the Kulubali dynasty coincided with one of the longest droughts of the century, which began in the 1740's and affected the sahel region of West Africa.[40] The severity of the drought doubtless weakened the state's capacity to launch wars. With fewer successful campaigns, the state could not contain its warriors' independence. Almost certainly, the drought affected the state's capability to collect taxes: there was much less available to collect. The state's herds were probably decimated during this period as well.

The death of Jekoro Kulubali at the hands of the slave warriors therefore signaled the end of Kulubali rule and led to a period of instability. Each leading warrior chief led his followers back to his corner of the central zone. Tonmassa Dembele, one of Mamari's original companions, attempted a reconciliation between the warlords, but neither Tonmassa nor the other warrior chiefs could control the centrifugal tendencies of the warrior aristocracy.

The collapse of the state affected the whole region. The Maraka towns of Sinsani and Nyamina remained important regional markets, but without the stimulation of the war economy and without the state's direct involvement in production, the level of commercial activity and specialization probably declined. The state had functionally disappeared, and the Maraka had to wait until Ngolo Jara reestablished the faama's role in the Segu warrior system and in the region's war economy.

The Maturation of the Segu State, 1765–1861

Ngolo Jara's rise to power and his reassertion of the *fanga* or power of the king ultimately depended on his ability to control the forces of decentralization inherent in the warrior state. As a young boy, Ngolo was among the slaves closely associated with Mamari. After apparently spending several years with an important Muslim cleric of Jenne, he returned to Segu to assume a position of considerable trust in Mamari's administration. Mamari probably wanted to test Ngolo's loyalty, since he appointed him guardian of the four cults of Segu, one of the principal posts of the Segu state and one that he retained during the interregnum. Around 1765 or 1766, Ngolo used his office to call a meeting of the slave warriors at the central religious shrine of Segu. Warriors customarily arrived unarmed, but during the course of the ceremonies, a cavalry troop under Ngolo's eldest son surrounded the meeting and forced the slave warriors to submit to Ngolo. His action put an end to their presumption of equality with their rulers. No longer was Ngolo merely one of the companions; he was now the faama. The humbling of the slave aristocracy through chicanery is often repeated in the traditions.[41]

Ngolo institutionalized his new power by reorganizing and rebuilding his army, and he reconquered much of the territory lost following the collapse of the Kulubali state. Without doubt, Ngolo's ability to lead successful campaigns strengthened his position in relation to the warrior chiefs. But no Segu king could count on absolute loyalty. When Mungo Park was in Sinsani in 1796, he heard the following account:

> When the present king of Bambara's father [Ngolo] desolated Maniana, the chief of Sai (almost opposite Segu) had two sons die in battle fighting for the king's cause. He had a third son living, and when the king de-

manded a further reinforcement of men, and this youth among the rest, the chief refused to send him. This conduct so enraged the king that when he returned from Maniana, about the beginning of the rainy season, and found the chief protected by the inhabitants, he laid siege to the town with his army and surrounded the town with trenches. . . . [The town was reduced by] horror of famine. . . . The rest of the town was carried away as captives, and sold as slaves to different Negro traders.[42]

Once the state's position within the central zone was reestablished and regional threats to his power were contained, Ngolo led his armies against Sidi Baba of Sokolo, against the Senufo, against the Mossi, into the Baninko, and toward the south. During his campaign in the Wasalu region of northern Ivory Coast, the important commercial towns of Tengrela and Tiongi submitted to Segu overlordship. He also pushed the borders of the state upstream into Kangaba, leading his armies as far as the gold-producing regions of Siguiri. Bambara presence was also felt in the western reaches of Upper Volta. The exiled ruler of Mossi, Naba Kango, sought refuge in Segu during a secession crisis, and he later led a Bambara mercenary army to reclaim his throne. Descendants of these Bambara troops are still discernible in Ouahiguya.[43]

Ngolo further undermined the power of the warrior chiefs through administrative reforms. He placed each of the five districts of the central zone under the command of his sons. The death of Ngolo's eldest son, N'Ji, in the campaign against Sokolo was the first in a complex string of events that led to civil war (Bambara: *fadenw kele,* war among brothers of the same father) and the next cycle of decomposing state power at Segu. Ngolo reigned for 25 years before he died in 1790 during the second war with the Mossi. Three of Ngolo's sons wanted to divide the succession. Only Monzon, eldest son and child of a slave mother, refused, citing the Bambara tradition of collateral succession. Nyankoro, Diokele, and Mamuru, sons of free women, challenged him. Only three divisions of the army, between 900 and 1,800 men, followed Monzon; the rest sided with Nyankoro and his brothers. Vastly outnumbered, Monzon sought allies among Muslim leaders and rich Maraka merchants. Traditions compare Monzon favorably with his brothers, who are portrayed as selfish tyrants. Monzon reaffirmed the camaraderie and reciprocity so cherished by the original Bambara association.

Nyankoro allied himself with Desekoro Kulubali, leader of the Kaarta Bambara, who marched to the banks of the Niger in 1792 and destroyed Nyamina. But Monzon's power continued to grow, and the turning point in the civil war came when Monzon demonstrated his goodwill toward rebellious warrior chiefs and they shifted alliances.[44] He reconquered Nyamina and struck deep into Kaarta, capturing at least 900 slaves. In 1794 or 1795, he finally destroyed his opposition and reestablished central authority at Segu.[45]

The extent of Monzon's authority remains unclear. Park, who arrived in the Middle Niger valley about two years after the civil war, is our best source for the first decade of Monzon's rule. Park returned again in 1805. What he was told about Monzon was certainly designed to impress the white stranger. Through an emissary, Monzon promised Park safe passage throughout all his domains: "Monzon says he will protect you." He was told "that a road is open for you everywhere, as far as his land extends. If you wish to go east, no one shall harm you from Segu until you pass Timbuktu. If you go west, you may travel through Foladoo and Manding, through Kassan and Bundu; the name of Monzon's stranger will be sufficient protection for you."[46] On the other hand, Monzon prevented Park from entering Segu town during both trips to the region, possibly because he could not guarantee his safety. Segu did not control the Malinke hinterland of Bamako, which meant that Kangaba, the large slave entrepôt on the Upper Niger, was not part of the Segu state. Banditry was widespread in the region southwest of Bamako.[47]

Muslims seem to have been more prominent in Ngolossi Segu than during the Kulubali era. According to Delafosse, Ngolo waged war with the Mossi to secure the return of several merchants who had earlier fled from Segu during the period of disorder. Traditions also credit Ngolo with placing all the Maraka commercial towns under direct state protection.[48] Muslims did not merely provide the commercial infrastructure that made the warrior state viable. They also provided powerful magic that even the most redoubtable traditionalists could not easily dismiss. After the battle of Noukuma, where Shehu Amadu defeated the Segu army, Da Monzon is said to have claimed that Amadu's magic from Muslim sources was more powerful than his: "Shaikh Amadu has in his gourd a talisman of victory more effective than all of the same type that I have from Sinsani, Walata, Timbuktu, and even Kong."[49]

Muslims also seem to have exerted a powerful influence at the court. In 1796 Monzon did not feel strong enough to publicly challenge the "Moorish inhabitants" of Segu, hinting at the important role a Muslim faction enjoyed at Segu. During his second visit to the region, Park was informed that "Modibinne is Monzon's prime minister; he is a Mohammaden, but not intolerant in his principles."[50] During this period, the Maraka towns apparently established an informal system of representation at Segu, in part to lobby for the interests of the Maraka in general, but also to protect the interests of individual merchants traveling through the realm and trading in Segu. This evidence of a powerful Muslim lobby suggests that court politics under Monzon were dominated by contending war and peace parties, represented respectively by warrior chiefs and Muslim merchants. Certainly this duality in state policy between waging war and aiding commercial activity formed part of the structure of the Segu state.[51] One of the central paradoxes of the Segu state was how the war economy related to economic growth in pre-industrial West Africa.

The Desert-Side Foundation to the Maraka Economy

The Segu Bambara war economy under both the Kulubali and the Ngolossi provided two important conditions to the expansion of Maraka commerce and production. First, it provided relatively long-term security within the context of perpetual warfare, and second, it yielded slaves, who were both commodities and units of labor. With slaves, the Maraka expanded their strategic location within the ecologically specialized trade of continental West Africa.

The Middle Niger valley abutted onto the economy of the southern Sahara and shared with it mutually beneficial economic relationships. These relationships, based on comparative advantage, had an innate capacity to expand, given propitious climatic and political conditions. Climate and security remained the two most important variables in the structure and growth of the desert-side economy. When the region enjoyed sustained periods of security along with good and reliable rainfall, herds increased dramatically and farmers amassed ever larger grain surpluses.[52] Such surpluses fostered interaction between the two specialized economies.

At the base of the Maraka economy was trade with the Moors of the western Sahara. The Maraka towns of the Middle Niger region stood astride an ecological frontier between the desert, the savanna, and the Niger River. Sinsani and Nyanima were not as far north as Sokolo, Gumbu, Nioro, or Murdia, nor as near the southern limit of nomadic movement as Bamako, but their location along the Niger river made them the terminus of the desert peoples' transhumance. Moreover, their riverside locations meant that they were less prone to the periodic sahelian droughts faced by market towns actually on the desert edge. The Moors of the western desert also chose not to cross the river, because they were concerned about losses to livestock in wetter zones.

The Moors arrived at the Maraka towns during the dry season and grazed their herds on recently harvested fields. The animals benefited from the cereal husks and other debris left in the fields and they provided the farmers with manure. Milk and livestock were traded for cereals and cotton cloth. Cereals were a necessary part of the Moors' diets, especially during the hot, dry periods of late spring when the herds' milk production declined.[53] Cloth from savanna farms was made into tents and clothing.

Out of this ecological exchange the Maraka developed a complex commercial and production strategy. They increased the scale of grain and cotton cloth production through slave labor. How early the first slave plantations emerged among the Maraka is difficult to determine, but by the late eighteenth century, slaves lived together on outlying plantations.[54] Some Maraka had only a few household slaves; by the early nineteenth century, successful Maraka planters had several hundred slaves working on a number of plantations at the same time. One of the leading merchants of Sinsani, Koromama Kuma, is remembered as having over 3,000 slaves.[55] Even the slaves the Maraka planned to trade were often put to work on the plantations before being sold. The procedure increased the available short-term labor supply and reduced the cost of slaves' upkeep until their sale. Slaves who proved themselves good workers were probably retained.

The Moors, who were both slave owners and slave traders, purchased large numbers of slaves. Many of the slaves were settled in agricultural communities and salt works deep within the desert, and the Moors, in turn, imported more salt, dates, horses, and livestock. A brokerage system emerged to handle the increased scale and complexity of trade. In Sinsani, each Moor family had its habitual host, a Maraka household head, on whose fields the Moor unit camped and grazed its animals. The *surakajaatigi* (Bambara: host of the Moors) provided his counterpart with cereals and condiments, housed him and his goods in his compound, and conducted all trade on behalf of his client. The Moor gave his host gifts of salt, dates, and dried meat. If the salt was not completely sold before the Moor retired to better pasture or to avoid the onset of the rains, he entrusted his Maraka host with what remained.[56]

Commercial trust was basic to this relationship and the surakajaatigi benefited in special ways. A price, or rather an assortment of goods, for all the unsold salt was usually agreed on in advance. Since the price of salt rose throughout the Western Sudan during the rainy season, the broker stood a good chance of reaping windfall profits. Because the Maraka host acquired salt on trust, he did not tie up his capital in salt purchases. Instead, he kept his own capital free to invest in other commercial or productive activities, including additional salt purchases. Sustained ties with Moor suppliers were therefore central to Maraka commercial strategies and forms of accumulation. To further cement their ties with the Moor suppliers, Maraka traders invested in plantations. Not surprisingly, surakajaatigiw were often the wealthiest and most powerful members of their communities.[57]

Despite the constant demand in the savanna for desert salts and other produce, political events influenced the volume of the trade and the spatial dimension of regional markets and routes. Since their slow-moving caravans were prime targets and provided rich rewards for pillage, Moors avoided unsettled areas. Most rock salt imported by the Moors into Sinsani came from the

Idjil mines in the western Sahara by way of Cenjetti, Tichit, and the northern sahel towns of Nioro, Walata, Gumbu, and Sokolo.

The Maraka referred to Idjil salt as *kogo jalon* (Bambara: black or mottled salt) because of its high concentration of minerals. Salt from Taodeni, whiter in color, competed to some extent with Idjil salt, although it fed different markets and had overlapping if somewhat different uses.[58] Taodeni salt arrived in Sinsani by one of several routes. Some was carried overland by way of the sahelian town of Bassikunu. Sometimes Maraka merchants went to Jenne, where Taodeni salt was cheaper than Idjil salt imported into Sinsani by the Moors. Caillié noted in 1828 that Moor caravans imported Taodeni salt directly to Sinsani in order to avoid Jenne, whose commercial situation had so badly declined because of the border conflict between Masina and Segu.[59] At mid-century, Barth remarked that Sinsani merchants bought salt in Timbuktu and shipped it via the river route.[60]

The desert-side dimension of Sinsani's economy also influenced the character of Maraka long-distance trade. First, the goods received from the Moors in exchange for local agricultural and handicraft products made up an important part of the assortment of goods the Maraka exported to markets further south. Second, some Maraka exports were derived directly from locally produced indigo-dyed textile production. Dyed cloth production was probably stimulated by the increased production of white cloth, although the two manufacturing processes were not identical. Third, the Maraka were unwilling to spend more than four months on their commercial voyages. Many of the characteristics of Maraka commercial strategies, including their small and mobile caravans and their preferences for wholesale trade, can be explained by their concern for managing and overseeing production on their farms and plantations. Nor is this surprising, since the Maraka invested a significant portion of their capital in agricultural production, mostly in the form of slaves.

Slavery dominated the economic and social life of the Maraka, even more so than for the other social groups of the Middle Niger valley. Although most Bambara, FulBe, and Somono households could aspire to slave ownership, only the Maraka underwent considerable change in the structure and organization of household relations and economic organization as a result.[61] This transformation occurred progressively throughout the eighteenth and nineteenth centuries, and by 1860 it is possible to discern an economic model of a cosmopolitan urban master class dependent on an expanding plantation sector. Umarian conquest eventually led to the collapse of Sinsani after 1865, but it did not destroy the Maraka social form. The Maraka model was a solution to certain economic and political variables, and when these conditions prevailed, the model was reproduced. This was true of the smaller Maraka towns to the west, which captured the bulk of the desert-side trade and developed a production sector virtually identical with the one developed in the riverine Maraka towns.

The desert-side trade stimulated trade and production throughout the regional economy. Bambara communities traded some of their grain reserves to the Moors and to the FulBe. Although the Bambara may not have planted extra fields merely to service this demand, they may well have used their normal surpluses for trade.[62] The arrival of the Moors at the end of the harvest cycle was a time for increased commercial activity. Periodic markets were eagerly attended, and more people probably had more goods to trade, even if most local producers supplied the same kind of products. The Maraka, on the other hand, used the goods received by the people of the desert to help transform their towns into central markets for the sale of local and exotic goods. In the following section I will examine the Maraka markets to see how the desert-side dimension and the political economy in the Middle Niger valley contributed to the growth of the regional economy, which also fed the larger continental economy of West Africa.

Maraka Markets and the Assortment of Goods

Within a decade, between 1796 and 1805, Mungo Park visited Sinsani twice. Despite the normal courtesy due "strangers," his first visit ended abruptly when the Moors, who were there for their annual trade, became hostile. He recognized that his host, the chief of Sinsani, was either unwilling or unable to guarantee his protection. The Moors' ability to influence public opinion in Sinsani indicates the importance of the desert-side trade to the Maraka. It may also indicate a renewed Islamic militancy that was just beginning to sweep the interior of West Africa. During his second visit, Park remained in Sinsani for over a month. This time, Park had official recognition as faama Monzon's "stranger." He was therefore assured both protection and subsistence.

Park nonetheless remained suspicious of Monzon's commitment and wary of the intricate court politics in Segu. He was aware of the growing sentiment against him in Segu, spurred by what appeared to be the Muslim party. When Park requested two canoes in order to follow the course of the Niger to its mouth, Monzon was under considerable pressure to resist his request. When the canoes finally arrived, they were in poor condition. Rather than risk asking for replacements, Park decided to buy his own canoes, and thus, on 8 October 1805, he entered the market as a trader and sold some of the goods he had brought with him.[63]

Park's observations on the market and the balance sheet of his sales provide some of the best data on early-nineteenth-century prices. Park's imported European goods may have sold especially well because of their scarcity value, but he also collected prices on selected local and regional produce. Unfortunately, these data do not offer much insight into the operation of the economy as a whole. Nor do they offer evidence on how prices affected producers and consumers. Surprisingly absent in Park's observations was mention of the two staples of the desert-side trade, grain and cloth. This neglect suggests that wholesale desert-side transactions were conducted behind the closed doors of the hosts' compounds.[64] Park's prices can be compared with those collected by other nineteenth-century visitors, and although there is no direct equivalence in goods (our observers were imperfect in this regard), Table 1 illustrates general price levels and the availability of imported goods in the Middle Niger valley.

Table 1 indicates some long-term changes in market prices for cloth, European imports, and firearms. Park's imported European goods fetched especially high prices, so that our earliest data may be skewed, but when nineteenth-century cowrie inflation is taken into account, prices for European manufactures tended to decline throughout the period.[65] Fluctuations in salt prices may have reflected political conditions more accurately than market demand. Prices of African goods, especially cloth, remained remarkably stable when cowrie inflation is taken into consideration. Firearms were the exception to these generalizations. The evidence clearly indicates that firearm prices increased. It may have been that over the course of the nineteenth century, firearms had become essential to the political economy of the Middle Niger valley, and that warriors would pay whatever the market demanded.

Sinsani had an active daily market, and on Tuesdays a large weekly market serviced the left bank from Farako to Niaro. Sinsani market impressed Park considerably:

> Sansanding contains, according to Koontie Mamadie's account, eleven thousand inhabitants. It has no public buildings, except the mosques, two of which, though built of mud, are by no means inelegant. The market place is a large square, and the different articles of merchandize are exposed for sale on stalls covered with mats, to shade them from the sun. The market is crowded with people from morning to night: some of the stalls contain nothing but beads; others indigo in balls; others wood ashes in balls; others Hausa and Jenne cloth. I observed one stall with nothing but antimony in small bits; another with sulfur, and a third with copper and silver rings and bracelets. In the house fronting the square is sold, scarlet, amber, silks from Morocco, and tobacco, which looks like Levant Tobacco, and comes by way of Timbuktu. Adjoining this is the salt market, part of which occupies one corner of the square. A slab of salt is commonly sold for eight thousand cowries; a larger butcher's stall, or shed, is in the center of the square, and as good and fat meat sold everyday as any in England. The beer market is at a little distance, under two large trees; and there are often exposed for sale eighty to one hundred calabashes of beer, each containing about two gallons. Near the beer market is the place where red and yellow leather is sold.
>
> Besides these market places, there is a very large space, which is appropriated for the great market every Tuesday. On this day astonishing crowds of people come from the country to purchase articles in wholesale, and retail them to the different villages, &c. There are commonly from sixteen to twenty large fat Moorish bullocks killed on the market morning.[66]

Shortly after making these observations, Park joined the transactions. Park's experiences as a trader, an occupation obviously not unfamiliar to him, are worth quoting. "I therefore opened shop in great style, and exhibited a choice assortment of Euro-

TABLE 1

Prices of Goods in the Middle Niger Valley, 1805–1885

(prices in cowries)

1805	1828	1864–66	1880	1887
		FIREARMS AND WEAPONS		
Musket: 6,000–7,000 Cutlass: 1,500–2,000 Flint: 40 Gunpowder, one bottle: 3,000		Knife: 1,000	One- or two-shot firearm: 25,000–30,000 Flints: 20 2-kg barrel gunpowder: 30,000	Double-barrel flintlock: 35,000–40,000 Pistol: 12,000–15,000 Revolver: 25,000–30,000 Flint: yellow quality, 140; black quality, 200 Knives: 800–1,800
		EUROPEAN AND INDIAN CLOTH		
Indian baft: 20,000 Scarlet, ten spans: 20,000 Light yellow cloth: c. 20,000 Blue cloth: as high as 20,000	Piece of colored cloth 18″ × 20″: 300		Blue calico (coudée):[a] 600 Guinée (coudée): 500 Various imported cloth, Baja, indienne (coudée): 600 Mousseline (coudée): 600	Calico (coudée):[a] 500 Guinée (coudée): 400 Heavily designed cloth: 600–700 Mixed cotton and wool: 600 Handkerchief (valued at 0.50F): 1,500 Indienne (coudée): 600
		AFRICAN CLOTH		
	Ordinary white bubu: 2,000 Ordinary white pants: 1,000	També sembé: 4,000	Bubu: 6,000–7,000 Pants: 5,000–6,000	Ducuruni-fin: 7,500 Kosso jé: 8,000

TABLE 1 (cont'd)

1805	1828	1864–66	1880	1887
		MISC. EUROPEAN GOODS AND CURRENCY		
One sheet of paper: 40 One dollar: 6,000–12,000 One arraloola, or five-bar piece: 8,000 One miktal gold: 3,000	Scissors, lengths of colored indienne, three sheets of paper, and necklace of glass beads: all at 15F	One sheet of paper: 50–100	Gross of gold (3.8g): 5,000–6,000 5F piece: 2,500–5,000 Glass bead: 20	Small bottle perfume (cost .50–.75F, St. Louis): 2,000 Small scissor: 1st quality, 2,500; 2nd quality, 1,500 Mirror: small, 800–1,000; round, 2,000 One needle: 50 Red chechia:[b] 3,000 Paper snuff box:[c] large, 1,000; medium, 500; small, 400 Wooden snuff box: 2,000–2,500 5F piece: 2,000[d]
		AFRICAN GOODS		
Salt bar: 8,000 Ivory tusk: large, 10,000; medium, 7,000; small, 3,000–4,000 Indigo ball (size of a fist): 40 Good beer for seven men in one day: 300	Salt bar: 10,000–12,000 normal price, up to 25,000 Kola: 15–18 along the route to Jenne; 8–10 in Jenne Load of wood for one meal: 10	Bafel Tichit salt: 10,000 in 1864; 40,000–60,000 in 1865–66[e]	Salt bar: 40,000–50,000, and up to 60,000 Muule of millet: 120 Muule of rice: 300	

TABLE 1 (cont'd)

1805	1828	1864–66	1880	1887
		LIVESTOCK		
Fat cow: 15,000 Good beef for seven men in one day: 620 Donkey: 17,000 Sheep: 3,000–5,000 Fowl: 250–300 Horse:[f] 40,000–80,000	Donkey: 11,000	Cattle: 1 slave or ½ slave Horse: 2–5 slaves, up to 7 slaves	Cattle: 60,000 Donkey: 40,000 Sheep: 2,500–6,000 Goat: 2,500–6,000 Chicken: 140–300 Horse: 200,000–300,000	

SOURCES: *1805*, Park, *Mission*, pp. 218-21. *1828*, Caillié, *Journal*. *1864–66*, Mage, *Voyage*. *1880*, Gallieni, *Mission*, pp. 436–37. *1887*, Caron, *De Saint Louis*, pp.326–29.

[a]Coudée at 0.50m (Gallieni) or 0.62m (Caron).

[b]A red cap worn by Muslims and usually made in Tunisia.

[c]Probably without tobacco.

[d]Caron noted that this exchange rate was 25 percent lower than normal. Five francs usually exchanged for 2,500 cowries. Thus all Caron's prices presented in francs are 25 percent higher than usual.

[e]This is apparently an inflated figure.

[f]Between 2 and 10 prime slaves.

pean articles to be sold wholesale or retail. I had of course a great run, which I suppose drew upon me the envy of my brother merchants."[67] Park earned enough to buy another canoe, and shortly thereafter he sailed down the Niger.

Between Park's visit to Sinsani at the beginning of the century and Caron's at the end, Sinsani's market expanded and contracted in direct relation to shifts in the political dynamic of the region. From the beginning of Monzon's rule to the arrival of the Umarians, Sinsani flourished. With the Maraka rebellion of 1863, Sinsani was effectively severed from the regional economy and declined abruptly. Nyamina and the new Maraka communities in Beledugu captured her share of trade. In 1863 two French explorers, Mage and Quinton, made the following observations of Nyamina, echoing Park's description of Sinsani nearly 60 years earlier.

> At Nyamina, as in all large cities, a market meets every day; but there is one day a week when there is a large market that attracts people from far and wide. Buyers and sellers crowd together. . . . The market is a large square. . . . Under the booths one sees one, two, or three merchants seated on straw; before them, also on straw, one finds their commercial objects: salt, glass beads, cloth, paper, sulfur, lead shot, rings of copper or silver for the ears, nose, hands, and toes, necklaces, local cotton cloth, pagnes, bubus, and burnus of the best quality. In one corner there is a public barber who uses a razor that comes from Sierra Leone . . . a salt merchant who . . . sets up very small heaps whose prices vary from five cowries up to 100 or 200. . . . The salt has just arrived from Segu, valued at 20,000 cowries, which is the price of a slave. Now we arrive at the butchers; all the butchers are on the same side of the market. . . . Much meat is grilled and smoked immediately. . . . Further on, one finds women in front of calabashes selling grain, baobab flour, maize, tamarind, herbs, beans, groundnuts, couscous, pimento, etc. There are also fish merchants who sell fresh fish or smoked fish; fish are bought to add to the sauce that goes on the cereal couscous.[68]

The descriptions of Maraka markets by Park and Mage reiterate the markets' commercial functions. They were centers for wholesale transactions, where traders bought the goods they retailed in the countless small hamlets of the savanna. They also acted as direct retail outlets. Maraka markets thus catered to the full range of consumers. Those "social islands of purchasing power," so central to Hopkins's analysis of West African economic history, bought luxuries, including large quantities of salt, slaves, horses, and imported cloth. Consumers with little cash, probably the majority, bought pinches of salt for five cowries, and equally small amounts of fresh or dried fish and other condiments. Certainly, these condiments were luxuries in their own right, since most household gardens had some spices and seasonings.

Trade alone cannot account for the economic character of Maraka towns or for their position within the larger economic system. Sinsani and Nyamina were at once entrepôts and production centers. Heinrich Barth, who traveled widely in the Central Sudan and the desert edge, recognized the difference between an entrepôt based solely on trade and a manufacturing center. "The great feature which distinguishes the market of Timbuktu from that of Kano is the fact that Timbuktu is not at all a manufacturing town, while the great emporium of Hausa fully deserves to be classed as such."[69] The life of the entrepôt, Barth wrote, was seasonal and followed the annual caravan trade. The manufacturing town was busy all year. Barth could also have added that the entrepôt and the manufacturing center had very different economic linkages and stimulated production in different ways. Although they differed in size and scope, the Maraka towns bore a greater resemblance to Kano than to Timbuktu. The economies of Kano and the Maraka cities rested on a mixture of commercial activity and manufacturing.

Towns like Sinsani and Kano also benefited from the peculiar forms of economic development generated by warfare. Warfare was at best a fickle engine for sustained economic growth. As a general proposition, it stimulated the regional economy by generating commodities and goods in demand within and outside of the regional economy. It also divorced from the market a sizeable number of potential producers and consumers who as slaves had only indirect influence on expanding the domestic market.[70] Commercial and political forces intervened constantly in the structure and form of the economy. The meteoric decline of Sinsani when it no longer participated in the state system is indicative of this interdependence. The next section traces the ebbs and flows of trade and routes leading into and emanating from the Middle Niger region.

Stability and Change in Trade and Trade Routes

The Middle Niger valley was surrounded by three export regions. Trade with the Maghrib, Senegambia, and the southern forest zones followed different routes, each with different mechanisms of trade. Each direction of trade required specific solutions to commercial and technical problems. I shall have more to say about these in the next section. Here I am concerned with the changing directions of trade over time.

The great commercial revolution stimulated by the transatlantic slave trade gradually spread deep into the interior of West Africa as African traders imported European manufactures and exported local produce and slaves. Throughout the Western Sudan, traders responded to new opportunities. During this period, the Gajaaga Soninke, the Jahanke, and the Malinke More of the Senegambian hinterland opened the commercial routes they eventually dominated. At about the beginning of the eighteenth century, Maraka traders began trading to Kankan, an important market on the edge of the Guinea–Sierra Leone corridor (see Map 3). Some informants claimed that Maraka traders took these routes to the river systems feeding the coast. They returned with firearms, flints, gunpowder, pearls and other fashionable minerals, manufactured goods, and guinée cloth. Still others went west through Kaarta and into the Upper Senegal commercial complex, where Maraka long-distance traders joined the routes dominated by the Gajaaga Soninke.[71]

Most Maraka traders, however, chose not to maximize retail profits through direct trade with the Europeans or their factors along the coasts or its immediate hinterland. Rather, they directed their trade to the secondary supply centers at the intersection of regional trade routes. In Kankan, for example, Maraka traders came in contact with the Malinke More, who controlled the routes to the headwaters of the Gambia, Faleme, and Senegal rivers. They also received goods from Sierra Leone. European merchants were concerned that the relay trade cut into their profits. In a letter addressed to the faama of Segu in 1848, Raffenel

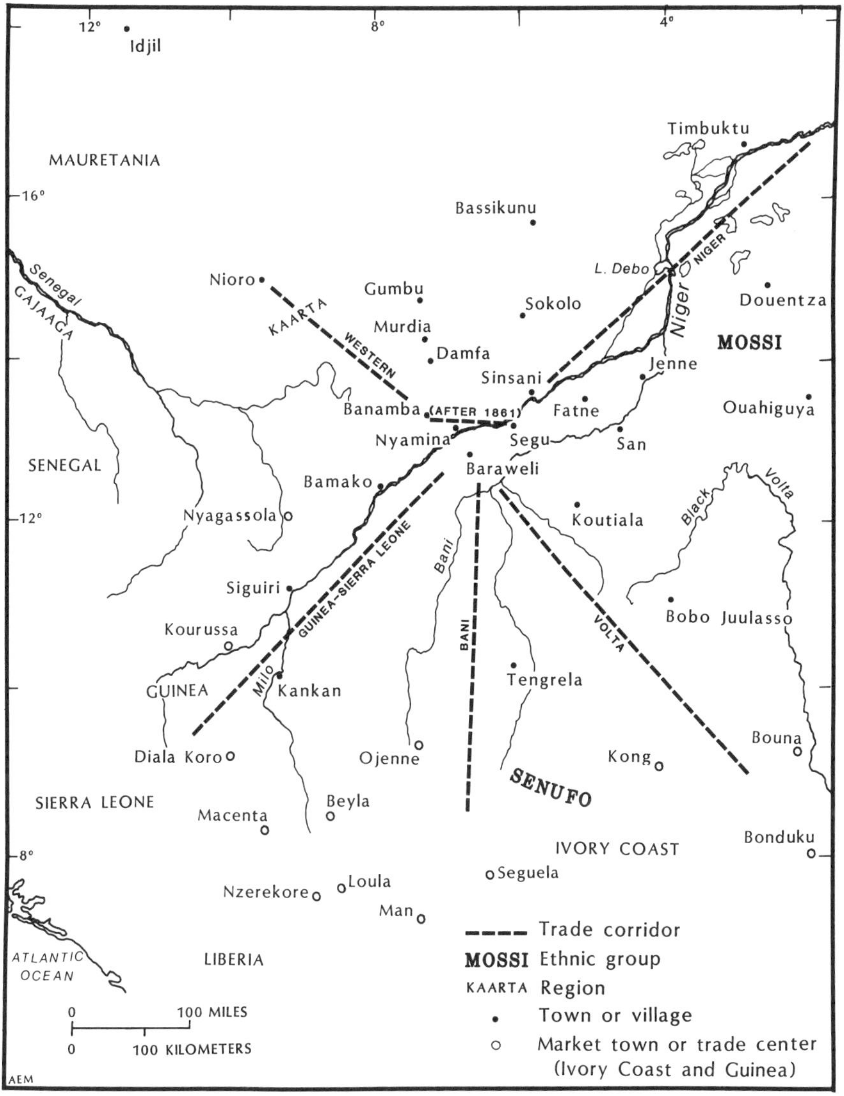

Map 3. Trade Routes of the Middle Niger Valley in the Nineteenth Century

tried to promote direct trade between the Middle Niger and the French factories of Senegambia. The 1828–29 Galam expedition to Segu was in direct response to these concerns. The Galam expedition failed and Maraka merchants resisted Raffenel's invitation.[72]

Despite the lack of direct contact with Europeans or their agents, the pull of the Atlantic trade on the Middle Niger valley remained strong. Certainly the demand for slaves in the New World stimulated predation in Africa. At least some of the slaves produced by the warriors of Segu found their way into the Atlantic economies. Even more direct, however, was the dependence of the Segu political economy on firearms, gunpowder, and other European manufactures, which could best be supplied through the Atlantic coastal trade. Demand for these commodities increased the importance of the westerly and southwesterly direction of trade. Most Maraka caravans that fed the Atlantic trade probably followed the Niger axis to the forest zone where they could obtain both European manufactures and kola. Perhaps part of the explanation of Maraka traders' resistance to direct trade with European factors was that despite the importance of imported manufactures to warriors, the Atlantic trade remained tangential to the ecozonal character of Maraka commerce.

Because commercial ties with desert and forest regions remained strong, the economy of the Middle Niger valley was resistant to the dramatic swings in the coastal export economy. To some extent, trans-Saharan trade competed with Atlantic imports. With the exception of war material, most consumer goods available through Atlantic trade could be supplied more cheaply through trans-Saharan routes. Manufactured goods occasionally arrived via trade routes along the desert edge from Senegambia.[73]

Until the Masina jihad of 1816, the routes used by the Maraka suggest both competition with Jenne for control over the regional trade and a certain division of labor. Jenne controlled the Niger-Bani axis to Bobo Juulasso and the connecting routes on to Kong, Bondouku, and Salaga. The Bani route to the gold and kola fields of the Volta river systems was well traveled and certainly profitable. Maraka traders, on the other hand, controlled the Niger route to Kankan and therefore the artery leading to the kola fields of Wasalu and the gold fields of Bure. By the mid 1830's, when

Jenne's share of the trade declined, Maraka merchants worked both the Niger and the Bani routes and they traded in the forest-edge entrepôts of Kankan, Sikasso, Bobo Juulasso, Ojenne, Man, and Tengrela. Although the commercial importance of individual towns changed during the nineteenth century, each one supplied the Maraka with a similar assortment of goods, in which firearms, guinée cloth, and pearls figured significantly.[74]

Along the Niger and Milo river routes to Kankan and the Wasulu markets, the Maraka were predominant. This predominance has considerable significance for our understanding of the operation of pre-industrial long-distance trade. Traders had virtual monopolies over goods and services within their home regions and often along the routes they commonly used. Here they could count on more secure and perhaps higher profits than along the routes where they had no commercial advantages over other traders.

Maraka merchants' decisions concerning destinations were contingent on market information but were finally determined by their desire to return home before the new agricultural cycle. The Maraka were not archetypical itinerant traders who bought and sold continuously along the routes, maximizing small profits by shrewd deals. Instead, they were sophisticated managers of complex production-commercial firms who constantly balanced commercial profit against investment in production. They exported an assortment of goods that reflected the particular comparative advantages of the Middle Niger valley in the continental trade of West Africa. To the desert-side, the Maraka exported grain, cloth, slaves, and occasionally kola. To the south, Maraka traders carried salt, dried fish, slaves, and locally produced indigo-dyed cloth. After the early nineteenth century, slaves from the Middle Niger valley no longer moved southward; usually they moved westward and northward into the desert and sahel. During Samori's state-building endeavors, the slave trade from Wasulu flowed northward to the Middle Niger valley along many of the same routes that had carried slaves southward 50 years earlier. Well into the twentieth century, slaves were traded to western markets of Senegambia and Guinea.[75]

The Maraka had two predominant forms of long-distance trade: they transported goods by caravans and canoes. While the two forms of transportation were mutually supportive, riverine transport was more efficient. A colonial official in 1892 estimated that it cost six times more to move a quantity of goods by caravan than by canoe.[76] The same was probably true in the earlier centuries as well, and canoes were therefore used whenever possible in long-distance trade. Significant constraints, however, had to be overcome before the potential of riverine transport could be achieved. Until the Segu state promoted a group of professional fishermen-transporters, riverine transport in the Middle Niger valley was relatively undeveloped.

The hydrology of the river posed its own restrictions on long-distance canoe travel. Sotuba rapids, in particular, marked the transition from narrow riverbed to wide riverine basin. As described by Mungo Park, Sotuba was not an insurmountable barrier: "The king of Bambara's canoes . . . frequently pass the rapids by keeping close to the left bank; persons [are] stationed on the shore with ropes fastened to the canoes, while others push it forward with long poles."[77] But this particular solution might not be available to all travelers of the river. Even when Sotuba was forded, canoes could only partially offset the costs of long-distance trade to the kola entrepôts of the forest zone, because merchants still needed to locate alternative forms of transport beyond the point accessible by canoe. Although canoes could provide reasonable security, passengers and cargo were prone to predators lying in wait by the side of the rivers. Because they had limited capacity to change routes around unhospitable regions, canoe transport was highly sensitive to political conditions.

Maraka traders therefore had some choice in how and where they were going to conduct their business. Depending on the itinerary of their expected trade, they could use either canoes or caravans. Canoes traded mostly downstream to Timbuktu; caravans went westward to the Gajaaga commercial centers, southwestward through Kankan and onto the Sierra Leone–Guinea corridors, and southeastward to the kola entrepôts of Wasulu and Bonduku. Each form of trading had to meet and resolve distinct problems. Each provided advantages the other did not. Each offered considerable profits, but also attendant risks.

Caravans

The caravan was the basic institution for moving goods overland. Curtin has argued that the caravan was a flexible unit capable of altering its size and destination in response to perceived dangers. Passing through politically unsettled areas, caravans were often large, thereby providing their members with mutual protection. Once the danger passed, the caravan divided into smaller units, giving flexibility to merchants dealing in different commodities or working on different commercial timetables. The caravan Caillié joined in 1828 en route from Tengrela to Jenne consisted of 500 to 600 members. Other caravans contained as many as 2,000 people. Hopkins described the caravan as "slow moving markets, selling some of their goods on the route and paying for foodstuffs and services as they went."[78] The Maraka caravans my informants described were significantly different.

Maraka caravans rarely had more than thirty or forty merchants. Since they were small, the caravans maintained a rapid pace to their destinations, often 750 kilometers away, and returned before the end of the dry season. Merchants usually packed enough dried and ground grain to last the first leg of the trip, which not only reduced overhead but allowed the self-sufficient caravans to avoid small villages whenever possible and minimize the daily effort to set up and break camp. The large slow-moving caravan that Caillié described actually spent much more time in villages than between them.[79]

In Caillié's caravan, most merchants headloaded. A few used donkeys. In Maraka caravans, donkeys were the most common form of transport. When necessary, poor Maraka traders headloaded a shipment of dried fish and indigo-dyed cloth and returned with a load or two of kola carried by slaves. Most Maraka merchants used one or several donkeys, rarely if ever using pack oxen or camels, which carried heavier loads but were more expensive and less appropriate for the often rugged terrain along the southern and southwestern routes. Curtin argued that 74 percent of the goods transported in the Western Sudan were carried by camels, 6 percent by pack oxen, and 20 percent by donkeys.[80] These figures may reflect the global movement of goods, but the actual composition of carriers along regional trade routes was probably very different. The merchants in caravans entering Bamako in 1890 and 1891 used an average of 4.2 donkeys for every pack ox. Since there were virtually no camels on the trade route through Bamako, about 80 percent of the goods carried by animals were carried by donkeys.[81] Most Maraka in the Middle Niger raised their own donkeys, but an active trade in donkeys took place between Maraka cities and the outlying Bambara villages. Locally, donkeys could be had for as little as several hundred cowries, although some sold for as much as 40,000 cowries.[82] Because the Maraka maintained a rapid pace on their commercial expeditions, animal losses were often quite high. Maraka were then obliged to buy donkeys at high prices along the route.

In addition to carrying their own food, Maraka merchants provided most of their own protection. Caillié remarked that "bandits always attacked the Malinke merchants who crossed the woods near Kankan, but never the Saracolet [Soninke or Maraka] caravans, because they know that the latter carry firearms and that the former are not armed as well. Before crossing the woods, the Saracolets take care to fire a volley of shot."[83] This tactic informed bandits that an ambush would cost them dearly. No matter how well armed, Maraka merchants maintained scrupulous relations with the rulers of the areas they traveled through. They could not protect themselves against the formal power of the state.

The ultimate safety and well-being of the Maraka caravan was in the hands of the *kulukuntigi* (Bambara: *kulu*, caravan; *kuntigi*, leader), who was always selected by mutual consent. Since the Maraka caravan was small, membership was usually limited to kinsmen and close friends. Whenever possible, traders were drawn from within one Maraka town. Only rarely was it necessary to seek additional members from kin and trusted acquaintances in another Maraka town. Trusted slaves could join a caravan, but only as agents for their masters.

The caravan leader was expected to be experienced in both the art of commerce and conciliation. Only an experienced trader with a reputation for integrity, a knowledge of the dialects along the caravan's route, and a history of commercial success was chosen to lead a caravan. On rare occasions, a marabout might lead a caravan, because his control over magical knowledge provided extra protection and the promise of good fortune. At the very least, a marabout was called on to provide proper sacrifices and prayers before the caravan departed.[84]

The kulukuntigi's leadership extended throughout the course of the voyage and encompassed several roles. He represented the caravan in dealings with local officials and he offered the necessary presents (tolls) for the right to cross territories safely. He was also responsible for gathering and evaluating market information. Whenever the caravan came in contact with other merchants, a lively exchange of information about prices, supplies, political conditions, and gossip took place. Not all the information was treated with equal respect, however. The Maraka paid most attention to information received from fellow Maraka or other merchants with reputations for honesty. After evaluating the information, the leader could alter the itinerary. He accepted final responsibility for his decisions, and if he made poor choices he did so at the price of his commercial reputation. For all this, the kulukuntigi was not paid a service fee. On the contrary, he was investing in less tangible rewards, since each successful voyage increased his commercial reputation. A solid commercial reputation was necessary to become a broker.[85]

The *jaatigi* (Bambara: broker) was crucial to the operation of the Maraka commercial system. Abner Cohen has argued that the trade diaspora emerged as a solution to numerous technical problems of pre-industrial trade across heterogeneous social environments. To fill the need for information, speedy dispatch and handling of perishable goods, credit, and adjudication, a trade diaspora comes into being. Cohen defines a trade diaspora as a dispersed but highly interrelated network of communities that maintains its self-consciousness through the manipulation of identity. Faced with the threat of assimilation in an alien environment, a trade diaspora continues to function only as long as it maintains a sense of ethnic exclusivity. A shared ethnic identity, crucial to the operation of diaspora, was often multilayered and could be adjusted to fit different situations. The Hausa kola merchants Lovejoy studied all considered themselves Hausa on the routes to Salaga, but in the Sokoto Caliphate they clearly differentiated among themselves.[86] Although the trade diaspora may define itself in ethnic terms, it does not necessarily limit itself to servicing members of the same ethnicity. The solutions to the technical problems of trade by one ethnic group were nearly the same as those of another. Curtin draws attention to the development of a sense of supranationalism among Muslim traders in the Western Sudan. Especially outside their home regions, where they no longer had significant commercial advantages to protect, all Muslim juula may have treated each other as comrades-in-arms.

For the Maraka, the ability to participate in an established commercial brokerage system was crucial for two reasons. First, the Maraka diaspora was constrained. A handful of Kuma had settled in Kankan in the eighteenth century. The Maraka who had established themselves in the kola city of Tengrela did so only after the troubles following the Maraka revolt of 1863–65. That the Maraka could conduct long-distance trade outside the limits of an ethnically exclusive network supports Curtin's argument that the functions of an established diaspora were open to all Muslim merchants.[87]

Second, brokerage services were crucial to the success of their trade because most Maraka merchants sold their goods wholesale. The broker housed visiting Maraka traders and stored their goods. He then conducted the exchange directly or used a *tefe* (Bambara: jobber or agent) to locate sellers with the goods the Maraka merchants wanted. Ideal transactions involved direct exchanges, for instance a load of salt for a load of kola. If the bargain involved assortments (perhaps salt, dried fish, and dyed cloth), several buyers were probably needed. The broker received a commission from each seller and was usually responsible for the jobber's commission. Maraka merchants were aware that wholesale transactions were not as profitable as retail, but they rarely wanted to spend time dealing with smaller quantities in an open market. For the Maraka, a rapid turnaround was basic to their overall commercial strategies.[88]

Nonetheless, profits from the Maraka kola trade could be considerable. For instance, one salt bar bought for as little as 3,000 cowries in Sinsani was worth three baskets of kola, each containing 1,000 nuts, at Tengrela. Returning to the towns of the Middle

Niger, the trader unloaded his goods wholesale to a local retailer at 4,000 cowries a basket on credit. On this transaction alone, the gross profit was 400 percent. Similar profits were probably standard for the entire assortment of goods the Maraka carried with them to the forest entrepôts. The Maraka assortment consisted of salt re-exported from the desert-side trade and several types of indigo-dyed cloth, including wraps, blankets, and other luxury attire. The Maraka also traded livestock, especially horses, although the southern livestock trade grew most rapidly during the last two decades of the nineteenth century. Another Maraka export was dried fish, acquired in transactions with the Somono of the Middle Niger. These goods were all exchanged for kola, cowries, and slaves. During the late nineteenth century, slaves acquired in Wasulu were incorporated in the Maraka plantation sector or supplied to the expanding domestic market for slaves in the Western Sudan.[89]

Against the potential profits derived from this ecozonal trade, the Maraka had discrete overhead costs, including transportation, food, brokerage fees, and tolls or taxes. Most of what the traders ate on the outward voyage was derived from the surplus of their own plantations. Unless they restocked in their destinations, Maraka needed to buy food on the return trip. Transport costs were probably not excessive, especially if the trader used local donkeys and crossed the river where passage was cheap. Brokerage fees were never fixed in proportion to the amount of goods in the transaction or the services rendered. Wealthier merchants probably paid more than poorer merchants. The cumulative expenses of tolls and taxes along the route could be significant, even though merchants avoided regions where tolls were considered excessive. In the Western Sudan, taxes usually did not correspond in exact proportion to the value of the goods carried as seems to have been the case in Senegambia. On the contrary, local officials probably followed a progressive tax system that required richer merchants to pay more. The system provided latitude for both the official and the caravan leader in negotiating safe passage.[90]

During the Bambara era, Maraka merchants informed the Segu kings either directly or through their representatives in Segu of their intention to embark on a commercial voyage. If the adventure proved successful, they gave the king presents upon their return. On the routes, the Maraka paid nothing unless it was demanded. My informants claimed that they did not pay taxes but only gave presents. This reveals something of the tensions in the rulers' concern with deriving revenue from taxes on the one hand and encouraging trade on the other. Most precolonial states did not have well-developed fiscal policies. The most powerful states did not necessarily receive the greatest sums from traders. The meanest did. In other words, the Maraka usually paid protection money: they paid not to be pillaged. By receiving payment, the officials implicitly recognized an obligation to protect the strangers. There appears to be no direct correlation between trade and taxation. Some states in the interior encouraged merchants by adjudicating commercial disputes in favor of merchants and by giving them presents. Whenever possible, merchants bypassed states where they felt taxes were too high; sometimes this was not possible. Part of the initial appeal of the new Islamic states of the nineteenth century to merchants was their claim to regularize tolls under the *wusuru*, an import-export tax of 10 percent.[91]

Maraka traders also moved goods northward along the Niger river system. This form of carriage was organized differently and had to resolve a different set of technical problems. A viable riverine transport system was based on the organization of the fishermen, who controlled canoes and the knowledge of the river.

Transport and State Intervention: The Case of the Somono

Even more direct than the state's intervention in the Maraka economy was its participation in the establishment of a specialized group of fishermen. The Segu state intervened in the riverine economy to fulfill its own institutional needs. The Somono, therefore, owed their origin and their social organization to the operation of the Segu Bambara political system, but they contributed to the dynamic of the entire regional economy.

The Niger and its waterfolk have been an important part of the logic of the Western Sudanese empire systems since at least the fifteenth century. Control over the river provided a reasonable system of communication, a reliable means of transport for both troops and traders, and a steady source of protein. The exact origins of the relationship between the Niger waterfolk and the state that dominated the riverbanks is no longer traceable. Sometime in the nineteenth century, Shehu Amadu of Masina tampered with the oral traditions recorded in the Tarikh el-Fettach. His motives are not known, but his actions established historical precedents for state intervention in the riverine economy.[92] To further compound the problem of tracing their social origins, fishermen's specialized occupation resembled the endogamous occupational castes widespread elsewhere in the Western Sudan. The origin of the Bozo is therefore less clear than that of the Somono.

Bozo is the name of an ethnic group. *Somono* is the Bambara term for fisherman, or more exactly, boatman.[93] The latter is clearly an occupational category, the former is not, although Bozo tend to fish. The Bozo claim to have been among the earliest inhabitants of the region, and they have maintained their language, their culture, and their religion against often severe compulsion. The Bozo are concentrated in the interior delta region. Downstream they entered delta zones fished primarily by the Sorko, who played an important part in the life of the Songhay state. In contrast, the Somono were a professional group composed of Soninke, Bambara, Malinke, Bobo, Minianka, Bozo, and other groups in the Western Sudan. All Somono speak Bambara and they became Muslims during the eighteenth and nineteenth centuries. The Somono were centered in the heartland of the Middle Niger valley around Segu and they established settlements along both banks of the river from Nyamina to Sinsani. During the early colonial era, Somono established a sprawling quarter along the riverbanks of Bamako.[94]

Somono traditions stress the circumstances of their insertion within the Segu Bambara state. Earlier in this chapter I applied the notion of a social contract to the relationship between the king and his slave warriors. The same concept, with slightly different connotations, can also be applied to the relationship between the king and the Somono. In essence, the state fostered the growth of the Somono in exchange for goods and services. But the notion of a social contract does not in this case imply a relationship between juridical equals. The Somono were originally slaves and therefore dependent on the state. In the Umarian political economy, the Somono retained their subordination to the state, but their forms of social production were much less dependent on state intervention.

In 1864, Mage recorded the basis of the social contract between the Somono and the state:

> The Somono are of Soninke origin. They maintain that they fell as slaves into the hands of the king of Segu, who proposed to them that they make canoes and fish for him. They succeeded very well and the king gave them slaves to teach their trade. Thus, after each expedition, he gave them a portion of his share of slaves. The Somono expanded along the littoral, forming in each village a type of corporation, which lives apart, works, and transports [goods and people] by canoes, of which they have a monopoly, and which provides them with many cowries, especially during market days.[95]

The Segu kings' success in developing a group of fishermen indicates cleary how the dynamics of reproduction in warrior states influenced the wider economy of the region. By the end of the Ngolossi era, the Somono had effectively colonized the river and in the process provided efficient transport and daily supplies of fish. In return for a steady stream of new recruits and the exclusive right to navigate and fish the river, the Somono paid a special tax directly to the king in cowries, fresh fish, and other produce. Moreover, the Somono also provided a ferry service for the movement of personnel and information, manufactured gunpowder and carried it into battle, and repaired and built the walls of the king's palace and other fortifications in the state. Because of the importance of their services, the Somono were under the direct protection of the king and were never re-enslaved.[96]

Through state intervention into the organization of the Somono, the fishermen of the Middle Niger altered the technical character of fishing and expanded production. Somono fishing was based on a mixture of small nets handled by individuals or a small group, and large nets requiring considerable management and manpower. Such large-scale fishing, called *basama*, was a complex cooperative venture that took advantage of the river's hydrology and the organized manpower available to the Somono. Basama groups used nets, of 300 meters or more, that spanned the river basin. This type of fishing was more productive than using small nets or blocking the streams or shores as the Bozo typically did. Basama were organized by Somono chiefs, who received a portion of each day's catch or the entire catch of the first day.[97]

The Segu state's control over the river came slowly. By the time of Park's second visit to the Middle Niger valley in 1805, the Somono were clearly part of the Segu state's forces, but other fisherfolk were not. Even within the heartland of the state, Park described how the owner of a canoe refused to comply with the orders of Monzon's agent to deliver the canoe:

> Bookari sent four of the Somonies over to the town on the opposite side of the river to . . . requisition a canoe for carrying part of our baggage. The people refused to give the canoe and sent the Somonies back without it. Bookari went immediately with all the Somonies; and having cut the owner of the canoe across the forehead with his sword and broken his brother's head with a canoe paddle, he seized one of his sons and brought him away as a slave with the canoe.[98]

Park's account made clear that not all the fishermen along the Middle Niger were equally dependent on the state. The Somono were clearly at one end of a continuum of state-community relations. They also did not form a homogeneous unit. Many were recruited from the king's share of his booty. Others, such as the Bozo of Banankoro, were resettled close to the Segu heartland during the reign of Da Monzon. Others chose to become Somono by submitting to the Somono chiefs and to the state, and by fishing in the waters of the Middle Niger valley. The social boundaries surrounding the Somono were therefore permeable; their ethnic identity was related to an occupation, a political relationship, and gradually, throughout the eighteenth and nineteenth centuries, an Islamic and pacific tradition. The Djire family, who consider themselves Somono, were the imams of Segu and acted as the king's marabouts.[99]

The pattern of Somono settlements also reveals the long arm of the state. Somono communities on the right bank of the Niger appeared with curious regularity about fifteen kilometers apart.[100] This regular pattern clearly represents a discipline imposed from above. It also indicates that Somono were largely responsible for intrastate communications. In 1863, when Mage and Quinton were taken by canoe from Nyamina to Segu, this network was organized as follows:

> Each of our canoes received a skipper and two crew members at Nyamina; besides, at each village one gets a [new] crew, which thus relays from station to station. This operation creates a certain loss of time, especially at night, when one must wake the boatmen. This service, however poor it may be, had been, I was told, organized by El Hadj [Umar] for his needs. This was the beginning of order, which I could only applaud. But later I learned that this, as all else, the conquerors took from the vanquished, and that this service had existed since the creation of the Somonos.[101]

In addition to the benefits already discussed, the Segu king received a share of the tariffs collected by the ferrymen. As early as 1796, Park remarked that the king of Segu used some of his slaves to carry people across the river. Park mused that the king's share of the tolls collected by the ferrymen, even if it was only ten cowries a person, amounted to a considerable annual income. A century later, the cost of simple passage was 80 cowries, and the patterns of revenue sharing were far more complex.

Among the numerous variants recorded, the standard model divided the revenue into two or three parts: if it was divided into two, the king or chief of the village received one part and the chief of the Somono the other; if it was divided into three, the king or village chief, the chief of the Somono, and the ferrymen each received one part. Another method was to give the entire proceeds of market-day ferrying to the boatmen. Boatmen most certainly laid claim to a portion of their labor, and although we have no indication of grievances during the Bambara period, the Somono did not hesitate to lodge complaints with French officials when they were not promptly paid. In the absence of more direct data for the Bambara state, we can only assume that the greater complexity of revenue sharing at the turn of the twentieth century reflected the decline of the state's hegemony over the river.[102]

Control over the river and greater access to riverine transportation translated into a commercial opportunity for Maraka merchants. River transport facilitated the movement of bulky cargoes over long distances, and led to an important opening for the surplus grains produced on Maraka plantations. Timbuktu depended almost wholly on imported cereals, and although most of its needs were met by the merchants of Jenne and the interior delta, Maraka traders entered this trade and offered strong competition. Maraka traders turned considerable profit from the movement of cereals and slaves downstream to Timbuktu and realized a sizeable return on the salt they imported on the return leg of their voyage.

It is not clear when the large-scale movement of cereals along the Niger began. By the sixteenth century, Leo Africanus described the canoe trade between Jenne and Timbuktu. In 1805, Park received a sketch of the river to Timbuktu from an old Somono who had made the trip seven times.[103] The trade was probably very old.

The advantages of riverine transport were considerable. In 1897, Dubois estimated that an average 20- to 30-ton freight canoe on the Niger could transport as much produce as a caravan of 1,000 porters, 200 camels, or 300 pack oxen.[104] The commercial use of the river was not without its costs, however. Initial investment in canoes and salaries for boatmen could be costly. Losses due to leakage were common, and the sudden fierce storms on Lake Debo put smaller craft in jeopardy.[105]

Riverine transportation developed out of the traditions of fishing but involved different forms of capital investment. Freight canoes were specialized vessels that were usually unsuitable for fishing. They were also constructed differently from smaller fishing canoes, although the construction techniques and material were certainly interchangeable. Fishing canoes were often dugouts and were still in use by the end of the nineteenth century. Though limited to the size of the trees used, dugouts could be large. Park was astonished when a dugout canoe, composed of two logs attached end to end, ferried four horses and several men across the Niger.[106] The technological breakthrough in building freight canoes came when craft were constructed from several planks, which overcame the dugout's size limitations. By the nineteenth century, most canoes that plied the Middle Niger were made of calcaidra, karite, or ebony planks, which resisted water damage. Usually the planks were sewn together in a mosaic fashion to accommodate the faults in the lumber.[107] Because the boat builders did not use resins or gums to patch the planks or the holes from sewing, the boats leaked, and to minimize damage to the cargo, one or two crewmembers constantly bailed. The more water-resistant goods, such as iron slug, blocks of karite, and jars, were stored lower in the hold; cloth and cereals were loaded higher. The larger the craft, the larger the crew. A boat of 30 tons often had a crew of sixteen to eighteen plus two mates and a captain. More common, however, was a canoe of six- to ten-ton capacity manned by two crewmembers and the captain.[108]

In response to the growing demand for riverine transport during the eighteenth and nineteenth centuries, Somono established regular freight services. Somono entrepreneurs and wealthy merchants invested considerable capital in cargo canoes. In the late nineteenth century, freight canoes cost between 200,000 and 300,000 cowries.[109] Such an investment was certainly within the resources of big Maraka planters. Most merchants, however, could not tie up so much capital, and the riverine transport system therefore provided passage to both individuals and groups. Individuals could purchase passage and cargo space; several merchants could rent an entire canoe.

In the late nineteenth century, passage from Jenne to Timbuktu cost 1,250 cowries, and a 100-kilogram load traveled the same route for 1,500 cowries. From Sinsani, passage cost 2,000 cowries and a 100-kilogram load cost 1,500 cowries.[110] The availability of both good transport and a steady market for grains, slaves, and other locally produced commodities stimulated in the Niger river commercial system a growth that had far-reaching implications for the structure of the Seguvian social formation. The viability of both the Maraka plantation sector and the river transport industry were intimately related.

The river, however, was always a central element in the political economy of the region, and political conditions severely influenced the operation of this commercial corridor. The establishment of the caliphate of Hamdullahi and its control over the river along the interior delta influenced the operation of the riverine system. Masina attempted to establish a regular system of import and export taxes, but it is otherwise unclear how actively it intervened in the riverine trade.[111]

* * *

The webs of relationships that characterized the economy of the Middle Niger valley and its place in the continental commerce of West Africa were determined by the actions of the state. The perpetual crisis of state power, under which the Segu Bambara state operated, led the state to intervene in the economy of the Middle Niger valley. The consequences of this intervention were experienced unevenly. On the fringes of the state, enslavement led to depopulation and to insecurity of investment. Within the central zone of the state, the war economy led to the articulation of specialized producers. The social organization of production sometimes changed considerably. The Maraka invested extensively in slaves, who formed the base of the complex commercial and productive enterprises the Maraka managed. The Somono emerged as a group of specialized fishermen and transporters. Webs of relationships expanded outward from the Middle Niger valley and linked producers across ecological zones. Despite the constant threat that state power would decompose and that slave warriors would pillage randomly, the Segu Bambara state coincided with a period of marked economic growth in the Middle Niger valley. Despite the persistence of many of the same institutional and social factors, the Umarians did not establish the same conditions for the reproduction of social relations of production.

THREE

The Umarian State and the Economy, 1861-1890

In 1861, Segu fell to the army of al hajj Umar Tal, a cleric from Futa Toro in the Senegal River valley. The Umarians established a warrior state significantly different from its Bambara predecessor. Umar, his advisors, and many of his followers were guided by the vision of a revitalized Islamic society. They failed, however, unable to bring this vision to reality. Their failure to control and direct state power and their failure either to replicate the forms of Bambara state intervention in the economy or to establish new patterns had profound effects on the economic and social history of the region.

Of the three states examined in this study, the Umarian example underlines most clearly the consequences of state intervention in the economy. Both the Bambara state and later the French colonial state encouraged economic expansion; the Umarian state discouraged investment in either production or commerce. The consequences of the Umarian system of state on the economy were not the product of misguided management. With the beginning of the widespread rebellions against the Umarians in 1863 and after the death of Umar in 1864, the Umarians in Segu were no longer able to use the resources of the state to control production directly.

The Maraka revolts of 1863–65 were central to the profound crisis in state power. Especially after the Umarians' failure to suppress the revolts, Umarian warriors depended for their subsistence on petty predation and direct extraction of surpluses from local communities. They seemed incapable of freeing themselves from this dependence, and the local communities never felt secure enough to risk capital investment in production or in easily appropriated trade goods. The Umarian forms of intervention in the economy led to downward cycles of economic investments throughout the Middle Niger valley. The patterns of accumulation for both the Umarians and the local populations reflected these patterns.

The state's influence on the economy was uneven throughout the region. Producers and traders along the river, which had been the center of commercial and productive activities during the Bambara period, suffered the most. Maraka who had moved to the Beledugu frontier towns of Banamba and Touba beginning in the 1840's benefited from the decline of the old established Maraka towns of Sinsani and Nyamina. Although the Umarians did what they could to discourage traders and producers alike, Banamba and Touba developed and refined the Maraka plantation system. The Beledugu Maraka communities owed their good fortune to their location along the crucial western corridor, which tied together the western and eastern parts of the Umarian state, and to the development of two new warrior states in the southern savanna led by Samori in Wasulu and Tieba in Kenedugu. Despite changes in local conditions, the nature of West African market demand continued to stimulate trade and production across ecological zones.

This chapter begins with a history of the Umarian conquest of Segu and its military organization. I examine how the Maraka, who were among the leading Muslim inhabitants of the Middle Niger valley, viewed the jihad and why they revolted against the Umarians in 1863. I then examine the nature of the Umarian intervention in the economy and explore what this meant for the structure and performance of the regional economy between 1861 and 1890.

The Umarian Conquest

Umar was one of the few political and religious leaders of the great nineteenth-century Islamic revival in West Africa to have actually made the pilgrimage to Mecca. His pilgrimage, which began in 1825 and lasted nearly a decade, exposed him to the debates and political struggles that were transforming the Islamic world.[1] On his return to West Africa, Umar helped disseminate the Tijaniyya message and participated in the state-building enterprises in the Central Sudan. He became a trusted advisor of Muhammed Bello, the caliph of the Sokoto Caliphate. When Bello died in 1837, Umar began his long homeward journey, passing through both Hamdullahi and Segu. In both states, Umar threatened the established political order. He eventually settled in Jegunko, in the foothills of the Futa Jalon in late 1840. This is where Umar began his own state-building enterprise.

Jegunko symbolically straddled the fringes of the Futa Jalon theocratic state and the pagan world of the savanna. The Jegunko settlement was a partial withdrawal from the temporal world demanded of Sufi followers, yet not the complete *hijra* that in the model of the Prophet usually preceded a more militarist phase of jihad. Umar spent nearly ten years in Jegunko. He traveled and preached widely, and wherever he went, he called on the people to abandon their insincere and incomplete ways. New followers flocked to Jegunko and Umar's community became a political threat to his neighbors, especially Almamy Umar of Futa Jalon, who had just returned to power after a bloody succession crisis. Umar Tal was forced to decide between possible reconciliation with the almamy or further withdrawal from the territories of Futa Jalon.[2]

In 1849, Umar moved his community from Jegunko to Dingiray. The move was modeled on Muhammed's flight from persecution and pollution, and it signaled the transition from peaceful to militant phases of jihad, marked by the further cleansing of the heart and soul before the excision of unbelief. Umar prepared for jihad by teaching, by military training for his *talaba* (Arabic: students, disciples; singular, *talib*), and by purchasing arms and ammunition. He continued to look toward Futa Toro, both for recruits and for steady supplies of arms.[3]

When Umar's neighbor the animist King Yimba Sako of Tamba, attacked Dingiray in 1852, Umar was ready to begin his jihad. The early victories of the jihad forces were instrumental in attracting additional followers and transforming Umar's students and followers into a powerful military force. By the time Umar brought his jihad to Bambuk, Bundu, and Khasso in 1854, his army numbered about 12,000 soldiers. In 1855, Umar conquered the Massassi Kulubali state of Kaarta, gaining Nioro, the Massassi capital and an important desert-edge town. Nioro remained the seat of his new state until he launched his campaign on Segu in 1859.[4]

The conquest of Kaarta had been swift, but transforming the region into an Islamic state proved difficult. Umar's talaba considered themselves conquerors, and they wanted to enjoy the fruits of their victory. The excesses of Umar's followers such as Alfa Umar, who was charged with destroying the pagan idols and converting the animists, enflamed the defeated Kaartans into widespread resistance. Throughout the Umarian empire, periodic rebellions and broken alliances made effective rule difficult. During the Nioro period, which lasted from 1855 to 1859, life was hard for the talaba; the material rewards they had expected from bringing Islam to pagan Kaarta proved illusory.

Had Umar called his jihad at another time or at another place, the history of the Western Sudan might have been different. He began building his state at exactly the same time that his French counterpart, Louis Faidherbe, began expanding French control over Senegal, and both empire builders claimed the same areas, the Upper Senegal, where they clashed in 1857. The encounter was a telling one. First, Umar failed to capture the French post of Medine, perhaps his first significant military defeat. Second, Umar learned the power of French military technology and managed to capture two French cannon, which provided tactical advantages in his conquests of the Middle Niger. Third, the French themselves learned to appreciate the military potential of Umar's troops and accordingly launched aggressive countermeasures that denied the Umarians access to the western bank of the Senegal. Finally, the failure of the Medine campaign led Umar to redirect his efforts eastward into the country of the animist Bambara of Segu. While recruiting heavily in Futa Toro in 1858–59, he and his followers looked eastward to the Middle Niger valley for a secure military and agricultural base and for the home of their new state (see Map 4).[5]

In early 1860, Umar marched triumphantly through the Beledugu towns of Merkoya and Damfa at the head of an army that probably consisted of 25,000 recruits and 10,000 women, children, and slaves. He met and defeated the Segu army under

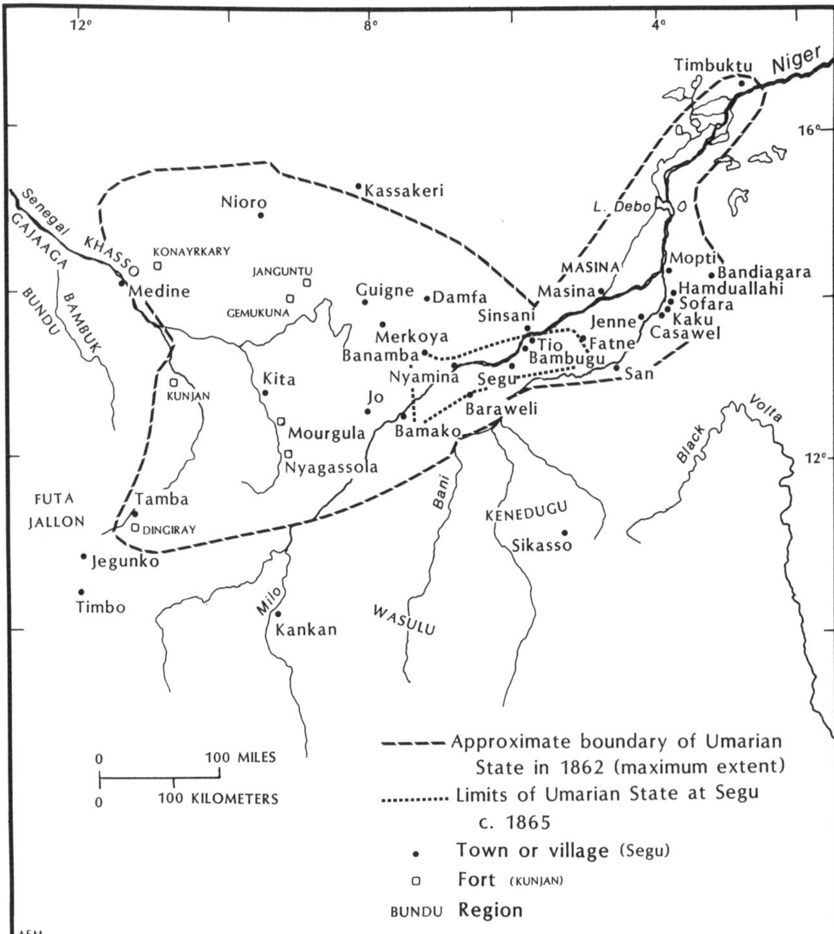

Map 4. The Umarian State, 1861–1890

Kaban Badji, the nephew of the Segu king, at Nganu in Beledugu. The Umarians marched into Banamba the next day.[6]

How the Umarians consolidated their hold over the seven Maraka cities of Beledugu is representative of their attempts to establish administration in conquered territories that were already Muslim. Umar bypassed Banamba, a market town, in favor of the neighboring town of Touba, a religious center. Perhaps his choice was prompted by his general disdain for merchants. In Touba, Umar installed a local cleric as both imam and cadi. That one man should have both these roles puzzled my informants, since the separation of their roles was basic to Islamic political theory. Umar's decision nevertheless reinforces the notion that the Umarians favored personal rule rather than new institutions as an administrative strategy. Not surprisingly, Touba and its chiefs remained loyal to the Umarians until the end.[7]

The march through Beledugu was exhausting. Shortages of food and water plagued the Umarians until they reached Nyamina. Between May and September 1860, Umar rested his troops and attracted additional followers. Among the new followers were the Maraka from Gulumba and Medine-Sako, located between Touba and Nyamina, who eventually settled in Baraweli at the head of the southern trade corridor leading to the kola and slave markets of the southern savanna. Fresh Futanke recruits from Nioro arrived on the eve of the major confrontation with Segu.[8]

The Bambara king of Segu, Bina Ali Jara, brought what force remained of the crumbling Segu state to bear at the left-bank garrison of Woitala. The excitement and fear of the impending struggle with the pagan forces of Segu are clearly portrayed in the Umarian chronicles. The armies were well matched. One of Umar's chroniclers, Cheikh Kamara, asserted that the Segu army under the command of the king's son Tata was 35,000 strong. Mage learned from Umarians active in that campaign that Segu's army was not larger than 20,000.[9] The superior weaponry of the Umarian forces, especially the cannon used to flatten the earthen walls of Woitala, turned the battle in their favor. Casualties on both sides were high; the Umarians captured 700 prisoners and 560 horses.[10]

In September 1860, Umar entered Sinsani as befitted a conqueror. He then prepared for the remaining tasks of defeating Segu and entered into a diplomatic and legalistic contest with Hamdullahi. During his five months in Sinsani, he exchanged a heated correspondence with Amadu III of Masina and with the al-Bekkay Kunta of Timbuktu.[11] The steady expansion of Umar's jihad in Kaarta worried Hamdullahi. Since its establishment,

Hamdullahi and Segu had been inveterate enemies. As late as 1855, Masina forces regularly raided the Segu state, often penetrating deeply into the central zone. Amadu III sought to capture Sinsani and use its resources against Segu. After the defeat of Hamdullahi's forces against the Umarians in the battle of Kassakeri in Kaarta, a leading Hamdullahi advisor, al hajj Seidou, proposed an alliance with Bina Ali, king of Segu. He argued that the people of Segu would prefer the rule of Amadu III, a neighbor, to that of an unknown marabout. Moreover, such an alliance would void Umar's justification for jihad, since the region would then be under Muslim influence. The correspondence between the Umarians and the Masinankes revolved around the central issue of whether Amadu III committed apostasy through his alliance with Segu. In defense of his actions, Umar maintained that Amadu's aid to the Segu armies during Umar's march to the Niger and his subsequent protection of the faama of Segu constituted reprehensible acts. In his response Amadu III argued that Ali of Segu had converted and destroyed the Segu idols, and that Segu was both Muslim and under Masina's protection. Therefore, Umar's military invasion of the Middle Niger region encroached on territory already under Muslim rule. In conclusion, Amadu III demanded that Umar immediately depart from the region. Umar continued to assert that any alliance with pagans reduced both parties to the state of nonbelievers.[12]

These are the Muslim perspectives on the alliance. But how did Segu view it? I have no evidence of how Bina Ali conceived of this alliance or of how he balanced what was certainly a very controversial position among his own warriors. Moreover, an alliance that demanded Segu's subordination threatened the centrality of state power at Segu. We should thus be skeptical about Bina Ali's conversion. Bina Ali may have consciously misled Hamdullahi's emissaries, who came to inspect Segu's commitment to Islam, by directing them to the Muslim Somono quarters, while he secretly protected the Segu idols.[13]

By January 1861, Hamdullahi mobilized its army. Under the military command of Balobbo, Amadu III's uncle and his unsuccessful rival for leadership of the Dina, Hamdullahi amassed 8,000 cavalry, 5,000 infantry, and 1,000 musketeers. The remnants of the Segu army joined Balobbo's forces at Tio on the right bank of the Niger opposite Sinsani. For two months neither side acted as they waited for the waters of the Niger to recede. Waiting probably became intolerable for Umar's talaba, who were still heady from their successful campaigns through Kaarta and the strategic victory at Woitala. They were anxious to continue onward. In the middle of February 1861, soldiers aboard two rival fleets of canoes began shooting at one another. Acting without Umar's permission, about 500 talaba attacked a village near Tio. The Masina army captured and massacred them. The next day Umar divided his army into two wings and under the cover of darkness crossed the Niger. Umar's army crushed the Bambara and Masina forces at Tio and marched to Segu. Before he left Sinsani, Umar posted a garrison of some 1,200 soldiers under the command of talib Bakary Tako and appointed Koromama Kuma chief.[14]

By March 1861, Umar was titular head of the Segu Bambara state. But his actual control was far from complete. Bina Ali, his family, the surviving slave warrior chiefs, and what remained of the Segu army dispersed. Some fled to the right bank of the Bani, others to the left bank of the Niger, and still others, including Bina Ali, toward Hamdullahi. At Segu, Umar found the Jara storehouses full of treasure, which he distributed among his army. The Jara gold alone was reportedly worth about twenty million francs.[15] Umar also discovered the Segu idols, which vindicated his argument against Amadu III.

In March, Balobbo reorganized the Masina army and moved toward Segu. The Masina army was again routed and Umar decided to secure his control over the Middle Niger region by conquering Hamdullahi. A decisive battle against Hamdullahi's forces was fought at Cayawel, in which Amadu III was seriously wounded. Jenne fell next, and Hamdullahi itself posed little threat to Umar's steady march. Many Masinanke changed sides and joined Umar's army. With the capture of Jenne and Hamdullahi, the Caliphate's military organization and power dissolved, at least temporarily.

Umar's victories over Segu and Hamdullahi had been swift. By early 1863, however, resistance to the Umarian conquest flared throughout the Middle Niger valley and Masina. In Masina, Sidi Ahmad al-Bekkay Kunta of Timbuktu led part of this new military activity. By June 1863, Umar's forces were under siege in Hamdullahi and suffering greatly. Umar and his companions fled an embattled Hamdullahi and sought refuge in the hills. There, in February 1864, Umar and his close followers met their end. Umar's death heralded a serious crisis in the extended Umarian state.[16] Uncertainty of succession, Amadu Shehu's early inability to command leadership, and endemic resistance created conditions that favored the decentralization of the Umarian state.

Local Perspectives on the Jihad: The Maraka

Most histories of the Umarian conquest of the Middle Niger valley view the events from the perspective of the Umarian community.[17] This is a history of the forward march of the Umarian experiment and of its successes and failures, but it remains one-sided in its appreciation of what that experiment actually meant to the non-Futanke actors involved. Oloruntimehin, for example, has argued that Umar manipulated internal political conflicts in the areas he conquered to his own advantage.[18] This view credits Umar with initiating political action. An analysis of events from the Maraka towns provides an alternative perspective. Instead of being passive recipients of political change imposed from without, well-developed political factions within Maraka towns manipulated the opportunities offered by Umar's conquest. Because the Maraka were Muslims, their experiences also provide insight into what Umar's movement promised and what it actually delivered. The jihad, after all, was legitimated by its commitment to further dar al-Islam.

The Maraka experience suggests that there was no uniform Muslim response to Umar's jihad. The events of 1859–65 were motivated as much by local ambitions and loyalties as by ideologies. Devotion and the promise of participating in a larger Islamic community play virtually no roles in the Maraka traditions of this era. To find the roots of the Maraka response to the Umarians, we need to return briefly to the Bambara period.

The Maraka never established nor sought political sovereignty. They were content to leave the political kingdom to the local ruling dynasties as long as their commercial and clerical activities were unhindered. The sustained commodity boom of the first half of the nineteenth century led to increased political activity and conflict over the office of the chief in Maraka towns, which had only local jurisdiction. That these conflicts were not resolved internally, but only through direct intervention of the state, reveals something about the place of these towns in the Segu Bambara political economy of the region.

Since the Bambara civil war of 1790, Kuma and Sise candidates had competed for the chieftaincy of Sinsani, a position that yielded considerable revenue in the form of market taxes, by trying to win the favor of the king and his court through lavish presents. Mage described the tactics of these two factions by saying that as Sinsani grew richer each year, it simultaneously enriched the kings of Segu.[19] The stakes increased dramatically during Kirango Ben's reign in the 1840's, as Koromama Kuma began to covet the chieftaincy. Koromama and his rival, Lamine Sise, were both wealthy merchants and large slaveowners. Koromama apparently heralded the death of the old Sise chief with no less than 3,000 slaves, as well as singers and dancers. During the three months in which Koromama and Lamine competed for the chieftaincy, the king and the slave warriors of the court "drank copiously," as the Bambara say, from the gifts they both presented.[20] Lamine Sise was eventually appointed chief. Koromama had to wait until the arrival of Umar for his next opportunity. A similar situation prevailed in Nyamina.

As early as Umar's march into Markoya in December 1859 or early 1860, Sumana Oulale, only lately of Nyamina, approached Umar. Koromama did the same when Umar was in Nyamina. Both saw in Umar an opportunity for their own political advancement. To Koromama, political power probably seemed the natural goal of one so fruitful in commerce and industry, and the natural outcome for one so generous in pious acts. Sumana Oulale, however, remains a more ambiguous figure. He was a newcomer to the Middle Niger valley. According to his family's tradition, he was a trader from Jenne who probably fled following the decline of Jenne under Hamdullahi. Other traditions point to his upper Guinean origins.[21] All traditions assert that he was a wealthy man who rather quickly became a trusted advisor to Nyamina's chief Betlen Sako. But Koromama's and Sumana's ambitions and actions were remarkably parallel.

Both men apparently sent luxurious presents and messages

welcoming Umar. In his letter Sumana claimed that the current chief of Nyamina was an animist and was married to a Bambara princess. He also let it be understood that he was an upright Muslim and would welcome Umar with open arms. Koromama's letter promised that he would open the gates of Sinsani and he underlined his longstanding and rightful claim to the chieftaincy.[22] Koromama's and Sumana's actions coincided with Umar's victories over the Segu army at Damfa and Nganu, when the prospects for continued military success seemed very bright indeed.

As Umar neared Nyamina in late May 1860, he sent a messenger to Betlen Sako demanding the city's submission. Betlen convened a meeting of Nyamina elders to discuss how best to respond to Umar's message. The city had maintained strong ties with the Bambara state and had, after its destruction in 1792 by Dese Kulubali, regained much of its commercial importance. Sumana Oulale and his friend Almamy Amara Berete convinced the council to abandon the city so that the Umarians would have no cause to stay. In so doing, they would neither sever their relationship with the Bambara nor resist the Umarians. They could, so it seemed, buy time to see what would transpire in the approaching confrontation between the Umarian and Seguvian forces. In a dramatic scene captured in the traditions, Betlen Sako left Nyamina by boat and thus renounced his claim to the chieftaincy only to see Sumana Oulale laughing on the shore. On his arrival, Umar demanded that the chief return, but to no avail. He then named Sumana chief. As a result, Betlen Sako and his followers allied themselves with the Bambara. Umar stayed in Nyamina, feasting on the wealth of the inhabitants for three months while he prepared for battle against Segu's forces.[23]

The conquest of Woitala in September 1860 opened the left bank of the Niger to the Umarians. Sinsani was certainly the prize of the region, and it was without doubt the most important commercial city to fall into their hands since the beginning of the jihad. From Woitala, Umar sent one of his talaba to Koromama to inform him of his intention to enter the city.[24] Koromama guaranteed that the gates would be opened. The chief, Lamine Sise, called a meeting of the Sinsani council and argued for combat. On discovering Koromama's secret strategy with Umar, Lamine pleaded with Koromama that resistance would be futile if the city was divided. Lamine eventually agreed to deliver the city to Umar to save it from destruction. His action resembled those of Betlen Sako in Nyamina. Both attempted to maintain cordial relations with the Bambara; both finally capitulated peacefully to the Umarians. The Maraka were certainly aware that at this point the Bambara cause was lost.[25]

Mage, who was an eyewitness to the Maraka revolts five years later, explained events differently. He argued that the wealthy merchants in both Nyamina and Sinsani initially welcomed Umar because they anticipated the introduction of Islamic law, a more orderly system of justice, and a decrease in taxes.[26] This is a reasonable perception of how Muslim merchants may have regarded the Umarian conquest. Although Islam is generally favorable to commerce, there is no functional relationship between the establishment of an Islamic state and the propagation of favorable commercial policies. The establishment of an Islamic state in northern Nigeria certainly encouraged commercial development there. Merchants in Jenne, however, felt the restrictions on trade and consumption imposed by a puritanical Islam.[27] Other variables are important, notably the establishment of a viable regional economy, its linkages within a larger interregional economy, and the level of internal security. The history of the Maraka cities within the Umarian state exemplifies the complex relationship between the state and economic growth.

The opportunism inherent in Koromama's actions was consistent with Sinsani's political orientation since the Bambara civil war. Quinton, who was Mage's companion at Segu, gave the following explanation of Sinsani's shift in allegiance:

> There are many ways of explaining the surrender of Sinsani, a village that had always lived in good relations with the king of Segu and was populated by a crowd of Bambara. The principal chiefs of Sinsani were, it was said, Soninke Muslims who would be happy to obey a chief who professed the same religion. The truth is that religion did not enter at all into this situation of changing alliances. When a situation involves wealth or property, religion plays no role in Africa as elsewhere.[28]

The Muslim revolutions of the nineteenth century obviously meant different things to different groups of Muslims. To the

Maraka, reared within a quietist tradition of Islamic practice, relatively undistinguished in their learning, and benefiting materially from their special prerogatives in commerce, the new age of Islamic militancy posed difficult questions. The Maraka had not considered a juula revolution, nor had they sought a political kingdom.[29]

Instead, they adapted themselves, chameleon-like, to changing fortunes that intruded on their commercial and productive activities. They looked forward to a continuity of state policy that would guarantee their established social and economic positions within the regional economy. As long as the Maraka felt that the state was providing an acceptable level of security, they supported the political status quo. When the Umarians fundamentally altered the regional political economy, the Maraka did not passively accept these new conditions. When the Maraka of Sinsani revolted against the Umarians in 1863, they took up arms against their fellow Muslims by forming an alliance with pagan Bambara warlords and the Muslim al-Bekkay Kunta.

But this is to anticipate developments. From the moment of Umar's arrival in Sinsani, clues about the future Umarian policy toward wealthy commercial centers began to reveal themselves. Before his entrance into Sinsani, Umar summoned Lamine Sise to request that the townspeople provide clothing for his army. The traditions attribute the following exchange to Umar, Lamine Sise, and Koromama Kuma.

> "Do you have another army besides the one here with you?" [asked the chief.]
>
> "No," replied the shaykh.
>
> "If I am incapable of clothing your army, how could I be chief of the village?" And he gave each soldier of the army, whether male or female, whether large or small, three pieces of clothing. And the shaykh was amazed. Umar's host was Koromama, who was not the chief of the village.
>
> "Do not be stunned by the chief's power. I can give to each of your soldiers a young girl together with a slave as a domestic, and all the costs of clothing will be borne by me; they will have need of nothing until my death."[30]

This dialogue is obviously allegorical, but it does reflect the ways in which the Umarians perceived the wealth of Sinsani. Without much delay, the Umarians began to harvest their rich catch. The experience of the Maraka proved how the structure of the new state, its forms of accumulation, and its reliance on warfare influenced local economic and social relations.

Warfare and the Umarian State

For Muslims, the world is divided into two parts: the abode of Islam (dar al-Islam) and the abode of warfare (dar al-harb). This duality—Islam versus unbelief and war versus non-war—was deeply embedded in the thinking and justification of Islamic statecraft. The state was called into being to bring belief to areas where unbelief reigned. Warfare thus lay at the very foundation of the ideology of state power because it justified the state's existence. Not surprisingly, warfare was a central institution in Islamic states.[31]

In both the Bambara and the Umarian cases, warfare and the division of booty were organically linked to the structure and organization of the state. But the links were different. In the Bambara case, the division of the booty was based on a set of individual contracts, each contract an affair between the faama and the warrior. That the faama claimed between half and two-thirds of the booty merely reflected the social organization of the Bambara military and the primacy of the state within it. Because of the individual nature of the contract between the state and the warriors, the faama was obligated to redistribute a handsome portion of his share to his warriors.

Islam defined a different sense of community. All Muslims were part of a larger community bound together by the *shari'a* (Islamic law). Thus the community already existed, at least in principle, and did not need to be built through judicious redistribution of resources. Moreover, it was the duty of all able-bodied free men without debts to respond to the call for jihad. They had no alternatives. Islamic law and traditions rewarded warriors through division of booty according to categories of participation and not by individual actions. Individual warriors did not receive a share of the booty they captured, as Bambara warriors did. Rather, Islamic law sanctioned a division of booty by military hierarchy: the cavalry received three times as much booty as foot soldiers.[32]

The division of booty merely reflected the costs of participation. Horses were expensive, they usually required grooms, and in Sudanese warfare horsemen were tactically superior to foot soldiers. Of the share horsemen received, however, two-thirds was destined for the care and replacement of the horse. Whereas the Bambara model encouraged individual performance, the Islamic model reinforced the fighting unit by division. As far as conditions permitted, Umarian warfare conformed to Islamic models of community and distribution of booty.

The incidence and forms of warfare therefore serve as a sensitive indicator of the complex interplay of social, political, and economic forces within the Umarian state. Forms of weaponry also indicated how well the Umarians were linked to the larger commercial world. Their sustained technological superiority over other Africans attested to the efficacy of their Senegambian recruitment network and commercial policies.

For the Umarians, a significant watershed in the political economy of the state and in the organization of warfare occurred between 1864 and 1865, which saw the demise of the Umarian army at Bandiagara and the failure of Amadu's campaigns against Sinsani. The Umarians had suffered defeat before, notably in the dramatic battle with the French at Medine in 1857, but Amadu's campaigns against Sinsani in 1863–65 revealed once and for all the fragility of the Umarian state. Until 1864, the predominant Umarian military form was the campaign, usually involving the full force of state resources. After the Sinsani campaigns, the predominant form of warfare in the Segu region was *razzia*, or small-scale and loosely structured military operations. This form of warfare scarcely promoted the centralization of state power.

The Umarian army was composed of elite cavalry troops who were largely of Futanke origin. These Futanke talaba formed an aristocracy both within the army and within the conquest state. At a time when horses were costly and in uncertain supply, the Futanke talaba occasionally fought on foot. Beyond this elite core were new Muslims who had responded to the call for conversion before the commencement of hostilities, and irregular FulBe cavalry armed with lances who were recruited from the local populations recently conquered by the Umarians. The irregulars included the forobafula, the state herders of the Segu Bambara before they joined the Umarians. The Umarian army also had contingents of animists, led by their chiefs who were allied to Umar or his successors. They were called *sofa,* to distinguish them from the mounted talaba elite.[33]

The sofa had formed the elite cavalry guard of the Segu king's troops, and were by definition "fathers of the horse." But most of the sofa in the Umarian army were foot soldiers. The subordination of the sofa to the talaba reflected a class division in the Umarian military organization. The use of the term *sofa,* which is of Malinke origin, also reflected how local traditions of warfare were grafted onto the Islamic model. In 1878, Soleillet described a sofa regiment composed of between 1,000 and 1,200 foot-soldiers divided into four wings and under the central command of a "colonel." The original core of the Umarian sofa may have been, as Saint-Martin argues, the domestic slaves of the talaba and grooms, who became warriors in their own right during the course of the campaigns.[34]

The size of the army fluctuated considerably in response to new immigrants from Futa Toro and Bundu and in response to military successes. Umar may have had only 1,100 troops at the beginning of his campaign against Bambuk in 1854. By the siege of Medine in 1857, he had 15,000 at his disposal. For his march on Hamdullahi in 1862, he had 30,000. While Umar relied heavily on the recruitment of troops from Futa Toro, his son, Amadu Shehu, made greater use of local recruits. In 1866, Amadu had 4,000 talaba and 11,000 sofa in his service. Amadu apparently did not hesitate to use animist warriors in his army.[35] After 1864 there may have been no more than 10,000-12,000 talaba under arms throughout the Umarian state. Most were isolated in their fortified garrisons. After 1865, when the conquest was over, they never again fought as a unified army.

Regular troops possessed firearms, and keeping them armed was big business. Merchants of Bakel and Medine competed with British agents from Bathurst and Sierra Leone to supply firearms and munitions to the Umarians. Amadu founded a trading fair at Guigne in 1872, midway between Segu and Nioro, probably to take advantage of the international trade in firearms and imported luxury goods. Guigne, situated in the heart of sparsely populated and hostile western Beledugu, was clearly not a natural location for commercial activity. It was at considerable risk from raids and in 1879 it was destroyed by rebellious Bambara.[36]

European military technology was rapidly changing during this period and the African markets absorbed huge quantities of obsolete weaponry.[37] Precisely because of the statewide coordination of the arms trade, the Umarian armies were usually better armed and equipped than their Bambara rivals. Soleillet described the Umarian army in 1878 in the following terms: "The troops do not have uniforms, but they are uniformly armed with flintlock European rifles in unusually good condition, and armed with power horns and leather sacks of balls. Officers have sabers and double-barreled piston-loaded firearms."[38] Irregular Umarian troops were armed with lances and assorted firearms. The rebellious Bambara also had firearms, but their equipment was often mediocre and in need of repair. When the Umarians faced African opponents, their greater firepower usually proved decisive.[39]

Before 1865, the Umarians' motivation was quite pronounced. Paul Holle, the French commander at Medine in 1857, remarked on the considerable courage of the Umarian attackers. The Umarians' courage was fostered by a belief that those who fell in jihad ascended directly to heaven.[40] But booty played no small role in assisting military ardor. In the early stages of the jihad, booty was used to reproduce the fighting unit as a whole. In most of northern and West Africa, the Maliki orthodoxy governed division of the spoils, although it is unclear how closely the Umarian army followed these dictates. Captured weapons, horses, and other strategic material were usually appropriated directly by the military command.

While the one-fifth share claimed by the *amir al-muminin* was the rule for the talaba, the same division of booty was not applied to the sofa. From the sofa, Amadu claimed half the booty, just as his Bambara predecessors had done. Among the newer troops under his command, many of them only superficially Muslim, Islamic laws of war may have been of little consequence. They often left the battle without giving up a share of the booty. But the preferential sharing of booty, which favored the talaba, sustained deep divisions within the Umarian army, profoundly affecting both the structure of the army and its operations.[41] In later stages of the jihad, as the army became disillusioned and as the state collapsed into autonomous provinces, the division of booty became even more difficult.

In the Segu region in particular, most talaba probably did not perceive themselves as permanent migrants. Some periodically returned home to Futa Toro where their families had remained. Others returned to Futa Toro when military successes became fewer and when they became disillusioned with Amadu's rule. As temporary residents, many Umarians did little if any farming or herding.[42] It is not surprising that even after a generation, the Futanke made little permanent mark on the ethnic composition of the Middle Niger valley, although this was also partly the consequence of the reverse migration of the Futanke ordered by the French after their conquest of Segu in 1890.

Islamic law and statecraft contained a more or less precise blueprint for a sophisticated public revenue system, but its implementation depended on the level and efficacy of state power and the capacity of the state to guarantee internal security. For the Umarians at Segu, a viable public revenue system remained largely unrealized because of their failure to pacify the region and control the Bambara warlords. Instead, a policy of razzia, structurally similar to the Bambara soboli, came to dominate Umarian military operations in the Middle Niger valley after 1865.[43]

In the mid-1860's and again in the 1880's, shortages of food and other goods became endemic in Segu. Mage, who accompanied the Umarians into the battle of Togo in February 1865, captured the sense of how hunger and greed motivated the Umarian army:

> The departure from the village was difficult. Each [talib and sofa] was loaded with baggage; several had sent for donkeys to carry the loot. This was a very curious spectacle: yesterday's warriors were transformed into scrap merchants. Everything appealed to them: some carried large calabashes, others sacks of millet, local lanterns that used a cotton wick soaked in karite or peanut oil; others have taken off a door, firearms, lances, or tools and equipment of the ironworker and the weaver. Others have taken cotton, tobacco, and balls of indigo; still others have a col-

umn or columns of captives. . . . About 3,500 women and children attached [to each other] by the neck are heavily laden and march under the blows of the sofa.[44]

Warriors ate well after this battle, but such victories were too infrequent. The failures of campaigns against Sinsani in 1863, 1864, and 1865 firmly entrenched the razzia as the predominant military form of the Segu Umarians after 1865.

Unlike the large campaign, razzias were usually organized spontaneously under the command of a military chief.[45] They were almost always productive. It was rare for a group not to return with a few women captives or other easily transferable booty. Mage noted that warriors hid as much booty as possible before returning to Segu. Anything marketable, such as slaves, amber, kola, firearms, and horses, was hidden and retrieved only after the formal division of booty. The concealment of firearms became commonplace. Amadu was able to redistribute only broken or poorly maintained firearms because the good ones were never delivered.[46]

As a form of military organization, razzia was well adapted to the internal tensions within the Umarian army. The army already lacked cohesiveness thanks to the uneven division of booty and the organization of ethnically segregated regiments. The talaba constituted the aristocracy of the state. Not only did they receive larger shares of the booty, but they were spared the obligation of paying taxes. Yet their privileged position did not make them consistently loyal to Amadu. Amadu accordingly tried to curtail their role by bringing more sofa into important military and civilian positions within his administration. Reliance on the sofa proved a mixed blessing, however. In 1884 Amadu's sofa troops conspired with Bambara rebels to block his march to Nioro.[47]

Both Umar and Amadu promoted the rivalry between the sofa and the talaba. While competition among the ranks had short-term rewards in increasing the fighting ability of the troops, it produced serious tensions within the army itself. Razzia, then, channeled the tensions by allowing groups to operate independently. Razzia also deflected discontent from the regime. A French administrator noted that "the [Futanke] who did not find much booty in their wars did not hesitate to show their dissatisfaction. . . . To calm them, Amadu occasionally sent them out to raid some villages."[48] Even during Amadu's flight eastward after the capture of Nioro by the French, razzia remained a basic expression of military and social organization.[49]

Finally, razzias became institutionalized in the Umarian state in response to the specific form of Bambara resistance. By 1864 or 1865 at the latest, the character of resistance in the Middle Niger valley had taken on a form that it was to retain thereafter.[50] Because most of the surviving Segu slave warriors became petty warlords, none had the organizational capacity to organize full-scale military campaigns. Their military actions were limited to razzia. A Bambara razzia could not be countered by a full-scale Umarian campaign; rather, it merely encouragd the Umarians to respond in like measure. These reciprocal raids spread disorder and insecurity throughout the Middle Niger valley.

Resistance

Throughout its 150-year history, the Segu Bambara political system barely contained the centrifugal tendencies of its warrior aristocracy. At every demonstration of political or managerial weakness, warriors asserted their independence at the expense of state power. Umar's victory over the Segu forces at Woitala and his defeat of the combined Segu-Masina forces at Tio destroyed the Segu state. The forces under Bina Ali Jara offered no resistance to the Umarian capture of Segu itself, and Bina Ali fled to Hamdullahi, where he was pursued and eventually killed. Bina Ali's death and the collapse of the Segu Bambara state freed the surviving slave warriors from participation in a coordinated military force. Yet the slave warriors survived, perhaps even thrived, in this new environment. The predominant characteristics of Bambara resistance to the Umarians were its small scale, its decentralized command, and its fluid alliances.

No warlord exerted enough influence to bully, threaten, or seduce the others into a united front. At times the warlords would fight on the same side, only to become bitter enemies shortly thereafter. It was not uncommon for one faction to leave the battle because it found another opportunity for pillage. In an era of declining returns on large-scale military investments, warlords could not rely on the loyalty of their followers, as Kegne Mari Jara was to discover during the battle of Sinsani. In reflecting on the history of Bambara resistance, the Resident of Segu in 1891 noted that "the slave warriors, captives of the faama of Segu, were for the Jaras less for reasons of real attachment than because of a community of tastes resulting from long years of pillaging and exactions accomplished together."[51] The problem of course was that a community of tastes was not enough to forge a powerful alternative to the Umarian conquest.

In 1863, Amadu had a chance to defuse Bambara resistance to his nascent political enterprise in Segu. He convened a meeting of slave warrior chiefs who had more or less allied themselves to the Umarians. When they arrived, he massacred them.[52] He probably hoped to avert a revolt, but if so he was disabused almost immediately. In late summer the inhabitants of Kaminiadugu and the left bank began a tax revolt that spread throughout the region. The 1863 revolts eventually defined both the form and character of the Umarian regime at Segu.

Over nearly 30 years, resistance in the Middle Niger valley took many forms. Perhaps the least dramatic but most damaging was the "subsistence response" taken by producers throughout the region. Farmers, herders, fishermen, and traders resisted the Umarian conquest and the subsequent forms of predation and exploitation by withdrawing from the market. They produced less, exchanged less, and therefore deprived the new state of a significant income through diminished tribute. In a region only 40 kilometers from Segu, many farmers hid their granaries deep in the bush to protect their surpluses from Umarian appropriation.[53]

Of all the forms of resistance, that of the Maraka was unanticipated. As one Umarian chronicler remarked, "the Maraka may wear wraps like women, but underneath they wear pants."[54] The Maraka of Sinsani, who had a reputation for pacifism, armed themselves and withstood the full thrust of the Umarian army at Segu for two years. Although Maraka resistance coincided with Bambara resistance, it stemmed from different causes. Maraka resistance raises important questions about the nature of the Islamic state Umar and his followers created.

For the Maraka, the great expectations of the rule of Islam promised by Umar's conquest proved ephemeral. As soon as Umar arrived, he confiscated all the revenue previously destined for the faama of Segu and the local chief.[55] After his departure, the Umarian garrison of 1,200 men remained behind to guard the rear flank. It was entirely supported and nourished by the community, and the talaba accepted no mean fare. The soldiers required the inhabitants to serve a rich meat sauce with each meal, and they commonly took anything that appealed to them. The Sinsani garrison was probably excluded from participation in the successful military campaigns of 1862 and 1863, and therefore from the booty; hence their desire for other forms of compensation.[56]

Tradition has it that Bakary Tako, the commander of the Sinsani garrison, desired not only to expropriate the wealth of the Maraka but also to humiliate them, an attitude that perhaps reflected the general disdain the Umarians had for merchants and subject peoples. Tako even demanded that the noble Maraka cultivate his personal land. To demand that the Maraka work someone else's land was to deny them the occupational characteristics of nobility and to reduce them to slaves. Bakary Tako further humiliated the Maraka by referring to them as the uncircumcised, thus denying them recognition as Muslims and justifying further extortions.[57]

In the spring of 1863, Amadu returned to Segu from the Masina campaigns because of rumors of a Bambara revolt. Once in Segu, he quickly discovered that he did not have the means to support his forces. Many Bambara had not paid any taxes that year and several regions were openly defiant. To generate revenue quickly, Amadu imposed on Sinsani a special tax in luxury indigo-dyed cloth valued at 800,000 cowries. Already humiliated by the Umarians yet fearful of military reprisals, Sinsani pleaded for a reduction in this tax. Amadu responded by doubling it, and Sinsani reluctantly paid.[58]

In August 1863, the tax revolt turned violent. The Kaminiadugu Bambara attacked a small Umarian garrison at Bambugu on the route from Segu to Sinsani; they killed forty talaba and carried off the women and children. Sarro revolted as well.[59] Three days later, the Maraka of Sinsani revolted. The Sinsani revolt was not, then, an isolated event. To the east and north the Kala Bambara had never recognized Umar or Amadu; on the right bank, the Kaminiadugu and Sarro revolts effectively cut the

Umarian forces at Segu and Masina in two. The FulBe of Masina under Balobbo and the al-Bekkay Kunta regrouped and began an offensive. By December 1863, Segu had become an island in a sea of rebellion. Widespread rebellion deprived the state of its much-needed revenue and left the soldiers hungry. Between 1864 and 1865, the cost of millet increased fivefold. By February 1864, the Umarian state in the east was reduced to two provinces, Segu and Gwenkala. In the context of the crisis within the Umarian state, the revolt of the Maraka appeared to make economic sense. The anticipated benefits of Umarian rule had not been forthcoming and the extortions leveled against the rich Maraka, the Bambara, and the Somono, revealed the collapse of the political safeguards so necessary for production and commerce.[60]

The Sinsani revolt lasted from the summer of 1863 to September 1865. In April 1864, following the Umarians' failure to capture Sinsani in the two campaigns of 1863 and 1864, the Maraka of Nyamina revolted as well. They were led by the deposed chief, Betlen Sako, who was allied with Kegne Mari, the surviving Jara leader.[61] In order to keep the crucial western corridor open, Amadu devoted his energies to suppressing the Nyamina revolt. It was the spring of 1865 before Amadu began to assemble his army for the final assault on Sinsani. The army, ten to twelve thousand strong, included talaba, Bambara sofa, and Amadu's FulBe allies. At the beginning of July, Amadu led his troops to the gates of Sinsani, where they laid siege. By September, the city had been all but reduced by famine. On September 17, just as the collapse of the Sinsani rebellion was imminent, the Umarian army lifted the siege and returned swiftly to Segu.[62]

Amadu's sudden retreat was prompted by a letter from Alassane Cierno, military commander of Segu, informing him that Kegne Mari had assembled a large army and had crossed the Bani to attack Segu. Amadu was forced to choose between Sinsani and Segu.[63] The Umarians were thus cheated of their victory and the rich booty they had hoped to gather. Despite the uneven military success of the Maraka revolts, they contributed in no small measure to the crisis of the Umarian state.

The Sinsani revolt offers a glimpse of the world of Bambara resistance and the politics of Bambara warlords. The Segu Bambara state system was based on the ability of the king to control the centrifugal tendencies of slave warriors who had their own weapons and their own followers. After 1861, the Segu king no longer controlled his warriors. When Kegne Mari dispatched his lieutenant, Mabere Kano, to aid the rebels on the left bank, he refused to return. Instead, he established his own autonomous command there.[64]

Whereas the slave warriors of the Segu state had formerly been lords of war, they now became warlords with small territorial bases. They also became highly suspicious of each other and fought the Umarians and their fellow warlords with equal abandon. Alliances were made to be broken and followers remained loyal only as long as their leaders brought them military success and booty. The small territorial bases each warlord sought to control were a new element in the Bambara warrior system, and they help explain the peculiar struggles among Bambara resistance leaders. Internecine conflicts were often waged over mere villages, since they provided their overlords with a source of food and recruits. The extent to which these areas were systematically ruled or exploited, we do not know. In 1887, Caron was struck by what he considered to be the feudal aspects of the region. "Nothing reminds me more of feudalism than the parceling of the land among Karamoko [Jara], N'To, and Mamfa."[65]

Bambara resistance and the Umarians' response had a profound effect on the regional economy and the development of state power. Widespread and decentralized resistance was hard to control, let alone defeat. Above all, uncontrolled warfare undermined the economy. It was no longer safe to accumulate wealth or invest capital, whether in trade goods, slaves, or cultivated land. Outside of selected and protected pockets of commercial vitality, trade remained severely dislocated throughout the Umarian era. The rich plantations which once surrounded Sinsani virtually disappeared. The Middle Niger valley lost its pivotal role in the commerce of the West African interior; it remained an important crossroads, but it contributed little to growth or development of the region.

The Umarians failed to control disorder within the borders of the state, let alone on its fringes. Everyone seemed to pillage everyone else. Whole villages lay in wait for caravans, ambushed them, and made off with captured goods, as the French lieutenant Gallieni was to discover in Jo. The collapse of state power was so widespread that talaba refused military commands they felt would yield little return or were hazardous. In 1880, for example, the Segu talaba refused a punitive mission against the Bambara of the Banamba region. By 1880, Umarian control over the Middle Niger valley was limited to a narrow band of land along the right bank of the Niger.[66] In these circumstances, the regional economy became sharply distorted.

Umarian State Policy and Intervention in the Economy

The Umarian state depended on commerce. The Umarians needed merchants to supply firearms, gunpowder, and luxury imports. But they also resented the wealth merchants accumulated. Merchant capital, manifested in possessions, trade goods, and productive investments, stood in marked contrast to the penury so many Futanke faced with the entrenchment of the jihad after 1865. With the institutionalization of warfare and predation within the state, the Futanke chose periodically to harvest the wealth of individuals and communities, drastically altering the established relationship between the state and the economy.

As a warrior state, the Umarians needed steady supplies of firearms and war matériel to support conquest and further the jihad. In the early years of the jihad, Futanke commercial policy was successful, providing the Futanke with sustained superiority in military technology over their African rivals. During the Nioro period (1852–59), firearms of both French and British origin were stockpiled. The French embargoes on further sales of arms to the Umarians in 1854, and again after the battle of Medine, succeeded primarily in further biasing Futanke trade and trade connections toward British factors and British sources. Mage recalled that when he arrived in Segu, Amadu Shehu gave him a cask of British sugar. As late as 1880, Gallieni stated bluntly that most goods in circulation in the Upper Senegal and Beledugu were of British origin. Throughout the 1870's and well into the 1880's, the British pursued an aggressive trade policy through their agents in Sierra Leone. The French, in turn, were anxious about British trade and British territorial designs on the interior. Only when the French resumed their conquest of Senegambia and the Western Sudan after 1879 did French goods challenge the predominant position of British goods in the Western Sudan.[67]

Maintaining commercial and kinship connections with the Futanke of the Upper Senegal remained crucial to Umarian activities in Segu. The lifeline of the state was the western corridor, which stretched from Nioro to Nyamina by way of Banamba and Touba. The trade fair the Futanke established briefly at Guigne was part of this western strategy, but its demise around 1879 exemplified the basic problems the Umarians had keeping this route open. Umarian garrisons were besieged by rebellious forces throughout Kaarta, Beledugu, and the Middle Niger. Only at considerable expense and with periodic military campaigns along the breadth of the western corridor did the Umarians manage to keep goods flowing at all. Two reports written by Gallieni in 1880 reflect the episodic character of trade along this route. He wrote from Nango that the "route from Nioro [to Segu] is the most secure and is habitually used by voyagers and traders."[68] Four months later he noted that "Amadu is always kept busy by the closure of his route through Kaarta by Bambara rebels."[69]

Security along the western corridor depended on Futanke forts, such as Gemukuna and Jangunte, and on Futanke garrisons whose duty it was to escort traders and travelers over dangerous terrain. One of the primary responsibilities of the almamy of Touba was to oversee the ferry service he provided between Banamba-Touba and Nyamina. Soleillet used this service in 1878 and left the following description:

> We arrived in a large field of the Bambara village of Sokolo, where some 150 to 200 voyagers pastured their donkeys and pack oxen waiting for the chief of the column. The chief arrived . . . mounted on a good white horse covered with a scarlet cloth richly embroidered with gold and silver braids. . . . The chief is quite young and a slave of the sultan. His name is Makhe Kanuba. He is dressed in white and armed with a sword and a rifle.[70]

Soleillet also noted that the almamy of Touba delayed the departure of the caravan as long as possible in order to increase both the numbers escorted and the revenue collected. Charging 100 to 300 cowries a load, he received considerable income.[71]

Because trade between Segu and the bulking stations of eastern Senegambia was crucial to the Umarian political economy, the Futanke could not rely entirely on independent merchants to supply their needs. If merchants were uneasy about making the perilous journey over the contested terrain between Nioro and Segu, official Futanke caravans, operating on behalf of the state, occasionally pushed through. These were predominantly royal caravans, with perhaps a handful of independent merchants tagging along to take advantage of the protection they offered. Mage noted the arrival of a caravan in Segu: "A caravan of people from Konayrkary arrived, coming to bring Amadu gunpowder and guns; several juula were with them, but the chiefs of this band were a Futanke called Amadi Boubukar [of] Tambo [and] Bakiri of Lanel."[72] Slaves often carried the loads in these royal caravans. They were not trusted, household slaves. In a caravan sent by Abibu in Dingiray to Amadu in Segu, each slave headloaded a large package, carried a firearm in each hand, and was shackled to other slaves.[73]

Amadu was not always willing or able to wait for his brothers or agents to send him supplies. He occasionally dispatched caravans from Segu with clear instructions. At Bakel, Soleillet saw a caravan led by one of Amadu's agents, Maka.

> Amadu instructed him to purchase from O'Quin, a . . . Bathurst trader, various objects in copper, including plates and cups, that are not found in our [French] factories; he will also buy, for a better price in Bathurst than in Senegal, blue calicot, which is in very high demand in Segu; [also] in Bathurst slaves sell for 100 gourds [500 francs]. . . . Having finished his purchases in the Gambia, he will return to Segu [via] Dakar and Saint-Louis and take the boat up the river route to Medine.[74]

It seems striking at first that firearms do not appear in this passage. But firearms were only part of the arsenal of the warrior state system. Periodic distribution of luxury goods, which helped give the talaba a sense of superiority vis-à-vis the inhabitants, was equally important to the viability of the Umarian state.

Juula from the Gajaaga were active on the western corridor in 1880. Some brought slaves from Segu to the markets of Senegambia. Others purchased salt in Nioro, sold it in Wasulu, and returned with slaves.[75] Merchants resident in the Middle Niger region did not trade along this corridor. They concentrated instead on the southern routes, which mushroomed with the state-building activities of Samori and Tieba. During the Segu Bambara period, the Maraka had predominated on the Niger-Milo route to Kankan, traveling on via the western highways to Sierra Leone and occasionally to the Gambia. Under the Umarians, however, they virtually abandoned this route in favor of trade with the central and eastern Wasulu. This commercial reorientation reflected a significant reorientation in the economy. Whereas during the Segu Bambara period the Middle Niger region was probably a net exporter of slaves, during the Umarian period it seems to have been a net importer of slaves. In both periods the Maraka were the principal purveyors.

Despite their need for trade and trade goods, the Futanke restricted trade. Banfo Tigana of Banamba, for example, was prevented from trading horses with Samori. He then took his load to Senegal, where he purchased "many beautiful things," which he presented to Amadu. Only then did Amadu permit Tigana to trade with Samori.[76] The example suggests a level of state intervention in commercial activity that was new to the political economy. Although their control was far from complete, the Umarians tried to designate who could trade and who could benefit. "Traders," Amadu is reputed to have said, "ought to be harvested at regular intervals in order to maintain their commercial virtues."[77] An account by Lieutenant Pietri, on the vanguard of French conquest, illustrates what Amadu had in mind:

> A Soninke, whose name was Douga, had amassed a certain fortune as a juula by trading between Nioro and the Niger. Having arrived at an age when his capacities no longer permitted these long and perilous voyages, he retired to his homeland in the neighborhood of Segu. He was not very rich, but his compatriots exaggerated the numbers of his slaves and his herds, and his renown reached the king. Douga had made enemies with several Futanke to whom he was not very generous. These intimates of the king used this pretext to slander him before the king, and awakened his cupidity and his easily provoked distrust. The Soninke was thus absolutely divested of his goods.[78]

One of my informants summed up the difference between Bambara and Umarian intervention in the economy in the form of a proverb: "There are those who say take the goods of the juula and those who say let them pass. Both are searching for a morsel of salt."[79] Rulers differed markedly in their orientation to merchants and the way they hoped to benefit from commerce. The proverb draws a distinction between rulers who preyed directly on merchants and those who benefited by encouraging commercial expansion. These were not just different styles; they were forms of state intervention that reflected profoundly different political economies and had considerable impact on the operation of the economy.

Commercial enterprise of any sort was a risky business in nineteenth-century West Africa. To add additional barriers to commerce at the level of direct state intervention, as the Futanke did, discouraged investment in mercantile and productive activities. The case of the Somono demonstrates clearly the new political economy.

The Somono had been nurtured by the Segu Bambara state, albeit for their particular contribution to its war economy, but their participation in transport and fishing had far-reaching implications for the economy as a whole. Once in control of Segu, the Futanke required the Somono to provide them with the services they had provided the Segu Bambara. But unlike the Bambara, they neither contributed new recruits nor guaranteed the Somono's economic privileges. Whereas the Segu Bambara state had intervened directly in the production process by increasing the manpower available to the Somono, the Futanke expected services and extracted surpluses. The Somono, wrote Mage,

> have the same obligations but not the same resources. They no longer receive slaves after the expeditions in which they carry the powder and the replacement firearms on their heads. But in contrast, when a Futanke prince has the need to "eat" a slave, in order to get the retail value to pay debts to an ironworker or leatherworker, he goes to a wealthy Somono and takes a slave he wants, and if the master complains or does not want to give the slave, he is beaten.[80]

Although the Somono were well enough ensconced along the river by 1861 to sustain their activities through natural reproduction, the Futanke created conditions inimical to long-term capital investment. The Somono had derived monopoly revenue from transport services and fish sales. According to Mage, who was held under house arrest in Segu during the formative years of

Futanke rule, the Somono were "in general very rich." Their prosperity was only relative, but they lived better than the conquering talaba. In addition to a supplementary tax of 20 cowries per household each week, the Somono were obliged to supply Amadu's residence with fresh fish each week.[81] They were also prey to talaba extortions. Two elderly Somono informants stated that "when a talib arrived at a village, he deposited his horse in one household [to be fed and cared for], his saddle in another, and his bridle in yet another. One could not wear elegant or richly embroidered clothes; if one did, a talib would simply take it and it became his."[82]

Not surprisingly, Amadu feared a rebellion of the Somono coincident with the Maraka revolts of 1863. As a precaution, "he deprived them of their canoes and their firearms, thereby depriving them of their means for escape, and also their principal means of existence; thereafter, they could only fish on dry land."[83] It is not clear how effective Amadu's prohibitions were, because the Somono were again ferrying troops and supplies in the middle of 1865.[84] Amadu may have had to rescind his order precisely because the Somono were so crucial to the organization of the warrior state. However, the speed with which the Somono abandoned the Futanke for the French in 1890 indicated how deep their resentments actually were.

Equally damaging to the economy of the Middle Niger valley were restrictions on riverine travel. Both Amadu and Tijani used the river politically. Amadu restricted canoe travel in areas that lay beyond his direct control. This meant that canoes rarely proceeded farther upstream than Nyamina, and almost never as far as Bamako.[85] Tijani established a military command at Mopti, near the confluence of the Niger and the Bani, where he berthed the state's military canoes. He restricted river trade with Timbuktu. Control over the river also provided the Futanke with readily accessible booty, though Lieutenant Jaime probably exaggerated when he reported that no boat could pass downstream from Segu without being stopped and its crew taken, killed, or enslaved. Too much intervention would stop the river traffic altogether, which was in neither Amadu's nor Tijani's interests. At Mopti, the one-tenth import-export tax was levied. In Masina, the river could be crossed only at Mourgula, which gave the state a high degree of control over trade and livestock. While short-term political rewards from controlling the river were substantial, the long-term consequences for the operation of the regional economy were disastrous. The viability of the Maraka plantation sector relied in part on cheap transport provided by freight canoes. In 1878, a Somono whose father had made the voyage to Timbuktu on numerous occasions complained that "relations with Timbuktu have ceased, to the severe detriment of the land."[86] The commerce of Sinsani, reported Jaime after his voyage down the Niger in a gunboat, was ruined when the Umarians stopped the river trade.[87]

Umarian economic policy, if we may call it that, reflected the prevailing ideology of state power. The land had been won for Islam and for the Futanke, and now it was time to reap the rewards. The Futanke were conquerors, but given the fragile nature of their control over the lands they had taken, they had little opportunity to enjoy the fruit of their labors. Instead, their failure to establish effective state power led to a crisis within the state that had severe economic consequences. Through both collective and individual actions, the Futanke ruling class created conditions that discouraged capital investment in commerce and production. Through their bid to control the river for political ends, they destroyed a sector of the economy that had led to significant agricultural and artisanal development along the banks of the river. In place of the well-established Niger towns and entrepôts, the fulcrum of commerce and production shifted along an east-west axis, giving a series of new towns along the desert edge a considerable economic boost. On the right bank, Baraweli assumed the role of production and commercial center. Despite the predominance of the western corridor for the political economy of the Umarian state at Segu, and the coincidental expansion of the seven Maraka towns of Beledugu, the core of Maraka commerce remained the north-south trade stimulated by demand for ecologically specialized goods.

Renewal of the Maraka Economy

Within five years of the Umarians' arrival along the Niger, their political economy had destroyed the economy of the Maraka riverine towns. Insecurity spawned by changes in both warfare and the war economy contributed to their decline. Umarian razzia and Bambara resistance considerably increased the risks associated with capital investments. Who would want to risk investing in trade goods or in plantations when the chances were high that they would be relieved of their property?

Maraka prosperity in the period before the Umarian conquest was based on a structural solution to the demands of an ecologically specialized market, which took the form of complex commercial and productive enterprises. The solution had been successfully refined over the course of the Segu Bambara period. With the collapse of the old Maraka riverine centers, it was not surprising that long-established and newly founded Maraka settlements on or near the western corridor adopted the Maraka model. In 40 years, the seven Maraka towns of Beledugu were transformed from a frontier outpost into the new commercial center of the Western Sudan.[88]

In the first half of the nineteenth century, Beledugu was contested terrain between Kaarta and Segu. Yet it was to this region, on the fringes of the Segu state, that immigrant Maraka first from Sokolo and later from the Soninke regions of Gajaaga and the Senegambian headwaters settled in the 1840's.[89] Desert-side commercial opportunities were especially promising here. Ecological conditions favored livestock, and herds of cattle, sheep, goats, donkeys, and horses were abundant. Few other regions in the Western Sudan were suited to raising horses. After 1870, horses supplied by the Maraka became a basic part of Samori's war economy.[90] Of the seven Maraka towns of Beledugu (Bambara: Marakaduguw wolonwula), Banamba and Touba were the most important.

Between 1864, when Mage passed through Banamba, and 1878, the year of Soleillet's visit, the fortunes of this part of Beledugu changed dramatically. In 1864, the town was already large by Western Sudanese standards, with a population of about 8,000. Mage, usually an astute observer, had little to say about the town except that it was surrounded by a six-meter wall, which indicated that Beledugu was still part of a rugged frontier. Fourteen years later, Soleillet noted that the plain around Banamba was "undulated, covered with magnificent fields of millet, indigo, lemon, and groundnuts." Banamba and Touba were now so crowded with merchants that lodgings were hard to find. At the end of the century, cultivated fields stretched 50 kilometers in all directions.[91]

The Umarian state did not offer Banamba special commercial prerogatives as the Bambara did to Sinsani and Nyamina. "We submitted [to the Futanke]," one informant in Banamba stated. "When the Futanke arrived, we declared ourselves Muslims, and they continued on to Segu. . . . There was no commerce between us. The only thing that existed between us and Segu was the payment of taxes."[92] In 1859 and 1860, when the Umarians first pushed through Kaarta, the Maraka of Beledugu were not yet wealthy. More lucrative prizes awaited harvesting further east.

In the early 1870's, when both Samori and Tieba of Kenedugu were actively building their states, the Maraka rapidly increased their holdings of slaves who cultivated the immense fields described by travelers. During the dry season, the slaves worked in the local cloth industry. Maraka traders were thus armed with virtually the same assortment of goods as their counterparts in Sinsani and Nyamina nearly a century before. Significant surpluses of grain and cloth helped funnel the desert-side trade into the Maraka towns of Beledugu. By the 1890's, nearly 1,500 Moors were in the vicinity of Banamba. Some settled there permanently.[93] In the process, they helped transform Banamba into the new desert-side emporium of the Western Sudan.

Samori's activities in Wasulu, even more than Tieba's in Kenedugu, provided the spark for the renaissance of Maraka trade and production. Samori began building his state in the confluence of the Niger and Milo rivers, an area where the Maraka had traditionally traded. Yves Person has described Samori as leading a "dyula revolution" by his ability to mobilize the small Muslim and commercial communities and their allies of the southern savannas into a warrior state committed to protecting commerce.[94] Like the Ngolossi and Umarians before him, Samori needed to replenish his supplies of weapons and cavalry mounts. The nearly insatiable demand for horses in Samori's camp provided a special opportunity for the Maraka. One informant described how Samori rewarded the leader who brought a caravan of horses to his camp:

> Upon arrival at Samori's camp, he gave a girl [slave] to the caravan leader as a welcoming present. Then he ordered his sofa to visit the horses, and they inspected the horses with utmost scrutiny. Each horse had its own price: some two slaves, others as much as five and ten slaves each. Samori went so far as to pay the price of a horse that died on the route to him, but the tail had to be cut in order to be presented to him.[95]

Maraka merchants did not deal exclusively with Samori, however. They also supplied Tieba, whose Senufo army fought against Samori in 1887–88. Tieba avoided dependence on the Beledugu horse trade by fostering trade with Masina and Mossi. Maraka traders supplied both armies with horses and other imports, but transactions were conducted somewhat differently in these two military camps. With Samori, horses were exchanged directly for slaves, in proportion to the value of the horse. In Sikasso, horses were bought with cowries. No slaves were available in Sikasso, since Tieba restricted slave sales to outlying villages.[96] Horses, although not exclusively controlled by the Maraka, gave them an advantage over other traders and contributed to the great expansion of the Maraka economy.

Besides horses, the Maraka imported desert salt into southern markets, along with various textiles (including a short indigo-dyed women's wrap known as *ducuruni-fin*), dried fish purchased from the Somono along the river banks, and livestock. Like their Sinsani and Nyamina predecessors, the Beledugu Maraka aggressively sought salt. Banamba and Touba had several brokers for the desert-side trade, and the concentration of Moors living in Banamba further attracted salt caravans. Ambitious traders used the brief lull in the agricultural cycle, between the first planting and the first weeding, to take kola stored from their southern expeditions northeast to Nioro, where salt was discounted at least 33 percent. Traveling conditions from Banamba at this early time of the rainy season were difficult, but the routes were still passable. At the desert-side entrepôts of Nioro and occasionally at Bassikunu to the east, the Maraka loaded donkeys with rock salt from Idjil and with *amersal*, a form of loose salt scraped from the higher strata of salt ponds located primarily at Tichit. These merchants then raced back to Beledugu for the harvest, threshing, and storage of the new grain crop. Only then did they assemble the caravans for their voyage to the markets of the forest edge. The mercantile rhythm of Beledugu Maraka, then, consisted of two active seasons.[97] By buying cheaply and selling dear, these Maraka absorbed not only regional differences in price, but also won considerable windfall profits from the annual price cycles of commodities. No new supplies of salt arrived with the onset of the rains, and whatever salt was stored was susceptible to losses due to moisture retention. Kola was also a perishable commodity, and even the best storage procedures were no guarantee against rapid deterioration.[98] Both salt and kola prices increased as the rainy season progressed.

Maraka traders were always sensitive to prevailing political conditions along the routes they followed. As the fortunes of Samori and Tieba fluctuated, so too did the directions and routes the Maraka followed. Maraka traders gradually abandoned the Guinea routes as Samori moved his capital to the right bank of the Milo river. Despite commercial connections on the left bank of the Milo, traders preferred to trade directly with Samori's camp because he offered traders protection. After unloading their supply of horses with Samori, Maraka merchants took what remained of their assortment of goods to the kola markets further south and east. In what is now northern Ivory Coast, Maraka merchants traded in Man, Makasouba, N'Fola-Dene, Bogola, and Ojenne. Several Maraka families had recently settled at Ojenne, following the Maraka revolts of 1863–65. Merchants from Touba still went to the Guinean markets of Sekela, Zergne, Soninkou, and Majanta, where they maintained normal ties with the Malinke-More, who dominated the western routes from Kankan. As a result of Samori's wars, however, Kankan declined in the 1870's, which made the kola markets to the east attractive even to Touba merchants. A few Maraka traders continued to work the old Guinean routes, especially those leading to Kouryssa and Loula, where gold and other goods could be had.[99]

In the course of 25 years, Banamba had developed from an insignificant and frightened frontier town into a flourishing commercial and agricultural center. It now dominated the commerce of Beledugu, Kaarta, and the western sahel. Even as the town became an important staging ground for the caravan trade, Banamba became the major crossroads of trade between the headwaters of the Senegambia and the markets of the forest edge. In

1894, the commandant of Bouguni wrote that "all caravans that pass Bouguni go to Banamba."[100] Most forest goods, including slaves and kola destined for Nioro and Medine, were transshipped through Banamba.[101] At the beginning of the century, a traveler explained to an audience in France that "one already knows the role of Nioro [in the commerce of the Western Sudan], but that of Banamba has until now gone completely unappreciated."[102] The governor of Haut-Senegal-Niger's annual report of 1895 did not equivocate on Banamba's place in the regional economy. It was, according to the report, the most important market in the Sudan.[103] With the coming of the French in 1883, the Maraka towns of Beledugu absorbed yet another important function: by 1894, they were the breadbaskets of the new French military outposts along the Niger.[104]

Banamba's rise coincided with a major commercial decline in the older commercial zones of the Middle Niger valley. On the right bank, in the heart of the new Futanke state of Segu, commercial life declined as a result of uncontrolled warfare. Only Baraweli managed to escape the predations of the talaba. Here Maraka invested in a sizeable plantation economy and controlled part of the trade southward. For the trade to the central and eastern kola markets, Baraweli's location offered distinct advantages over its rivals farther west. Merchants from Baraweli did not need to cross the Niger and they could follow the Niger-Bani routes directly to Sikasso, Bouguni, Man, and the other markets of the region.

Baraweli was a product of the Umarian conquest. It was founded by immigrant Maraka from Gulumba, on the outskirts of Nyamina, who converted to Tijaniyya when Umar arrived in Nyamina.[105] They followed Umar through his conquest of Segu and settled in Baraweli with the permission of Amadu. In their dealings with Baraweli, the Umarians scrupulously applied Islamic norms as they understood them. "We were all Tijani," the chief of Baraweli explained, "that is what brought the favor of al hajj Umar."[106] The Futanke collected only the *zakat*, the alms payable by all Muslims, and only in times of full state campaigns did they requisition horses.

Maraka merchants of Baraweli traded horses, dyed cloth, reexported salt, and dried fish with Samori, with Tieba and his successor Babemba, and with the kola wholesalers.[107] Some slaves were sold, but many were incorporated in the expanding plantations of grain, cotton, and indigo that ringed the town. In this respect, the experience of the Baraweli Maraka was similar to that of their Banamba counterparts. In other ways, their experiences differed. In Baraweli, the Maraka probably erected a plantation economy immediately upon their arrival in the mid-1860's. According to one informant, "[our ancestors] arrived with many slaves. They were more numerous than free Maraka."[108] Baraweli brought the commercialization of indigo-dyed cloth to a new level and emerged as the most important producer of indigo in the region, even selling indigo to dyers in the other Maraka towns, where it had once been a staple crop.[109] Despite its plantations and the advantages of its southern location, Baraweli never developed the same commercial importance as Banamba. It could not. Political and economic conditions remained far from favorable on the right bank of the Niger.

Slaves, the Slave Trade, and the Maraka Plantation Economy

Slave villages resembling plantations had been part of the social landscape of the Western Sudan since at least the fifteenth century, but they seem to have developed among the Maraka first in the Niger towns of Sinsani and Nyamina. Because the plantations of Banamba and Baraweli developed later, we know more about them. But they also represented a further historical development of the Maraka plantation economy. The rhythm of work and the character of daily life on the plantations surrounding Banamba and Baraweli reflected the consequences of the Maraka commercial response to an era of expanded commodity production. Most Maraka slaves lived and worked in slave villages (Bambara: *jonbuguw*), which contained between 50 and 500 slaves. Most slaves eventually lived in fairly stable family units. Work on the central fields (Bambara: *forowba*) of millet, sorghum, and cotton was regimented and supervised by slave overseers. Although they were not exactly analogous to their New World counterparts, Maraka slave villages were plantations.[110] The Maraka thus traded slaves as commodities and invested in slave labor.

It is commonly held that slave traders trailed behind African armies ready to relieve warriors of their share of booty. Maraka informants firmly refuted this view. They insisted that slaves were bought openly in local markets or directly from warriors only after they had returned from the battlefield. Sometimes merchants and warriors conducted their transactions quickly and quietly, either in the home of the warrior or in that of the merchant. Transactions involving slaves belonging to the state were controlled carefully. Monzon, for example, regularly sold part of his share of booty in Kangaba on the fringes of the Segu state. Tieba prohibited slave sales in Sikasso and relegated these transactions to outlying villages. Samori tried to regulate slave transactions even more fully. In each sizeable town, a slave representative was charged with overseeing the fields of the crown, with organizing food transport to the front, and with selling war captives for horses, salt, and other imports. Slaves were sometimes concentrated in large markets. In 1880, Keniera had between two and three thousand slaves for sale. Because sales of slaves provided warriors with income and imported goods, even the best-laid controls on the slave trade were not always successful.[111]

Between the early 1870's and the late 1890's, the most important source of new slaves was the wide band of the southern savannas from the Upper Niger-Milo confluence through the upper reaches of the Volta rivers. This was a well-populated zone, in which communities tended to be small and states fragile if they existed at all. Samori and Tieba carved their states out of this area; well into the 1880's, the Umarians raided southward into the Geniekalari, and toward the Bani and Wasulu regions.[112] Wars were the most productive form of enslavement, and wars were continuous in the southern savannas in this period.

In 1880, Lieutenant Vallière, a member of the Gallieni mission, had the opportunity to discuss the slave trade from Wasulu with the leader of a slave caravan.

> The juula told me that the land of the slaves covers an immense region between the primary affluents of the Niger. Wasulu had one of the densest populations in the area. To explain how close the villages are, the king can without leaving his capital have his orders shouted from village to village to the extreme limits of his immense empire. The inhabitants . . . conduct incessant warfare. The only object of these incessant com-

bats is to capture women, children, and young men in order to sell them at the famous markets of Tengrela, Dialakoro, Kankan, Keniera, and so on. The chiefs sell their proper subjects in order to replenish their supplies of firearms and gunpowder and to buy beautiful ornaments. As soon as the harvests are completed, the young men form armed bands and raid their neighbors to earn a little extra.[113]

Although wars and armed raids were the most productive form of enslavement, kidnapping was widespread. In the early 1880's, women and children were kidnapped daily even in the area around the French post of Medine on the Upper Senegal. Merchants had the opportunity, the motivation, and the cover to kidnap a lone woman or child. Many were already leading caravans of slaves and a few additional captives included along the way probably went unnoticed. Most merchants, however, operated as the Maraka did. They benefited from their roles as purveyors and slaveowners, not as enslavers.[114]

Profits from the slave trade could be considerable. Departing from the French factories on the Upper Senegal or British factories on the Gambia, juula in the 1880's often went first to the salt market of Kerigui near Nioro with imported guinée cloth to exchange for salt. When salt was plentiful, two pieces of guinée were worth three bars of salt. Loading the salt on donkeys, the merchants descended to Kita or Nyagassola and thence to the markets of Wasulu. At Keniera, one bar of salt was exchanged for one slave. In this particular exchange, an initial investment of 25 francs in the form of two pieces of guinée was converted into three slaves. At Dialakoro, slaves were even cheaper. Returning to the burgeoning market for slaves in Senegambia, stimulated by the expanding market for labor on the peanut fields, slaves were sold for between 100 and 250 francs each. Other merchants followed an alternative route to the slave markets of the southern savannas. They first acquired firearms along the upper Guinea coast and then traveled inland via Futa Jalon, Timbo, and Tengrela, where slaves and kola were purchased.[115]

In reconstructing the spatial patterns of slave distribution, we need to distinguish between primary slave markets, secondary redistribution points, and final destinations. While warriors were willing to face the risks of the battle, they were usually reluctant to confront the risks of the market. They preferred to unload slaves as quickly as possible. In his brilliant discussion of the economics of enslavement, Curtin has argued that a slave had no value at the point of capture.[116] Costs of supervision and ease of escape made the local slave a risky investment; separation from home and kin was basic to the commercialization of slaves.

Primary slave markets corresponded to the primary zones of enslavement. In the 1880's, these were concentrated within or near the borders of Samori's and Tieba's states. Important merchant towns to the east, including Bouna, Bonduku, Kintampo, and Kong, were active centers of the slave trade. Slaves from these towns were primarily exported to Asante, which remained a ready market for slaves, and to the Mossi country, where some were retained and others transshipped to the desert edge. With the fall of most of these juula towns to Samori after 1886, the patterns of distribution shifted and more slaves probably made their way westward.[117]

Secondary redistribution centers corresponded to the major trade routes and to patterns of slave purchase and retention. Within the zone in which the Maraka were active, Kita became an important slave redistribution point. From Kita, slaves were directed to Soninke buyers in Kaarta and in the Upper Senegal, to Futanke consumers in Bundu and Futa Toro, and to the Moors of the western desert. West of Kita, the Jahanke and Gajaaga Soninke were active traders. Within the commercial zone drained by the Middle Niger, the most important slave markets of the Umarian period were at Baraweli, Segu, and Fatene on the right bank, at San, Sofara, Kaka, Jenne, and Bandiagara in Masina, and at Banamba and Touba on the left bank. Certain towns developed distinct reputations. Niaro, located on the left bank of the Niger between Sinsani and Sokolo, was called *jon te goila*, which meant that no slave remained unsold, and Niaro had the lowest slave prices in that region.[118]

Intimately tied to the commercialization of slaves was the specialized role of the slave jobber. The preferred method of trading was a direct transaction between buyer and seller. When this was not possible, traders used a *jontefe* (Bambara· slave jobber or agent). The jontefe rarely traveled far from the market he was associated with. He helped to unite buyers and sellers when business was slow, or when a master wanted to unload an old or recalcitrant slave and did not want to be associated directly with this transaction. A slave jobber, whose occupation came to symbolize dishonest market practices, was not above rubbing an old slave's skin with karite butter and his hair with charcoal to disguise his real condition.[119]

Slave prices corresponded only imperfectly to supply. Curtin has argued that slaves produced by the "political model of enslavement" did not conform to "real" market prices since no rational man would sell a slave for the low prices actually paid.[120] This model, however, is not fully applicable to the political economy of warrior states. For warriors, slaves were commodities produced to be exchanged for their means of production and their means of subsistence. Warriors had little desire to retain slaves, except for a few female slaves and young children they incorporated in their households.

In the Middle Niger valley, prices for slaves fluctuated throughout the nineteenth century. Part of the increase in prices was related to the general inflationary spiral of cowrie currencies, but this cannot account for all the changes. It is quite possible that the absurdly low prices cited by Mage for slaves available in Nyamina in 1864 reflected the decline in local demand during the Maraka revolt of 1863–65. Such low prices may help explain the Umarian propensity for executing male prisoners rather than selling them. Because the Umarian state no longer supplied consistently large numbers of slaves to the market, the slave markets active during the Segu Bambara period declined precipitously.

Although a normal price for slaves was known by buyers and sellers alike, actual prices reflected the sex, age, and physical condition of the slave. Before engaging in any transaction, the slave was subjected to a careful and minute inspection. A list of faults was then drawn up, and if the buyer was still interested, bargaining would begin. All slave purchases involved uncertainty. One could test muscles, but never the willingness to work. As one of my informants put it, "there are men who can read the *tere* (Bambara: fortune, spirit) of animals, but what man can read the *tere* of another man?"[121]

The price data in Table 2 were collected by European travelers and administrators between 1805 and 1906. My informants provided more detail on slave prices, but their evidence corresponds

TABLE 2
Recorded Slave Prices in the Middle Niger Valley, 1805–1906
(K, cowries; F, francs)

Year	Salt	Male slave	Female slave	Girl	Boy
1805	8,000K	40,000K	80,000–100,000K		40,000K
1828	10,000–15,000K		25,000–40,000K[a]		
1864	10,000K	40,000K	4,000–40,000K		
1878			40,000–160,000K		
1880	40,000–60,000K		100,000–140,000K		
1894 (1)		150F	200F	130–200F	130F
1894 (2)		50,000K[b]		150,000K[c]	50,000K
1904	40F	(110–240F)[d]	(110–240F)[d]		
1906			60–250F		

SOURCES: *1805*, Park, *Mission*, p. 221. *1828*, Caillié, *Journal*, 2: 212 (Jenne prices; slaves were cheaper further south, ibid., 1: 414–14, 466). *1864*, Mage, *Voyage*, p. 192. *1878*, Soleillet, Rapport no. 1, 15 Oct. 1878, Segu Sikoro, ANS-AOF 1 G 46. *1880*, Gallieni, *Mission*, p. 436. *1894*, Etude sur la captivité, (1) Segu, (2) Sokolo, 1894, ANS-AOF K 14. *1904*, Brevié, Rapport sur l'esclavage, Bamako, 1904, ANS-AOF K 19. *1906*, Deherme, L'esclavage en AOF, part 2, ch. 3, 1906, ANS-AOF K 25 (prices paid in Jenne and Bandiagara).

[a] Depending on age.
[b] Old slave.
[c] Aged 14 to 16.
[d] Average price, all male and female slaves. The highest prices were paid for slaves most recently acquired by the seller. An old slave woman could be bought for as little as 7F. In Bouguni, a slave could be bought for 40F.

only imperfectly to prevailing conditions in the late nineteenth century. My informants maintained that young women were consistently at the upper end of the price range in most of Africa. The Maraka planters, however, paid virtually the same prices for healthy young women as for healthy young men. Even a homely young woman rarely cost less than 60,000 cowries, whereas a less-than-prime male slave could be had for 40,000. A child capable of some work sold for 10,000–30,000 cowries; a baby on its mother's back, for 5,000 cowries. Old men and women brought their sellers 15,000–20,000 cowries. A deaf-mute who was capable of working also brought a good price. Pregnant women cost somewhat more because they carried additional value. Despite occasional dips over the nineteenth century as a whole, prices for slaves increased. "Slaves," mentioned one informant, "had become indispensable."[122]

Maraka planters' willingness to pay virtually the same for healthy males and females suggests a significant departure from the slave price trends elsewhere on the continent. Recent studies of slavery in Africa have indicated an overall preference for female slaves. Women were valued for both their productive and reproductive capacities. Female slaves were often concubines and some became junior wives. Their offspring either belonged to the master's lineage or formed dependent slave lineages. In all African societies, the presence of slaves always accentuated struggles for power and control within the master class and between masters and dependents. But where slaves composed larger proportions of the total population, these struggles were often fiercer and the outcome more politicized.[123]

Quantitative data on slave populations in the Western Sudan are poor, but they do exist. In 1894, Governor Grodet instructed local administrators to respond to a questionnaire on slavery.[124] In 1904, Lieutenant Governor Ponty again asked administrators questions regarding slavery. The quality of these reports is quite variable. Breviè's excellent report on slavery in the Maraka cities of Beledugu reveals some of the problems involved. "The household heads of Banamba told us," he recorded, "that there were no more than 300 slaves in the city. Slaves told us there were at least five times as many. At Touba, masters say there are 500 slaves; the slaves claim there are between 6,000 and 7,000. At Kiba, masters claim there were only 500 slaves; the slaves say there are 5,000."[125] Breviè understood the problems involved in collecting population data. Results depended on the pool one selected and whom one asked. Some masters may not have known the exact number of slaves they owned, especially if they owned several plantations. Others consciously lowered their estimates because they were distrustful of the French and because they were ultimately responsible for the taxes assessed on their slaves.[126]

A decade separated the two surveys of slavery in the Western Sudan. These were eventful years during which the French colonial state matured and changed. Administrators' attitudes toward slavery also changed. Why this occurred is the subject for a later chapter, but attitudes influenced the ways in which data were collected, presented, and analyzed. This helps account for some of the marked discrepancies in the evidence, but not all. In 1898, the two largest enslavers, Samori and Babemba, the heir to the Sikasso kingdom, were crushed by the French. The end of their military activities eliminated the major source of new slaves that had fed the demand for slave labor throughout the Western Sudan. Consequently, slave supply networks and existing plantation economies were thrown into crisis.

In his report, the commandant of Segu in 1894 estimated that slaves made up 53 percent of the total population. Using the 1899 census as a base, we can assume that there were about 70,000 slaves in the Segu cercle, the French administrative unit. By 1904, another Segu commandant counted 25,161 slaves out of a total population of 160,000. According to his report, slaves accounted for only 15.6 percent of the population. This decline is remarkable, and the commandant must have recognized the disparity between his findings and those of his predecessor, for he wrote that the relative decline in numbers of slaves was consistent with the process of emancipation whereby slaveowners liberated all slaves born of slave parents.[127] This was indeed part of the ideology of Bambara slavery, even if it was not the actual practice. It is possible that the two Segu commandants simply counted differently, or that the commandant in 1904 manipulated the evidence to indicate a smaller overall slave population and suggest that slavery was an insignificant issue in his district.[128]

Reports from the left bank provide a contrast to the Segu case. Sokolo had a much sparser population than Segu, yet slaves outnumbered freemen in 1894. In 1904, Sokolo had 13,343 slaves. The same year, the region around Sinsani, which had been the center of plantation economy in the middle years of the nineteenth century, had a slave population equivalent to 31 percent of the total. This population was probably not evenly distributed throughout the region but concentrated in and around the town itself. Since the town had 2,005 people in 1904 and the total slave population of the region was 6,436, the proportion surrounding Sinsani was probably much greater than the 31 percent presented in the French report. Despite the serious economic decline the region experienced following the Maraka revolts, Sinsani was likely to have had a larger concentration of slaves than neighboring non-Maraka communities.[129]

Even Brevié's data for the Banamba area contain significant inconsistencies. Much depended on whether the outlying slave villages, which sometimes ringed the Maraka towns of Beledugu for 50 kilometers, were actually counted. For example, Brevié estimated that there were between six and seven thousand slaves in Touba in 1904, although the population of Touba was estimated to be only 3,000 in the general census of 1899. Kiba in 1899 had a total population of 2,300; by 1904, Kiba was said to have 5,000 slaves.[130] It may be that Maraka planters anticipated a drastic decline in the numbers of new slaves available after 1898 and stockpiled supplies instead of selling them.

Evidence for the sexual distribution of slave populations in these samples is equally suspect. If only town slaves among the Maraka were counted, the numbers of children and female slaves would probably have been larger than in a representative sample in outlying slave plantations, where one would expect to find more able-bodied men. Similarly, Bambara communities might demonstrate a marked preference for female slaves, since the Bambara seem to have used slavery as a means for household expansion and may have assimilated female slaves more rapidly than males. In 1894, there were 4.5 female slaves to every male slave in the Segu cercle, which meant that there were approximately 54,500 females to 15,500 males. By 1904, male slaves outnumbered female slaves. This evidence is consistent with the gradual emancipation assumed by the Segu commandant, but it was far more rapid than the gradual multigenerational process practiced by the Bambara. In 1904, male slaves made up 44 percent of the slave population of Sinsani, including children. The same year, males made up 58 percent of the total slaves in Sokolo cercle.[131]

It is possible that female slaves were more numerous than male slaves in the 1894 surveys, and that with declining recruitment of new slaves, males predominated by 1904. This interpretation of the evidence is only possible if the host societies practiced rapid assimilation of female slaves and if the proportions of female and male slaves were already fairly close. This solution does not, in any case, apply to the Maraka. The Maraka did not regularly practice assimilation. Although masters took concubines and young Maraka experimented sexually with female slaves, the birth of a child fathered by a freeborn Maraka did not automatically liberate the slave mother or the child. Manumission of any sort was quite rare among Maraka slaves. Considering the sexual distribution of the slave population, the lack of assimilation, and the comparable prices paid for healthy males and healthy females, it is reasonable to suppose that Maraka valued slaves primarily for their labor power. Maraka slaves were above all workers whose labor contributed to the growth of a plantation economy designed to produce commodities.

The large number of slaves in Maraka society during the last half of the nineteenth century led to a divergence between the theory and practice of Maraka slavery, for the interests of masters and those of slaves were further apart than ever. Even then, Maraka slavery contained both paternalistic and exploitative elements. The two elements were not mutually exclusive, since paternalism was based on a perceived ability to coerce dependents and slaves without the use of force. Paternalism was an ideology that permitted exploitation, but one that also set limits on the extent of that exploitation. Slaves seemed to have accepted the ideology of paternalism because it provided them with safeguards. The term "moral economy" has been used to describe similar exploitative relations in precapitalist societies.[132] The concept emphasizes the existence of a conscious, ideological framework that contributes to the stability of servile relations.

For most of the nineteenth century, the stability of Maraka slavery rested on a set of mutually understood obligations between masters and slaves. These obligations were not rigidly defined, but revolved around a set of institutions that gave substance to the ideology of paternalism. Maraka slavery evolved around a shifting perception of what slaves and masters thought ought to be the nature of their relationship. During the course of the century, both masters and slaves pushed and pulled at the structure of their relationship in response to changes in economic and social conditions.

The contrast between slavery as perceived and practiced by the Maraka and by the Bambara peasants highlights the ways in which plantation slavery departed from the domestic model of the Bambara. The contrast between the two is particularly striking because the Maraka and Bambara spoke the same language, lived in the same ecological zone, and participated in the same social formation. A slave owned by a Bambara family tended to be assimilated more fully and more quickly than one owned by a Maraka family.[133] Despite changes in the economy and society during the nineteenth century, the Bambara remained peasant cultivators, and masters usually worked side by side with their slaves. In contrast, Maraka society was transformed through a progressive reliance on slave labor. Farming became a degraded occupation. "We do not know how to work," Maraka planters told Breviè in 1904.[134] Slavery not only freed the Maraka from the exertion and care of hard manual work; it had become the foundation for the cosmopolitan and religious life of the Maraka towns.

The Bambara distinguished between *jonfin* and *jonba*, between marketable and non-marketable slaves. Further distinctions could be made between enslaved freemen who stood a good chance of being ransomed and those who were recently enslaved but not yet settled with a new master. While these distinctions reflected subtle differences in slave status, the moment a slave entered the market, he or she suffered a profound social degradation. The *sanjon* (Bambara: slave of the market) had no rights whatsoever. The trader invested little in the sanjon's clothing and food, although this slave was often put to work while awaiting shipment. Slave traders had total sexual liberty with their female sanjonw. Moreover, the trade slave could be bought and sold repeatedly. Even a trade slave who remained with a family for many years could be sold. The Bambara identified slaves by one of four generations, and by such reckoning it usually took four generations for the last vestiges of slave status to be eradicated.[135]

In contrast to the Bambara, the Maraka designated all slaves entering Maraka society as trade slaves. They only distinguished between *jonw* and *wolosow*, between first- and second-generation slaves. This did not mean that the Maraka quickly assimilated slaves. On the contrary, the woloso status was generic. It was applied to all slaves who were born into captivity, and even a slave of the tenth generation remained a woloso. The implications are important. If assimilation meant the gradual erosion of the slave's marginal status, then the Maraka did not practice what Kopytoff and Miers identify as the critical aspect of African slavery.[136]

Despite these normative status distinctions, once a slave was settled for several years, was given a spouse, and raised a family, the slave could not help but develop some sense of stability. Although slaves and masters may not have shared the same expectations about life and work, they usually understood and shared a set of mutual obligations. In 1895, a French administrator wrote that the obligations between a master and his slave were exactly the same as those between a household head and his son.[137] One Maraka informant summed up the master-slave relationship as follows. In response to my question "What did you do for your slaves in return for what they did for you?" he replied: "We fed them and their children; they were clothed by the head of the family. All their needs were met."[138] The response is striking not only for the paternalism it manifests, but because it demonstrates how the oral traditions of the master class preserved this paternalism despite the shattering events of 1905.

The master was obliged to feed his slaves in direct proportion to the time they worked for him. On the days his slaves worked for him, the master supplied the main meal. Slaves provided all additional food themselves. Thus, if a slave worked for his master only three days a week, the slave had to fend for himself the other four days. If the slave worked the full seven days of the week, as Brevié found was common in Banamba, the master was obliged to supply his slave with all his food needs.[139] This labor-subsistence obligation was central to the master-slave relationship. The obvious reciprocity of the master-slave relationship should not, however, obscure the fact that the relationship was above all dictated by class distinctions. Masters had property rights to the means of production and to their slaves' labor. Because masters were part of a social system based on violence and domination, they could extract surplus labor from their slaves with relative impunity. Only when the traditional political economy was undermined by the colonial state, did masters' power to coerce their slaves decline.

Masters did not have nor could they ever have total power over their slaves. Slaves resisted in many overt and covert ways. Some escaped, despite the hazards involved. Trade slaves were usually far from their homes and either did not know how to return or stood a very high risk of being re-enslaved if they fled. Lack of food was always a problem for fugitives, and whenever they sought food they risked being questioned. Some, perhaps most, neighboring communities established mutual slave-retrieval pacts. Finally, unsuccessful escapes were severely punished. Slaves who feared to attempt an escape might appeal to the village elders, using public opinion to exert moral pressure on a master who was exceeding the limits of acceptable treatment. Slaves could thus use the very same ideology of paternalism to enforce limits on exploitation.[140] Slaves could also alter the rhythm of work, and occasionally they stopped working altogether.

The plantation system of Banamba and Baraweli, however, ruptured whatever remained of the personal relationship between masters and slaves. Many masters of Banamba visited their plantations only once or twice a year.[141] While limiting the possibilities of assimilation into the host society, the plantation system also provided slaves with some control over their daily lives beyond the supervised work period. It almost certainly increased their sense of corporate identity. The organization of the Maraka plantations, designed to increase production, therefore fostered collective resistance by the slaves.

It was not in the interests of masters to treat their slaves harshly. Both slaves and masters benefited when labor obligations and harsh working conditions were moderated. Slaves became less inclined to escape, and masters had to expend less effort on supervision. Slaves gained from their masters' protection and from their leniency. Moreover, they benefited from living in a community, even one composed only of slaves, where they could marry and raise a family and could develop an emotional stake in the society. In all Muslim societies, the manumission of slaves was considered a pious act; among the Maraka, however, it was rarely practiced. The Maraka plantation economy was thus a flexible system that offered both masters and slaves room to shape and define their relationships. It was also a system in which masters and slaves subtly redefined customary practices in response to changes in the larger regional economy and prevailing political conditions.[142]

Part of the struggle between masters and slaves revolved around fitting local and traditional patterns of work into the new plantation economy, its regime of work, and the new ideologies of social relations. Masters sought to mold these patterns to fit their aims of increased productivity and accumulation; slaves found in the patterns and institutions of work a means for resisting the loss of control over the labor process. Although the process of enslavement, the slave trade, and the slaves' insertion into a new society were designed to minimize the slaves' cultural heritage, slaves often retained many of their original traditions and practices, especially on plantations, where assimilation was rare. On the plantations, pre-servile traditions of work were often incompatible with the tendency for Maraka planters to rationalize their slaves' labor. For example, in most West African savanna societies agricultural work was divided into male and female tasks; on the plantations, men and women worked side by side at the same tasks.[143]

Most practices, however, did not interfere with the operation of Maraka slavery, and many served to facilitate slaves' acceptance of their situation. I have identified four practices that, on the one hand, gave substance to the struggle between masters and slaves but, on the other, reinforced the ideology of reciprocity. First, slaves had the right to free time. Second, they had the right to work their own fields (Bambara: *jonforow*). Third, they had the right to retain a portion of the product of work they performed for a third party. And fourth, they had the right to purchase and retain property, including slaves of their own (Bambara: *jonwmajon*).

The rhythm of daily life on Maraka plantations followed the seasons. Work was heavier and longer just before and during the rainy season, but slaves worked for their Maraka masters the entire year. During the peak agricultural times of weeding and harvesting, slaves worked long hours every day of the week. During this period, they also received full subsistence from their masters. At other times, slaves customarily had one or two days free each week, and they were free when the work on the main field ended late in the afternoon. At such times, they slept, rested, played, maintained their households, or worked on their own plots. Typical of many plantation systems, the slaves' gardens were a means of cutting the masters' overhead costs, but an energetic slave could amass some wealth from them.[144]

During the dry season, most slaves engaged in trade or a craft, particularly textile production. Virtually all second-generation male slaves wove, and probably many trade slaves did as well. Female slaves carded and spun cotton into thread, which was part of women's domestic labor. Despite the Maraka's propensity for regarding both male and female slaves as units of labor, the low level of productivity in carding and spinning meant that the demand for female slaves was always high. Even elderly female slaves, who were reputed to be good spinners, fetched high prices on the market. Slaves who did not weave made bricks, built and repaired houses, wove straw mats, cleared fields, and performed the host of other activities required by a farming system. Others packed goods for long-distance trade, and some even traded on their masters' account. Still others were artisans, who plied their crafts during the dry season. One Maraka informant claimed that his father had a plantation composed exclusively of ironworkers. During the dry season, however, slaves generally had more free time and worked less intensely.[145]

As a consequence of the Maraka production strategies, slaves developed skills in agriculture, craft production, and commerce, marketable skills that provided them with actual earning power. Slave weavers, for example, wove for third parties during the height of the dry season after they had exhausted their masters' supply of thread. It is unclear how much of their income the slaves actually retained. Slaves also marketed surpluses from their own plots.[146]

In periods of crisis, however, masters could invoke the good of the community to appropriate the earnings derived from the slaves' private plots. In times of famine, slaves were the first to suffer, even to the point of starvation.[147] Although a slave could acquire goods, he did not have the legal right to pass his possessions on to his children. On the death of a slave, his goods technically reverted to the master. In a strictly legal sense, the slave had usufruct only, and therefore his master could appropriate his property at any time. Usually, however, slaves were permitted to bequeath their small livestock and other possessions to their children.[148] Slaves occasionally bought small luxuries including kola, condiments, and cloth.

The condition of slavery has been defined as the negation of freedom.[149] Such a definition ignores both the complex ideologies associated with slavery and the varied strategies of survival developed by slaves. Self-redemption was available to Maraka slaves. Many slaves had income and could buy their freedom from their masters. A slave, however, could seldom afford the price of both his own freedom and his family's. And even if he did win the freedom of his entire family, his actual condition changed very little. In an environment where enslavement was widespread, people needed protection. A freedman would of necessity establish some form of clientage that may not have differed considerably from slavery itself.[150] Mage recorded a very telling conversation he had with the female slaves he and Quinton received while in Segu. When asked whether they wanted to accompany the travelers back to Senegal, "they replied," says Mage, that "they chose to remain slaves, but said to me: 'You are our master; if you want, we will follow you, but what we prefer is to remain [in Segu].' This preference did not shock me. For slaves of birth, daughters of slaves in a land of slaves, the word freedom does not awaken in them any inspiration. What consequence Bakel, Medine, or liberty?"[151]

In a social environment where the precariousness of daily life was constantly reiterated, it was not surprising that slaves sought to maximize their security. Among the Maraka, slaves sometimes bought their own slaves. Such a purchase may shock our sensibilities, but it enabled a slave to improve his situation materially without endangering his links to his community. The slave and his jonmajon worked side by side on the Maraka master's fields and side by side on the field of the slave master. The slave of a slave, then, contributed both to the well-being of his master and to that of his master's master. More important, the slave of a slave would care for his slave master in old age. When a slave's children belonged to the master of the mother, a slave could not look to them for aid. Nor was the Maraka master responsible for the well-being of a slave who was too old to sustain the labor-subsistence exchange. Hence, the slave of a slave provided his slave master with a degree of security during both his active life and his old age. In conformity with the patterns of slave inheritance, the jonmajon reverted to the Maraka master on the death of the slave master.[152]

Slaves owning other slaves was a peculiar institution. But it was not a solution unique to Maraka slaves. It appeared elsewhere in Africa, including Gumbu, Bouna, and the Sokoto Caliphate.[153] It also existed in the Americas, although its extent remains to be determined.[154] Where it existed, however, the institution demonstrates slaves' ability to establish complex and contradictory solutions to pressing problems of survival. Yet if owning slaves proved to be a solution to slaves' personal needs, it also helped perpetuate the entire system of slavery. In their relations with their own slaves, Maraka slaves reproduced relations of servility, reinforcing their own subordination to their Maraka masters.

The struggles between masters and slaves occurred against the background of the larger political economy of which Maraka slavery was a part. The Maraka revolts, which pitched merchant against warrior, undercut the processes by which the state intervened in the economy to support long-term economic investments and guarantee exploitative social relations. Hence the decline of the plantations surrounding Sinsani and Nyamina. Hence the decline of the previously flourishing regional markets of the riverine basin and the reciprocal decline of economic activity throughout the Middle Niger valley. All of this in turn contributed to the peculiar patterns of warfare in Segu under the Umarians.

Warriors needed merchants. They benefited from their services and from the economic environment that helped producers and promoted market activity throughout the Middle Niger valley. The warriors of the Segu Bambara state had benefited in exactly this manner. The Umarians failed to do so. The revolts of the Maraka in the early 1860's, along with those of the Somono and the Bambara, contributed to the Umarians' failure to establish effective state power and thus re-establish the state's role in the economy. The patterns of accumulation among Umarian warriors illustrate the consequences of this failure.

Predation, Production, and Accumulation in the Umarian State

The history of the Umarian period at Segu underlines the centrality of the state to the economic and social history of the region. The state's failure to control and guide productive activities reinforced predation as the sole expression of state power. With little direct control over its own subsistence, the Umarian population of Segu suffered constant uncertainty. In the late 1860's, conditions in Segu were grave and the Umarians were suffering. The late 1870's brought relief, and the Segu market was well supplied and active. Though European goods were scarce, food and local cloth were quite abundant. But the good fortune did not last. In the 1880's, as the French expanded their territorial conquest, conditions worsened and supplies along the western corridor became irregular. Amadu looked to Tieba of Kenedugu for assistance. Tieba promised emergency supplies of food in exchange for Amadu's support in his ongoing conflict with Samori and for occasional shipments of military equipment. In 1887, during an especially severe shortage in Segu, rebellious Bambara intercepted food supplies sent by Tieba. By 1889, a muule of millet cost an astronomical 500–600 cowries. Even the normally secure and well-fed royal household suffered, and three of Amadu's concubines died of starvation.[155]

Compared to the Bambara system of warfare, which stimulated trade and production throughout the Middle Niger region, the Umarian system of predation does not seem to have had a long-term logic. Divisiveness within the army, caused by ethnically segregated regiments and unequal division of booty, fostered razzia as the expression of state power. Instead of stimulating state management of resources, logistics, and manpower, razzia encouraged petty predation and decentralization.

Umar built his state on conquest. He held it together by his prestige and his patronage, which tied the loyalty of his talaba and his slaves to him by individual strands. Umar charged his state with defending and advancing Islam. The zakat was collected, whenever possible, and the Umarian state established customs duties—the 10 percent wusuru—signifying its sovereign right to impose and collect such taxes. Yet there was no centralized Umarian state. Instead, more or less isolated provincial capitals emerged, each constituting a *ribat*. The ribat, a fortified enclosure housing a Futanke garrison, was the predominant form of Umarian political architecture. At the western fringes of the state, at Dingiray, Kunjan, Gemukuna, and Jangunte, the Umarian system worked admirably. Mage, who traveled in the area en route to Segu in 1864, remarked that "order, or nearly that, reigns all over," and a tax in kind was scrupulously collected and stored in the fort.[156]

With Umar's death in 1864, any semblance of unity evaporated and the state effectively divided into three and later four zones. The first extended triangularly from Nioro to Kunjan and Konayrkary. Here Umar's sons, nephews, and appointed followers exerted considerable influence. The second was Dingiray, the original military camp. Dingiray constituted an isolated component of the Umarian state, and rather atypically for the Umarians, it had established peaceful relations with the subject peoples. Dingiray eventually seceded from a temporarily revitalized Umarian state in 1887, when Aguibu, one of Umar's sons, made a separate peace with the French.[157] The third zone was Segu. It was separated from the rest by a zone of rebellious Bambara known as Beleris of Grand Beledugu. After 1864, a fourth zone was established when Tijani led the Umarian forces in the reconquest of Masina. The relations between Tijani and Amadu were strained and Tijani never recognized Amadu's succession. By 1870, provincial garrisons throughout the conquered lands had become semi-autonomous, and Amadu struggled to bring these areas back into the semblance of a unified state. In the 1870's and 1880's, Amadu was battling, not against slave governors, but against his half-brothers, who had come of age since their father's death and who now demanded their share of the political inheritance.[158]

Personal loyalty and periodic redistribution remained the cornerstones of the Umarian system. Loyalty was occasionally fostered by grants of what may be termed fiefs. In Bandiagara, the village of Hegou belonged to a Futanke talib, Tbia Tabi.

> This was one of a large number of villages of captives who belonged to diverse Futanke living in Bandiagara. But the village of Hegou cannot properly be called a village of captives; it is inhabited by Bambara whose ancestors were already established there. When Tijani became the master of the land, he gave [these villages] in fief to one of his [people]; the people pay rents, but are not captives.[159]

The fiefs did not resemble those of medieval Europe. Land was not the productive resource involved in the transactions. These fiefs were grants of control over people, and thus the resources of those people. They resembled the patterns established by the Songhay empire and by the Masinankes during the era of the Caliphate.[160]

Establishing a temporal administration and rewarding loyal followers dampened the military ardor of the original adventurers who had been essential to the jihad. Moreover, some of the unmarried talaba who followed Umar's call promptly married or took as concubines local women and female slaves captured during the campaigns. The elite of the Umarian army was thus rapidly transformed by administrative and household concerns into a well-entrenched ruling class. This trend imperiled the Umarian state in two ways, undermining the elite's personal loyalty to a single leader and a single cause and prompting them to turn to more immediate, more local concerns. The system of personal loyalty so basic to the shaikh-talaba relationship of the Sufi orders was difficult to maintain, especially over wide distances. Amadu may have been Umar's political heir, but he did not inherit his father's saintliness; he needed to demonstrate his own political and spiritual abilities, and he never convinced all of Umar's followers or Umar's other children. Moreover, widely separated local garrisons were primarily concerned with local issues, often at the expense of recognizing central authority. The children of the talaba ruling class were not necessarily as committed to the jihadist goal as their elders had been. Military ardor and missionary zeal gradually lessened.[161]

After 1864, the state involuted into regional sub-polities. The patterns of involution varied from region to region, as did the Umarians' accumulation strategies. In the west, where the Futanke were much closer physically and socially to their homes, they often settled down and established permanent communities. In Segu, however, the talaba had few opportunities to do so. They took local wives and concubines, but Amadu's failure to establish a viable fiscal policy in Segu forced them to remain warriors. In Segu, warfare remained the principal form of social reproduction for the Umarian warrior class. Because of the structural legacy of warfare for the political economy of the state, many Futanke in Segu probably felt like the ex-sailor from the Senegal River who told Soleillet that he wanted to return home but could not do so until he made his fortune.[162]

Nonetheless, the Umarian state provided some of the talaba and members of Umar's family with a powerful means for accumulation. They could manipulate taxes to their advantage and

TABLE 3
The Household of Maki, Almamy of Dingiray, 1899

Member of household	No.	Member of household	No.
Mother	1	Clients[a]	2
Brothers	4	Personal male slave retainers	3
Sisters	1	Married male slaves	8
Sons and daughters	3	Wives of slaves[b]	11
Noble wives	3	Dependents of married slaves:	
Female slave retainers for		Boys	13
noble wives	5	Girls	2
Slave wives and concubines	10	Unmarried male slaves	5

SOURCE: Etat nominatif des captifs, Siguiri, 4 Aug. 1899, ANM B 77.
[a]One secretary and one bard.
[b]Three male slaves had two wives each.

appropriate certain goods captured in warfare. Amadu accumulated a fortune, which he was reluctant to spend on his followers even as late as his flight from Nioro. For other Futanke, especially members of the royal household, accumulation took the form of control over clients and slaves. This was the case for Maki, the almamy of Dingiray after Aguibu's move to Bandiagara. Maki's household was large; it was composed of numerous dependents, including wives, concubines, and slaves, who could be mobilized for many tasks including political support and production (see Table 3). In 1899, when Maki was placed under house arrest and sent to Bamako, his household was permitted to accompany him. He almost certainly left behind his agricultural slaves.[163]

For most Futanke in Segu, however, the expectations of material and spiritual rewards for participating in the expansion of dar-al-Islam remained unrealized. Talaba and sofa were, above all, warriors, created by and perpetuated by the operation of the Umarian political system. As warriors, they saw in war both the means of subsistence and the means of surplus accumulation. As the young Futanke talaba departed their garrisons, they would announce that they were going "to eat the land."[164] For the Futanke, land was the subject, not the instrument, of labor.[165]

In the absence of a long-term logic and sustained linkages to the economy, warfare in the Middle Niger region from 1865 to 1890 led to the reciprocal collapse of both the state and the regional economy. In the absence of a strategy for promoting economic expansion, the Umarians maintained fiscal viability by harvesting the rich. The Futanke resented the wealth of the Maraka and the Somono, especially when they compared it with their own penury. Oral traditions consistently refer to the Umarians' readiness to take whatever pleased them and their general disregard for due process. For local Muslims, who probably anticipated a systematic implementation of taxes and shari'a law under a Muslim state, it must have been shocking to have talaba confiscate whatever appealed to them under the guise of collecting the zakat.[166]

The ubiquity of pillage had both short-term and long-term effects on capital investment. Especially hard hit were the two forms of economic activity most basic to the Maraka's role in the regional economy, namely commerce and plantation production. Talaba predations undermined the Somono's willingness to invest in canoes and nets. The FulBe and the Moors became less inclined to invest in livestock, and they changed their patterns of transhumance. Villagers hid all their possessions.[167] Cattle, slaves, crops, and all other visible forms of investment and accumulation were targets for raids.

The arrival of the Umarians did not change the interregional nature of West African trade and production. What changed in the 30 years after the fall of the Segu Bambara state was the form of state intervention in the economy. As a consequence of the collapse of state power and the revolts incited by Umarian rule, the center of commercial and productive activity shifted from the banks of the Niger to the desert edge of Beledugu. The economic functions dominated by the Maraka of Sinsani and Nyamina were absorbed by recently founded Maraka towns on the desert edge of Beledugu and one new Maraka town on the right bank of the Niger. Towns like Banamba, Touba, Keruane, Damfe, Murdia, and Baraweli developed a commercial-production complex that replicated almost exactly the form established by the Maraka in Sinsani and Nyamina during the previous century. These new Maraka towns brought to fruition the plantation model established first along the Niger.

The Umarian period thus had very uneven consequences for the operation of the Middle Niger economy. It contributed to the maturation of the Maraka plantation economy, especially in the newer Maraka settlements in Beledugu and Baraweli. At the same time, however, it led to the decline of commerce and production in the Segu heartland. Banamba owed its fortunes not to the Umarian state, which did what it could to discourage mercantile and productive investments, but to the operation of a market determined by ecological demand and to the internal dynamic of the new warrior states in the southern savannas.

The economic history of the Umarian state was perhaps best expressed by Kami Kuma, the chief of Sinsani. In 1887, complaining of the state of the economy, he recalled the once-flourishing plantation sector, which was the basis of the Maraka economic model: "Previously, each household head had between one thousand and two thousand slaves working for him; now, he has hardly more than forty or fifty."[168] In 1890, on the eve of the French conquest of Segu, Kami wrote to Archinard, commander of the French forces, pledging his support to the new colonial endeavor and explaining how Sinsani had fared in the Umarian political economy. Sinsani, he wrote, "is too isolated as a result of the war. Most of the population has left. . . . [We have nothing] but weariness and poverty . . . we have nothing in our hands but hunger."[169]

The peculiar political economy of the Umarian warrior state, and its inability to reproduce the Bambara institutional and structural supports for the economy, led to a sustained crisis within the state and within the economy. The French, who established a military outpost on the banks of the Niger at Bamako in 1883, were also a warrior state, but their intervention in the economy had different consequences.

FOUR

The Colonial State and the Economy, 1883-1905

In 1881, Colonel Borgnis-Desbordes of the French Marines assembled an army and began preparations for a march toward the Niger. The army bore striking similarities to the army that Umar had led in the same direction just over twenty years earlier. In Desbordes' army, as in Umar's, officers were drawn almost exclusively from a single ethnic group; recruits in both armies were drawn from a variety of local populations. Both armies offered social mobility, material benefits, and spiritual rewards to the officer corps and the recruits alike. Both armies were subject to similar technical concerns of supply, organization, and survival in a partially conquered environment. Both armies distributed captured booty as a regular part of their enterprise. More significant, however, is the essential difference between the two armies. For the Futanke, as for the Segu Bambara before them, the army was virtually equivalent to the state. In the Western Sudan, the French colonial army was admittedly the most visible aspect of the state, at least in the first two decades of conquest, yet it was but a transient form of state power. The transmutation of the colonial state was basic to the colonial endeavor.

In 1893, the Minister of Marine, who had jurisdiction over colonial matters, attempted, with the approval of leading members of the French National Assembly, to establish greater control over the freewheeling military commanders in the Western Sudan. To reclaim the political terrain of the new territories for civilian and metropolitan rule, they appointed a civilian governor. Owing to resistance from French officers in the field, they were unsuccessful, and Alfred Grodet left in 1895 without having tamed the military. Before he left, however, he had identified the military's participation in slavery as an essential weakness in the military's hold over the structure of the colonial state. Grodet started an assault on the perpetuation of the slave trade that would eventually erode the precolonial foundations of the colonial state.

Between 1898, when the conquest of the Western Sudan was virtually completed, and 1905, when the slaves of the region began a massive and spontaneous exodus from their masters, the colonial state confronted the contradictions inherent in the military form of state power. As the Umarian case demonstrated, military tactics and organization alone could not ensure effective state power and control over the productive processes in the economy. By 1898, however, the very success of their warfare gave the French a monopoly of military power, a monopoly that ultimately led to transformations in both the state and the economy. The monopoly of war undermined warrior domination of the state because the social reproduction of warriors was no longer crucial to the survival of the state. The monopoly of war transformed the economy because the state no longer intervened directly in the reproduction of precolonial production processes. The ideologies of free trade and anti-slavery contributed to the military's eventual loss of control over state power and altered the nature of state intervention in the economy. In 1899, when civilian administrators seized control of the state, military officers remained powerful only at the district level. Ultimately, in 1905, the forces shaping the political economy of the Middle Niger valley passed into the hands of Africans, particularly slaves.

In this chapter, I will examine the military's goals during the conquest and the role of the state in the structure of the economy. I will examine how the French military tried to mold the economy to fit its needs, and then how it molded the institutions of the states it conquered to fit administrative and economic needs as it defined them. I will conclude by examining how both the state and the metropolitan commercial interests failed to penetrate the economy before 1905.

Conquest of the Middle Niger Valley

The conquest of the interior of West Africa involved two agenda, military issues and political and economic ones. Conquest was first of all a military issue, and each year, with the arrival of the dry season, the army justified new campaigns by claiming the need for greater territorial consolidation and security. The French officers brought with them a clear notion of military authority and a set of goals that influenced the entire political and economic experiment of state building until the end of the century. If the military men thought about the state at all, it was in terms of their needs in a harsh and combative terrain. These military men hardly distinguished between the army and the state, and in the process of conquest they built yet another warrior state on the banks of the Niger. Reared under tutors like Faidherbe, Borgnis-Desbordes, and Archinard, they had as their goals military effectiveness, conquest, and glory. These goals demanded that the military men in the field maintain a certain autonomy, which they jealously guarded.

Conquest, which preceded significant metropolitan commercial penetration, had another side. Debates about the economy and the state were part of the new aggressive colonial expansion that coincided with Faidherbe's governorship in Senegal in 1854–61 and 1863–65. As a consequence of European industrialization, older principles of colonial political economy were under assault. Free markets and free labor were championed over protection and privilege. In Senegal, the attack was leveled at the gum trade. By informal but complex rules between traders and rulers, access to gum acacia trees and to markets was granted in return for revenue paid to African rulers who controlled either the main commercial artery, the Senegal River, or the commodity. On the European side, the gum trade was in the hands of the Afro-French *habitants* who were prepared to accept the imperfections of the market. In 1851 and 1853, a group of major French traders led by the Maurel family petitioned the Senegalese governor for help in promoting free trade. They argued for an end to restrictions on the marketplace and for the right of everyone to buy and sell year-round. Their complaints were forwarded to Paris, where they were well received by the government of Louis Napoleon.[1]

The concerns expressed by these merchants, who operated out of Saint-Louis but were based in Bordeaux, were consonant with the prevailing concepts of free trade in metropolitan France. During the Second Empire and well into the Third Republic, the

French state did not waver in its commitment to free trade, although it never abrogated a role for itself in the workings of the economy. The state was a champion of free trade, but as a protector of French commerce and industry, it was willing to influence the marketplace to achieve that end.[2] In 1854, with Faidherbe's appointment to Senegal, the state could feel fully justified intervening in the regional economy there to remove restrictions that belonged to a different political economy. Faidherbe's willingness to use military force was basic to this ideology of free trade.[3]

Since the 1830's, peanut cultivation had been expanding steadily throughout west-central Senegal. By the 1870's, the peanut was the leading Senegambian export and metropolitan demand showed no sign of declining. Moreover, the peanut was a crop that had all the characteristics necessary for a regime based on free trade, since it was virtually impossible to limit the numbers of producers. Peanut cultivation did not require sizeable investment of capital. Labor was the only factor of production in short supply, and this was remedied through the traditional slave supply mechanisms. Instead of being exported overseas, African labor could now be retained within the continent and in the process help the development of the colonial hinterland.[4] The issues surrounding the continuation of slavery in West Africa were ones that most administrators preferred to leave unattended.

When Governor Brière de l'Isle launched an era of renewed military expansion in 1876, the army marched first into regions of peanut cultivation. Brière also secured a mandate from Paris to construct a railway from Saint-Louis to the new capital of Dakar. Another line was to run from Medine on the Upper Senegal to Kayes, and it was planned that the railway would eventually reach the banks of the Niger. French control over the Niger had been part of the dream fostered in the days of Faidherbe. Brière actively pursued this dream: in 1878, he sent Paul Soleillet on a fact-finding mission to Segu, and in 1880, he sent a young Corsican officer, Joseph Simone Gallieni, to explore a route to Bamako that avoided the Futanke-controlled Mourgula-Nyagassola corridor. Gallieni was instructed to seek a treaty with Amadu. Gallieni explored the route, but failed to secure a treaty with the Umarians. Probably the most important result of the mission was Gallieni's conviction that the Umarian state was in an advanced state of decay. He now advocated its complete destruction.[5] The French, however, not yet ready to engage the Umarian state in military combat, chose instead to concentrate their eastward strategy along the difficult terrain of the Bakhoy-Kita-Bamako route, which skirted the southern flank of the Umarian state. The French advanced militarily along this route, and they built their railway along it.

As one of his final acts during the 1880–81 campaign, Brière appointed Borgnis-Desbordes to the new position of military commander of the Upper Rivers, and thus guaranteed that his aggressive policies would continue. Desbordes' appointment marked the opening of the formal phase of conquest in the Western Sudan.[6] Desbordes received a new battalion of Tirailleurs Sénégalais, but was held in check (at least temporarily) by orders not to advance beyond Kita. French officers like Desbordes, whose forward march was halted not by African or environmental adversaries but by administrative fiat, felt the constraints on their prerogatives keenly. The conquest of the Western Sudan occurred at a time when the relationship between the military officers in the field, the governor in Senegal, and the Ministry in Paris was often strained. Paris exerted control indirectly through the power of recall and the purse.

In February 1883, Desbordes finally led his troops to the banks of the Niger and established a fort at Bamako. Once there, however, even the intrepid Desbordes was finally forced to admit the extreme precariousness of supplies and called for negotiations with the Futanke. In the process of the campaign, officers refined the principle of not accepting orders when they did not fit their interests. Insubordination, when it brought desired results, was rewarded. For bringing the French to Bamako in the face of orders to the contrary, Desbordes himself was promoted to colonel.[7]

The French arrival in Bamako in 1883 effectively halted further eastward expansion until Archinard led the march on Segu in 1890. The intervening years, 1883–90, provide a glimpse into the operation of the colonial state in its nascent and military phase. These years offered the commandants of Bamako an opportunity to establish a rudimentary state and intervene in the economy along lines defined by the nature of their power.

For the officers who established the first French post on the banks of the Niger in 1883, the economy was a means of sustaining the army and a tool to further their political and military aims. This was a state modeled on the barracks, a state in which the economy was to be administered through established forms of requisitioning. But though the officers might exhort, cajole, threaten, and bribe, the nascent colonial state at first made little impact on the structure and performance of the economy. Only when the state entered the market as a purchaser did it begin to fashion the economy to its needs, buying large and sustained quantities of grain, which was crucial to the survival of the military.

The barracks model proved to be a failure. It could neither accomplish the goals established in France for the new colony nor fulfill the agenda of the military officers. Glory and advancement awaited the bold and brazen officer in battle, and the conquests accordingly resumed in 1890 with the capture of Segu. Then the theater for action shifted briefly westward to the Upper Rivers and Nioro. Widespread revolts throughout the Middle Niger Valley in 1891–92 effectively forestalled further conquest until 1893, when Masina fell. Only then did the Middle Niger region again form one political economy. With more territory to be controlled, the barracks model of state was now discarded. In its place, Louis Archinard, the senior military commander and the architect of the conquest, used the power of the colonial state to resurrect three "traditional" African states, modeled, however, around an obligation to respect free trade. Archinard was probably unaware of the nature of the region's precolonial political economy. As the French were to find out in 1891, free trade was incompatible with the economy of the old warrior states. But Archinard had little choice. Republican France could no longer support a state and economy that rested on continued enslavement and slavery.

Bamako Interlude, 1883–1890

In 1883, Bamako was a small town with a population of six or seven hundred. It was not at all the great commercial and political center the French had wanted as a site for their new outpost on the banks of the Niger. But it had not always been so undistinguished. During the first half of the nineteenth century, Bamako had a considerable market. Its proximity to the gold and kola markets of the forest offered certain advantages not found in the Maraka towns farther down the river. Bamako also offered Moorish traders an opportunity to establish brokerage facilities independent of the Maraka commercial networks. This is what probably attracted the Oule of Tichit, who settled in Bamako around the beginning of the nineteenth century and traded in salt and kola.[8]

In 1795, during his first voyage, Park was disappointed with Bamako. Ten years later, for all his preoccupation with the catastrophic outward part of his second journey, Park had little to say about Bamako.[9] The town's brief commercial importance coincided with the general expansion of the regional economy following the Bambara civil war. "The Bambara kings of Segu," Gallieni wrote about Bamako, "protected commercial transactions there," just as they did in the Maraka towns.[10] With the arrival of the Umarians, however, the commercial environment changed. The Futanke conquest of Kaarta and the Bambara resistance severed the desert-side connection. An occasional salt caravan evaded the Umarians and arrived in Bamako, but the increased costs posed by insecurity sapped the brief vitality the Bamako market had enjoyed. In an action replicated throughout the Western Sudan, Karamoko Oule, son of the founder of Bamako's Moorish community, joined the Niare, the Bamako chiefs who were his hosts, and the Bambara of Beledugu against the Umarians. With the coming of the Umarians, Bamako's weekly market was ruined and the population dispersed to other towns or rural hamlets.[11]

Despite Bamako's diminished and unpromising condition in 1880, Gallieni was convinced that it was well suited to the geopolitical concerns of the French. "Bamako," he wrote to the governor, "where we would expect to find not only a very active center of commerce but also a place capable of resisting the enterprise of the son of the prophet, is obviously [well] designed as the location where we ought to establish our pavilion."[12] Gallieni's arguments must have been persuasive, for the ministerial instructions to Desbordes in October 1882 reflected the commitment to a Bamako fort: "The post of Bamako should have exceptional importance, because it is destined to assure us a post located directly on the Djoliba [Bambara: Niger River]."[13]

On their arrival in Bamako, the French quickly realized their vulnerability there. In the absence of a special detachment from the corps of engineers, Desbordes ordered his French officers, the African troops, and the irregular African auxiliaries alike to help build the new fort. "Because nothing now threatens us, officers and soldiers, we will become engineers, masons, or carpenters; we will, in two months, erect a fort that is habitable and capable of victoriously resisting any attack."[14] The fort was built before the rains, and even if it was not exactly comfortable, it protected the fledgling military enterprise.

The French anticipated some resistance to their arrival, not from the Bambara as one might expect, but from the Moorish traders and the African agents of British firms in Sierra Leone or the Gambia, who had vested interests in the established north-south lines of trade.[15] In April 1883, the northern arm of Samori's army attacked the French fort. Samori's forces won the first encounter, but ten days later the French defeated Samori's forces at Weyanko Valley.[16] These battles were not the first French encounter with Samori's army, but they set the tone of relations with Samori for the next dozen years.

After the battles, the French accused three leading Moorish merchants of complicity with Samori and executed them.[17] Whether the French had sufficient evidence of the Moors' alleged treachery remains unclear. The execution clearly stated that the French were prepared to stay in Bamako, that their protectorate over Bamako gave them certain prerogatives, and that they were prepared to impose their understanding of military justice on civilians. How the Bamako notables reacted to the French assumption of judicial power is not known.

For all the French military's determination to remain in Bamako, its survival there was not easy to ensure. The principal preoccupation of the military command was steady supplies of food, weapons, and matériel. Supplies had to be carried over tortuous terrain from the river stations on the Upper Senegal more than 500 kilometers away. Convoys could be sent from Kayes, but as the yellow fever epidemic of 1881–82 demonstrated, they were subject to natural conditions that the military had little control over. It was thus essential to secure local sources of food. The ministerial instructions to Desbordes in 1882 make this clear. Efforts were to be made, argued the Minister of Marine, to find local supplies of animals, rice, millet, peanuts, and other consumables.[18] The need for food shaped the initial engagement between the Bamako barracks and the economy of the Middle Niger region.

The commander of the Bamako fort was responsible for feeding the company of cavalry, its horses, and the African troops under his command. Whenever they could, French officers ate imported canned and processed foods. Their diets were usually augmented by local meat, vegetables, and rice. Captain Ruault, who was left in charge of the fort after the departure of Desbordes, also understood the necessity of storing sufficient food for the annual military expedition dispatched to the fort from Kayes. He wrote to Lieutenant-Colonel Boilève, the new military commander, in September 1883:

> It will be necessary, before the arrival of the column, to establish at the fort a considerable supply of millet. I estimate no less than 50,000 kilograms. Even if we can pay at least half with cloth, this will represent an expense of 6,250 francs. Finally, I think that the fort could be supplied locally, at least in part, with rice that will be necessary for the next campaign. One must pay one franc per kilogram, which is in any case less than the cost of sending it from France.[19]

Ruault overestimated both his power to influence the regional economy and the producers' readiness to respond to the demand for products not usually found in markets as far south as Bamako. For the Bambara and Malinke farmers, in particular, whose food economy was intimately associated with established forms of social reproduction, selling grain on the market posed significant cultural and social problems. The Bamako grain market therefore had to be nurtured, prodded, and engineered. Problems of local supply continued to plague Ruault's successors, and it was not until 1889 that Bamako could regularly meet its own requirements.[20]

The commandant of Bamako did not have to invent solutions to the local supply problems, for the French military had learned how to survive in hostile territory from its experiences in Algeria and especially the Senegalese post of Saint-Louis. In Saint-Louis, the French colonial authorities could hire out, under the auspices of the comptroller, contracts for the supply of grain, and the

Saint-Louis barracks were indeed adequately supplied with local grains. Saint-Louis was of course a much larger community than Bamako, but it demonstrated that a local economy could, given sufficient incentives, respond to the new market for food. Faidherbe, during his first term as governor, tried another solution to the problems of a food market; he captured enemy grain stores and livestock herds. Finally, a certain amount of consumables, including grain, fish, and livestock, flowed into the French posts in payment of taxes.[21] Official purchases of food could also be made to appear part of the imperial *mission civilisatrice*. Gallieni anticipated that once the French were firmly established in the Middle Niger, an increase in prices paid for local crops would help make the Bambara less ragged and savage.[22]

Saint-Louis and Bamako were very different, nonetheless. Saint-Louis was an ocean port and could receive supplies from France throughout the year. The French posts on the Senegal River, Bakel and Medine, probably more nearly resembled Bamako in the logistical problems they faced. These forts relied on the annual flood of the Senegal River for supplies. Supplying Bamako was also seasonal, but it posed more difficult technical problems. First, the distances, while not necessarily greater than the leg from Saint-Louis to Medine, were effectively doubled. Goods moving to Medine or Kayes could use water carriage, and especially the new steamboat service along the Senegal; the route from Medine to Bamako, with the exception of the leg between Kayes and Bafoulabe, went overland (see Map 5).[23]

This overland movement of goods required virtually an army of its own. Convoys of porters marched alongside colonial troops. Porters were usually recruited locally and worked segments of the *route de ravitaillement*, as the line from Kayes to Bamako through Bafoulabe and Kita was called. Porters rarely came forward voluntarily; most were more or less impressed from communities along the way. The *villages de liberté*, founded by the colonial authorities as a measure to protect freed slaves, were strategically positioned along the supply line.[24] Although the porters were compensated for their labor, sometimes as much as one meter of guinée cloth a day plus a liter of rice, the work was grueling and took a high toll on the porters. Porters carried loads of 25 to 30 kilograms each. A report by the commandant of Ba-

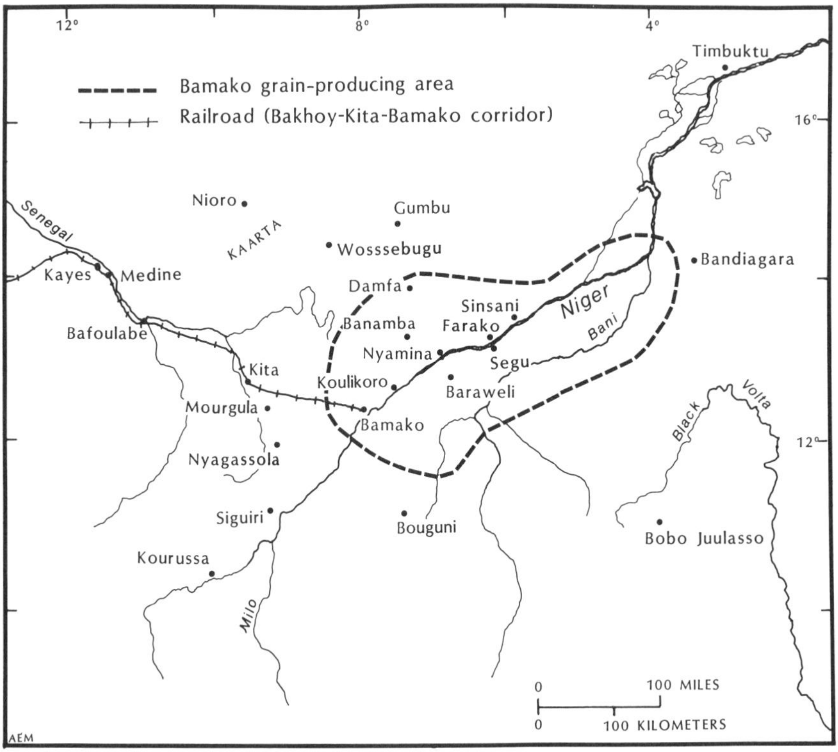

Map 5. The Grain Market of the Middle Niger Valley, ca. 1900

mako in May 1886 made this clear: "Captain Tautain has sent a convoy of 200 [porters] to Kita to supply the column. They returned on the 15th [April], almost half were incapable of doing any service for many days."[25] Porters also resented the work, which was often required during crucial periods of the agrarian calendar.

Second, the cost of moving goods over difficult terrain was very high. Even when the railway finally connected Bamako to Kayes in 1904, moving a ton of rice between Saint-Louis and the Middle Niger doubled the original price.[26] Donkey carriage or headloading could only have been more expensive. The main technological innovation in the supply system was the Lefèvre wagon, built especially for African conditions. Lefèvre wagons were designed to be airtight, which meant that they could float across rivers and streams without losing time to the burdensome off- and on-loading of pack animals. They could transport 250 to 300 kilograms each.[27] Lefèvre wagons seemed to solve many of the pressing supply problems, but they also created technical difficulties of their own. The combined weight of the metal casing, which assured watertightness, and the actual load made these wagons heavy indeed. Baillaud's description of the direct and indirect costs involved is worth recording:

> What an extraordinary idea to think that these heavy mechanisms would be ideally constructed for the colonies or for the transport of whatever. A round metal casing (of the sort that wastes much space) is supported by enormous iron wheels, whose maintenance requires almost daily replacement of the hubs; it is provided with iron axles, whose weight is almost equal to that of the entire wagon. . . . In the [Western] Sudan they are not used, because of the costs of maintenance and repair. One can easily understand how the Lefèvre wagons could become the sinister instruments of torture for the poor soldiers charged with bringing them up the ravines of Madagascar.[28]

It was obvious to the French military command that the supply route could be used only to transport essential matériel. Transporting food, not to mention having to provide for the subsistence of the army of porters, was neither practical nor economically feasible. Local sources of subsistence were critical to the survival of the colonial military in the Western Sudan.

The way the military commanders of Bamako stimulated the market for food indicated the manner of their intervention in the economy. To requisition grain from neighboring communities, which would only solve temporary shortfalls, would leave deep resentments and ultimately hinder the diplomatic goals of the Bamako fort. And it was impossible to contract grain purchases on the open market, as was done in Senegal, since there was no market yet capable of meeting the needs of the military.

The Bamako commandants tinkered with market forces through a variety of economic and extra-economic mechanisms for developing an active commerce in Bamako. They had first to identify and eliminate the obstacles to commerce. Some of the obstacles clearly remained beyond their control. For one thing, the entire edifice of the Umarian state contributed to the decline in regional commercial activity, and even if a Bamako commandant wanted to combat it, the military leadership of the Western Sudan was under orders from Paris not to do battle with the *grands noirs* of the region, namely Amadu, Samori, and Tieba.[29] Such actions as the French contemplated would have to be carried out at the local level. The case of Titi Niare, chief of Bamako, illustrates the obstacles the French encountered. Sensing a new opportunity to extract revenue, he raised market taxes and doubled some ferry tariffs for the Niger crossing immediately after the French arrived. Traders regularly passed through Bamako, but they did not sell their goods locally. "Bamako," reported the commandant in August 1885, "is bypassed in favor of the high prices received on the right bank."[30]

A gunboat mission later in 1885 helped draw attention to the French presence in the region, and by the end of the year the commandant was able to report that transit across the river had more than tripled and that Bamako had become much more important.[31] The grain market, however, responded more slowly than traders to changes in the commercial environment. Some progress was made during 1885, although it remained doubtful whether the fort could provision itself with rice. By mid-1885, market forces unleashed by the presence of non-farming residents contributed to the emergence of a special Wednesday produce market to complement the regular Saturday market. The Wednesday market was held near the fort and sufficed to meet the needs of the garrison and the wives of the African troops.[32] It was clear that African producers were prepared to respond to market demand, although both climatic and political considerations influenced their capacity and willingness to bring goods to the Bamako market.

The Bamako Saturday market increased slowly but steadily. By the end of 1885, however, the French delivered a blow to the very market forces they had helped to unleash. Prompted by military considerations, they took an action that severely damaged the operation of the local economy.

> Between December 1885 and January 1886, there has been a significant drop in trade through Bamako. The cause is simple: we have prohibited commerce with the right bank, which is intent on provisioning our enemy Samori. Horses, munitions, salt, etc.—all were stopped in Bamako.

> These orders, communicated to our friendly neighboring villages are also known to the majority of juulus and Maraka. They know that it is not useful to come to Bamako with the intention of getting a good price on the right bank, because they know they will be retained in our village for an uncertain length of time. Most of these merchants have redirected their animals to our supply service.[33]

The prohibition on trade with Samori, which constituted the bulk of the transit trade through Bamako, was felt deeply in the town. Merchants avoided Bamako. They crossed the river further downstream at Nyamina, Segu, and Sinsani. Changes in routes necessarily influenced the service industries in Bamako and disrupted local commerce. Following the decline in local commerce, Captain Loyer, the commandant of Bamako in 1886–87, began construction of a new marketplace, much grander than the rough traditional location. It was to be a symbol of the renewed quest for commerce. Loyer also sought to encourage more traders to Bamako by prohibiting them passage across the Niger at Sinsani, Nyamina, Koulikoro, and Kangaba.[34] His replacement, Doctor Tautain, sent out a request to 49 neighboring villages to return to Bamako for the Saturday market.[35]

French intervention in the economy was directed by contradictory motives. They wanted a marketplace solution to their food supply needs and they saw the economy as a tool in the arsenal of weapons against their enemies. Prohibiting the movement of horses to Samori's troops was similar to the embargo on arms sales to the Umarians. Both were attempts to mold the market to fit the political aims of the military state. The problem, however, was that the local Bamako market remained tangential to the major commercial currents in the region. By merely avoiding the zone where the French could influence trade, merchants still responded to demand for regionally specialized trade. Samori still received his horses, and the French could stop this trade only by paying higher prices, sending out raiding parties, or bringing a larger area under their direct control. They eventually did resort to further conquest, but not until the next decade.

If the military in West Africa remained convinced of its glorious role as conqueror of the Western Sudan, Paris did not. The Ministers of the Marine, most of whom were military men in their own right, assumed the dominant ideologies of progress and free trade. They also understood, even if they did not condone, the military's agenda, and while they could accept the need to maintain a militant posture, they stressed that the underlining objectives of French occupation were not simply conquest. "Vis-à-vis the Futanke in general," Minister Rousseau wrote to the governor of Senegal in the summer of 1885, "observe an attitude that is defiant but not hostile." He went on to develop what he took to be the objectives of the French endeavor:

> Time, foresight, consistency, and above all equity are the arms with which we will triumph effectively against all resistance that we encounter at the beginning of our influence. [Our] loyal partisans, who might now be small in number, rapidly increase once they recognize that far from exploiting them, we want only to establish a situation in which they can tranquilly cultivate their land, profit from the progress of our industry in refining their [techniques of] production, permit the free exchange of their products for ours, and help them appreciate the value of [our products].[36]

This vision, replete with its paternalist assumptions, did not exclude force as a tool for the advancement of French influence. It merely subordinated its importance. Paris accepted the fine line between preserving security and gratuitous adventure. This was clear in the instructions Minister Peyron sent to Colonel Frey, the new military commander. "Only in the case of direct attack by Amadu, or in the case of his ravaging the land that furnishes us with subsistence for our garrisons and other indispensable resources, only then push Amadu beyond Beledugu, without going too far."[37] Archinard, military commander during the conquest of the Middle Niger valley, pushed to the limit the implications of "security," as his letter makes clear:

> To respond to an aggression by pushing directly back to the old line will not produce success for us. The enemy will return, he will have with him the booty taken from our villages, and he will not wait for us. Amadu's lands and ours share too large a space for our small number of soldiers and partisans not to see that by attacking only in self-defense [we] will not stop the ruin of our people. . . . The necessity of one day taking Segu is recognized everywhere. . . . I am talking of an eventuality, and I am not asking for an order to take Segu, I am asking only to

conserve a little liberty of action with all the responsibility it implies for a military leader on campaign, but I ask for permission to decline all responsibility if my freedom of action is taken away.[38]

Archinard's letter was written on the eve of his assembling the conquest force for the capture of Segu in 1890, but it clearly reflects his frustration. Archinard, one of the central actors in the conquest of the Western Sudan, raised to new heights the problem of military insubordination. His threats about the fragility of the colonial enterprise barely veiled his intention of conquering a larger area and eliminating the territorial and political obstacles to a viable colonial economy. By destroying the Umarians, Archinard hoped to deliver the entire Middle Niger to the new colonial state.

Archinard conquered the Middle Niger valley in the spring of 1890. His success was made possible by the increased ability of the Bamako grain market to provide sufficient stores for the annual military campaign. For years the French commandants had struggled with ambivalent and contradictory goals, but by December 1889 the grain market provided the Bamako fort 21 metric tons of millet and 17 metric tons of rice. In January 1890, the Bamako commandant bought 35 metric tons of millet and 21.5 metric tons of rice. This was the first time since its founding that the fort of Bamako could fully meet its anticipated food requirements and also those of the forthcoming campaign.[39]

But if farmers were now willing to part with their grain, herders were still reluctant to part with their animals. "The post cannot," wrote the Bamako commandant in February 1890, "procure the number of beef it desires. The cattle that have arrived from Timbuktu and the north are weak and of poor quality."[40] The French had made strategic mistakes in their efforts to foster a livestock market. All along the route de ravitaillement, the French officials requisitioned both labor and cattle. In 1889, Lieutenant-Colonel Peroz condemned these practices: "It has come to be that the villages staggered along that line, villages that we ought to have had an interest in nurturing in order to see them develop, instead become depopulated each day. . . . If the villagers want to reconstitute their herds, they disappear into the forest, because we do not always leave them sufficient animals to reproduce [their herds]."[41] The requisitional model, which the

French avoided when building the grain market, seems to have been applied rather freely to the purchase of animals. The long-term implications of this policy hindered the development of commercial livestock sales.

The market in grains and other foodstuffs, nurtured by official military intervention in the economy, yielded large profits for the metropolitan commercial houses that established themselves in Bamako. By the turn of the century, the grain harvest became central to the regional economy and an indicator of its performance. "Commercial traffic," wrote William Ponty in the annual report on the colony's trade in 1900, "has been directly proportional to the quality of the harvests."[42] In 1903, the Bamako commandant estimated that participating in the grain market and speculating in a futures market yielded French traders and some metropolitan commercial houses about as much revenue as they earned during the entire year from other sources.[43] The expansion of the colonial economy after 1890, however, had to await further conquest and further consolidation of the French colonial presence.

Ideology and Politics in Building the Colonial State

In conquering Segu, Archinard clearly exceeded his ministerial orders, but dismantling the Umarian state had become an overpowering objective for him. For almost a year in advance, Archinard made secret arrangements for the march to Segu. Stores of munitions and food had to be on hand, bridges built along the proposed route, auxiliaries recruited, and negotiations pursued with the Bambara rebels. Captain Marchand reported from his mission in 1889 to Farako, the headquarters of Jara resistance on the left bank opposite Segu, that the Futanke capital was heavily fortified, and that any attack on the city would require considerable firepower.[44]

The march to Segu began nearly two months in advance of the actual storming of the city. Archinard left Kayes, the usual staging point for the annual military campaign, and followed the supply route to Bamako. Along the route Archinard recruited additional tirailleurs and auxiliaries. The two gunboats, berthed at Koulikoro, joined the procession as it departed for Farako. A flotilla of canoes from Somono villages on the left bank joined to make this expedition a colorful affair, and a logistical nightmare. Archinard's African army was transmuted only superficially by 720 regular soldiers and 32 French officers.[45] The 1,500 auxiliaries were eager for battle. For them, glory was probably less important than the allure of the rich booty reportedly stored within the Futanke capital. Twenty-five years earlier, Mage had reported on the fabulous treasure captured from the Bambara and hoarded by the Futanke.[46] Early on the morning of 6 April 1890, troops and artillery were ferried across the Niger on canoes supplied by the Somono from Nyamina. After Archinard promised that their villages would be respected, the Segu Somono also aided the French. By early afternoon, Segu belonged to the French. Lieutenant Sensarric quickly occupied the treasury, but it proved to be almost bare. To halt the auxiliaries' wild scramble for booty, Archinard ordered the tirailleurs to chase them out of Segu.[47]

Segu fell without resistance, much as it had fallen to the Umarians nearly 30 years earlier. Although Amadu had managed to strengthen his position within the Umarian leadership in 1884, Segu remained a weak link. It had never been fully integrated into a larger Futanke state, nor did it control the countryside. In 1887, Lieutenant Caron had reported that Segu was suffering from drought, and that her former enemy, Sinsani, was supplying her with grain.[48] By 1890, the situation had worsened. Madani, Amadu's son, did not even try to face the French, but fled with a handful of talaba. Archinard, not satisfied with Segu, reassembled his troops and marched on the Futanke fortress of Wossebugu. Much to his chagrin, the French managed to capture the stronghold only after a difficult street-by-street battle. Wossebugu was a reminder that the Futanke were not yet ready to acquiesce in French rule over the land.

The capture of Segu sent clear signals of French intentions to dismantle what remained of the Umarian state. Nioro was taken in 1891 and Masina and Bandiagara followed in 1893. Amadu fled from Nioro to Bandiagara, and from Bandiagara eastward to Sokoto, where he died in 1897 surrounded by a handful of faithful talaba. In 1891, Archinard's plans were interrupted by a severe case of blood flukes, which necessitated his return to France. He was replaced by Colonel Humbert. Humbert tried to emulate Archinard's style, but he was neither as skillful nor as lucky and he was recalled in disgrace.[49] Archinard returned in 1893 to complete his endeavor, but with a strong warning from Paris. His initiatives had exceeded the tolerance of the Ministry and had incurred the ire of his opponents in the French National Assembly. The Assembly, preoccupied with budgetary considerations, had had enough of military independence and escalating expenses in the Western Sudan. Moreover, the Boulanger crisis of 1888–90 had raised serious questions about the loyalty of some military officers, if not the entire military establishment. In 1893 Albert Grodet became the first civilian governor, and in 1894 a separate Ministry of Colonies was established.

Grodet was appointed to curb military independence and to adhere more closely to directives from Paris. One of his first acts was to dismiss Archinard. Still a popular hero, Archinard returned to France, where he later secured an appointment in the new Ministry of Colonies. Grodet was an able administrator, but his pronounced anti-military inclinations meant that he was probably not the best candidate for the governorship. The military men in the field resented his intrusion and resisted his policies. Grodet could never be sure whether his orders would be implemented.[50]

Glory still awaited the rash and successful soldier. In 1894, Lieutenant-Colonel Bonnier, disregarding orders from Paris and from his superiors, captured Timbuktu. After his heady victory, Bonnier let his defenses lapse and he died an ignoble death at night at the hands of rebellious Tuareg. Punitive action against the Tuareg was sanctioned, but further military activities were curtailed.

Grodet returned to France on leave in 1895 and never returned. He was succeeded by Colonel Trentinian. Trentinian was committed to principles of commercial predominance over accumulated conquest, but his power to shape the colonial enterprise was limited. Military officers continued to monopolize administrative posts at the district level, even though they were probably uninterested in mundane affairs of state. Many still firmly believed that Archinard's implicit promise of combat duties in exchange for administrative duties should be honored. They received their opportunity in 1896, when the Ministry of Colonies authorized the completion of the conquest of the Western Sudan.

To secure their control over the interior of West Africa, the French marched against Babemba, who had succeeded Tieba as faama of Kenedugu, and Samori, who had been pushed further eastward to the frontiers of Asante. With the conquest of Sikasso and the capture of Samori in 1898, the French won their last major military victory in the region.[51]

The larger state that Archinard erected in the Middle Niger valley between 1890 and 1893 could not be sustained merely on an enlarged version of the barracks model developed at Bamako. It demanded a different organization. Archinard, who may not have thought about the long-term implications of his policies, sought legitimacy for the new state in what he understood to be traditional African forms.

Since 1889, Captain Underberg in Bamako had been following Archinard's instructions to entice the Jara leader to join the French cause. Archinard's goal was to restore the Ngolossi, the former Bambara rulers of Segu. The vision of a renewed Segu Bambara state was appealing to both the Jara and the French. For the Jara, an alliance with the French might provide a means of rising above the competing loyalties of the resistance movement; for the French, a Jara leader in Segu would provide legitimacy to a French protectorate without the costs of direct administration.[52] Archinard crowned the Jara leader king of Segu in April 1890. We have no way of knowing whether Archinard saw the coronation as a long-term commitment to African institutions of state, or as a temporary expedient. He did, at any rate, crown three additional Africans kings during the next three years. Clearly, Archinard saw in African kingship an adequate solution to the problems of building a new state on the ashes of Futanke rule and inserting French power in strategic sectors of the new polity.

On 11 April, Archinard set the mortar to the new structures of state power in the Middle Niger valley. He told the assembled chiefs of the larger villages of the Segu heartland that

> Frenchmen have not come to Segu to take the land and to govern themselves, but with the intention of giving to the Bambara that which was stolen by the Futanke.
>
> One of the reasons that influenced the French to come is that the

Futanke were insolent bandits, barriers to free trade. But I know that the Bambara are bandits too, and that they pillaged not only the city but also the goods of other Bambara. This is not good.

I will give Segu to the son of your previous kings: your faama will be, beginning today, Mari Jara, but under certain conditions that will guarantee that the happiness of the land will be assured, that trade will be free, and that the Bambara of the right bank will not pillage those of the left bank. . . . To that end, the Commandant Supérieur will leave a white officer with his troops here. This Resident will reside in the Jonfutu [Amadu's palace]. The French Resident will not occupy himself with the administrative affairs between the faama and his neighboring villages. The faama will fully exercise his rights and nominate or change his chiefs according to his views, but the Resident has the right to be informed of all that takes place.[53]

Archinard built guarantees for commerce into this contract for a new state. He could do no less. Metropolitan opinion and the French government were committed to the principles of free trade. He therefore insisted that the new king not interfere with trade or the free navigation of the river. Only the French Resident was to have the power to deliver travel permits to traders, ostensibly to ensure that they not be unduly burdened by taxes. A similar division occurred in fiscal administration. All revenue, traditionally derived from Bambara villages and from the state herds, was exclusively the king's. Taxes derived from marketing or transporting goods by caravans and canoes were to be shared between the king and the French treasury. "All the routes are open," insisted Archinard at the meeting. "The Bozo and the Somono, who are, in fact, traders, will be exclusively under the orders of the Resident."[54] All disputes concerning trade were to be mediated by the Resident. No longer could the Bambara kings mold commerce to their ends. Archinard's decisions fundamentally altered the precolonial forms of state intervention in the economy.

The state as conceived by Archinard was instrumentalist. Segu under the Jara was a means of detaching part of the Umarian state and establishing a loyal African opposition.[55] He offered no evidence of planning for a state with a distinctive colonial character. He further complicated the organization of the new state by creating two islands in the Segu heartland that were outside of Mari Jara's jurisdiction. Bojan, a claimant to the rival Massassi Bambara throne of Kaarta, was made chief of Nango and its outlying agricultural hamlets, which were populated mainly by Bambara slaves from Kaarta. Bojan had been a principal leader of auxiliary troops during the recent Sudanese campaigns, and Archinard wanted to reward him. But placing Bojan at Nango, only 40 kilometers from Segu, made him a direct threat to Mari Jara's legitimacy. The other island was Sinsani, which included an imprecise zone on the left bank. In 1891, Archinard would select a trusted Senegalese Futanke agent as king.

The states Archinard created rested on a basic contradiction. Archinard imposed on Mari Jara tasks that he was clearly unwilling or unable to complete. The king had only recently held leadership over the Jara loyalist faction of the Bambara resistance movement. He had had little chance to prove himself in battle. Nor could his legitimacy be founded on rank alone. The social contract between the Bambara faama and his warriors depended on his ability to offer them rewards. Mari Jara's coronation may have given him legitimacy in the eyes of the French, but he still had to prove himself to his followers. Warfare was crucial to his relationship with them, and warfare the French tolerated only on their own terms. Through April and May following his coronation, Mari Jara did not or could not control his tonjonw followers, who continued to pillage both sides of the river.[56]

At the end of May 1890, the French accused Mari Jara and his advisers of conspiring to assassinate the French Resident and his troops and declare themselves independent. They were summarily executed. The executions revealed the weakness in Archinard's model of traditional African states, for state power among the Segu Bambara depended on a complex relationship between the king and his warriors, which in turn depended on the state's involvement in warfare. Archinard obviously had something else in mind.

Following the executions, the surviving members of the royal family and their loyal warriors fled into the Baninko, the traditional refuge of the Bambara. There the Bambara staged a general rebellion, which taxed to the limit the small reserves of troops left to the Segu Resident and the Bamako commandant. In the summer of 1890, Bojan and Mademba Sy, both leading African auxiliaries, moved into the Baninko to suppress the rebellion and were held at bay for nearly a year. At the end of April 1891, they finally crushed the Baninko rebellion.

The Baninko rebellion sobered Archinard, for it revealed the immediate weakness of his version of indirect rule. Although his commitment to African kingship was not shaken, he would now only appoint Africans who had proven themselves loyal collaborators, regardless of their traditional claims on kingship. In 1891, he crowned Bojan king in Segu, but worried about future rebellions. Archinard wrote to Eugène Etienne, the powerful undersecretary of state for the colonies, that Bojan's kingdom was much too large and unstable for Africans to govern. They constantly produced revolts, and revolts, Archinard did not have to say, raised ever greater financial demands on the Ministry. "I have thought," he reported, "that it will be good to establish a second kingdom next to that of Segu, a kingdom that will be powerful and devoted and that could extend toward Jenne, where it will eventually place its capital. This kingdom will be formed out of the land of the left bank of the Niger. . . . The new chief will reside in Sinsani." Archinard concluded that the only problem with this model of the state was to find a suitable candidate. He then proposed Mademba Sy, whose devotion and leadership were clearly proven.[57] Mademba was crowned king of Sinsani in 1891. In his letter of investiture he was instructed to work with all his might "for the development in the land of French influence, of our ideas of civilization, and of commerce."[58]

These instructions were more than mere platitudes to Mademba, who had been an employee in the Senegalese colonial post and telegraph service since 1869, an active participant in the Sudan campaigns since 1879, and Desbordes' political officer in 1882–83. Mademba had also become a French citizen during the brief period when France practiced assimilation in the four communes of Senegal. He had been to France and was demonstrably Francophile. If Mademba warranted Archinard's hopes and expectations for a viable and reliable African kingdom, Archinard's disappointment must have been all the greater when in 1891 a revolt against Mademba flared throughout the left bank. By early 1892, Mademba was a prisoner in his palace and had to be rescued by Bonnier.[59]

The results of the 1892–93 campaign to suppress African resistance were ambiguous in terms of Archinard's model of a traditional African state. On his way through Segu to Minianka and Jenne, Archinard retired Bojan as king of Segu. Segu became an administrative entity similar to the other cercles in the Western Sudan, the Resident became commandant, and all traditional taxes were abolished in favor of a regular system of taxation.[60] The suppression of the Segu Bambara state, however, was not the end of Archinard's experiment. Once in Bandiagara, the Futanke capital of Masina, he crowned Aguibu, one of Umar's sons, king, just as he had crowned Mari Jara, Bojan, and Mademba. This appointment was a significant political maneuver, since Aguibu remained a respected member of the Umarian community. Amid the pomp and ceremony at Bandiagara on 4 May 1893, Archinard read his letter of investiture, perhaps unaware of the paradox: "By virtue of the power given me by the Government of France, I make you king of Masina and I install you at Bandiagara as its capital."[61] Despite lingering monarchist sentiment scattered throughout the French military, France's Third Republic was well established in the early 1890's. The colonies, however, seem to have provided a fertile environment in which to implement at least some of the fancies of French conquerors.[62]

Archinard continued to worry about the viability of his model of state power. From Bandiagara, he passed through Sinsani with the object of completing the administrative reorganization of the Middle Niger valley. To Mademba he wrote, "The small amount of success you have had, the desertions of your sofa, and the measures you have taken to create order and discipline indicate that I have given you a task that was too heavy. I have abandoned the idea of seeing you command one day in Bandiagara."[63] The political experiment of building state power along traditional lines interpreted and channeled through a French colonial military mentality had uneven results. Throughout the Middle Niger, the dynamic of state power remained the active involvement of the French military in governance.

One of the major questions Archinard and his successors faced after conquest was how to ensure fiscal liquidity without hindering trade. Taxes were a legitimate concern of state, and in the

Third Republic taxes were used to promote and protect commerce and industry. The recent debates in France about tariffs permeated the West African savanna and informed the context of colonial taxation policies. Taxes on traders were to be minimal, although the exact linkages to traditional practice remained vague. Lieutenant-Colonel Humbert, who succeeded Archinard in 1891, grappled with the vague mandate Archinard left to the Segu Resident. He focused the debate on the wusuru, the 10 percent import-export duty applied by the Umarians as part of the public revenue system of Islamic states. Humbert's arguments, which were far from unique to him, clearly express the tensions between taxes as instruments of state power, forms of fiscal administration, and means of intervening in the economy. In a letter to the Segu commandant, he wrote:

> The wusuru is virtually prohibitive. . . . The merchandise of the Moors, for example, in moving to Kenedugu will pay 1/10 on entering our territories, 1/10 on entering Segu, and 1/10 on leaving Segu. This equals 3/10, and the same is payable on the return. That is more than 50/100.
>
> I think as you do that the wusuru is an affirmative right of sovereignty and not an instrument to feed the finances of the state, even at the risk, because of its repetition or because its tariffs are too high, of diminishing in notable proportions the commercial movement of the region.
>
> There are two solutions: either to suppress one of our customs zones or to reduce the tariff. You propose with reason the lowering of the tariffs because even partial suppression of this right would reduce the prestige and finances of the regions.[64]

Humbert's solution was not very imaginative. He proposed retaining all customs zones but reducing the wusuru to one-twentieth the value of the goods imported. His only innovation was to abandon export duties.

Humbert's proposals on fiscal policy reflected an ambivalence shared by other military commanders. For the early administrators, the aims of colonialism were fairly simple: to seek peace and stability and to foster commerce. The means to achieve these ends, however, led to the marriage of African institutions to military barracks practice, often with peculiar results. The following was the situation in Segu, for example: "The Bozo and the Somono are by reason of their usual occupations placed under the exclusive authority of the French. If the faama has something to request of the Bozo or Somono, he can only do so through the French [Resident], who may accept or reject the request."[65]

Archinard understood the important role the Somono could play in the military organization of the state through their control of transport and communication. He was careful to claim traditional precedents, and in the process he inserted the French barracks model at the very core of the reproduction of the state and the Somono. In his instructions to the Segu Resident, he outlined the services the Somono were to render: "In addition to the revenues due to the French government in exchange for the protection it accords the Bozo, they are charged, as it is their practice, to provide [fresh food] for the palace of the Resident."[66] The French reproduced the form if not content of the social contract with the Somono and ensured that they were placed under the direct authority of the French at every major riverine town.[67] This relationship entailed special privileges for the Somono, but also special obligations in terms of provisioning of goods and services.

The French reproduced their share in the relationship as they understood Bambara practice. The Futanke had not provided the Somono with the same support as the Segu Bambara had, but they expected the same services. This had led to a crisis for the Somono and the riverine economy. The Resident of Segu explained how in the first year of the new state he had fostered the Somono-state relationship. Of the five to six thousand captives the Futanke left behind them when they left the town in 1890, one thousand "were given to the Somono, and the rest separated in villages of the province of Segu in groups commanded by a chief."[68] At about the same time, Sinsani notables asked Archinard for state assistance in reconstituting the Somono along the river: "We would like to request [that you] give us several of Amadu's canoes that are at Segu, to put at the personal disposal [of the Somono of Sinsani] and to put at your service. This had been the practice of the first Bambara who inhabited Segu."[69]

Accounts of the early colonial experiment in state building on the Niger reveal the strands woven together by the military commanders to establish the legitimacy of their new rule through traditional African institutions. But in their commitment to liberating trade and commerce from what they thought were restrictive practices, the new colonial rulers excluded a huge terrain from their political apparatus of state. Their actions would eventually negate the precolonial African model of state power. By eliminating the state's established form of intervention in the economy, they deprived the state of its established role as reproducer of relations of production. If the economy was to be free, any constraints on access to resources had to be removed. The new ideology of free trade was therefore difficult for the military builders of state to uphold. For them, precolonial institutions such as the state-Somono relationship remained vital to the maintenance of military effectiveness. The French tried to reproduce a traditional relationship, but they were (or would be, especially after 1905) intolerant of any judicial restrictions on access to resources. The very basis of the state-Somono relationship was the guarantee of exclusive privilege. The crisis of the new colonial state over the next fifteen years is directly related to the incompatibility of certain precolonial economic institutions with the French commitment to a free economy.

Commerce and the Colonial State, 1883–1905

The colonial economy was fashioned slowly. As the Bamako interlude of 1883–90 clearly demonstrated, the state had a limited capacity to forge a new economy. Even with the expansion of the colonial state following the conquest of Segu in 1890, the regional economy remained fundamentally precolonial. French metropolitan commercial houses established themselves in Bamako with reluctance, and their share of long-distance trade remained insignificant. The survival of most commercial houses depended on their success in inserting themselves into local and regional patterns of trade.

From the standpoint of metropolitan commerce, Bamako remained a commercial backwater well into the first years of the new century. Built originally to aid military conquest, the railway, which arrived in Bamako in 1904, grafted a colonial layer onto the regional economy. The railway ended the isolation of the Bamako fort, provided a new point of departure for metropolitan commerce, made possible the comparatively cheap export of agricultural products, and created employment. Export crops like rubber, grain, peanuts, and cotton offered peasants a fairly reliable income. Grain exports increased dramatically after 1905. Sales of peanuts expanded rapidly after 1907. Cotton production, encouraged directly by the administration from 1898, also expanded, if somewhat more gradually.[70] Metropolitan commerce finally discovered a set of profitable operations. But if the railway provided a viability for the colonial economy of the Middle Niger valley for the first time, it did not assure its success.

As the railhead inched its way from Kayes to Bamako over more than 25 years, the center of colonial commercial and administrative activity shifted with it. Kayes was both the commercial center, until it was displaced by Kita, and the seat of administration for the Western Sudan until 1907, when the colonial administration was moved to Bamako. In the late 1880's and 1890's, Kita became the hub of the colonial economy. As late as 1898, Bamako had only one permanent commercial house, Gilium, Pillet, and Colas. In addition, seven or eight other companies were represented in Bamako, but most of them, according to Baillaud, "do but appear and disappear. They arrive with a stock of merchandise, which they exhaust and do not renew."[71] According to the Bamako commandant in 1891, large European traders and their agents all returned to Medine in August.[72] The colonial economy of the 1890's thus reflected a seasonality determined more by the precolonial economy than by interests of French commerce. By 1900, however, there were nine metropolitan commercial houses located in Bamako.

Merchandise from France was offloaded at Saint-Louis or Dakar, brought by river to Medine, and then transshipped by rail from Kayes to Kita. Supplies from Kita were brought overland to Bamako and the mining regions of Upper Guinea. Gilium, Pillet, and Colas was remarkable among French commercial houses because it organized its own supply system. While Gilium invested in wagons, modeled on the Lefèvre wagon, but lighter and more maneuverable, and in river craft to supply its affiliate in Timbuktu, most other European commercial concerns relied on the services of administrative ravitaillement or local Moor transporters to carry their goods, for a fee of course. The Moors, who charged a more or less regular tariff, captured most of the commercial carriage of goods between the railhead and Bamako. In 1903, Moors charged eight to ten francs per load on the 196-kilometer journey from Kita to Bamako; they charged five francs per load on the 130-kilometer trip from Bamako to Banamba. In Segu the rate was assessed per unit-day rather than for the voyage. Donkeys were hired at one franc a day.[73]

In the minds of colonial administrators, the railway had come to embody the colonial economy. In his annual economic report for 1904, the lieutenant-governor noted a causal link between the railway and European commerce. "Kita," the report noted, "attained its commercial apogee while it was the terminus of the railway under construction. The progressive distancing of the terminus has resulted in a diminution of its commerce. At the present time, it is almost totally abandoned. . . . The rapid routing of merchandise toward the interior [allows] merchants the possibility of renewing their stock three times each year, thus tripling their transactions."[74] In 1908, the Bamako commandant could write that "railway traffic is the principal element in the increase of economic activity of the cercle."[75]

There is no question that the railway provided metropolitan commercial houses with a means of expanding the trade of the Western Sudan. A mere increase in quantities imported or exported did not, however, determine the structural viability of the colonial economy. The organizational and managerial weaknesses of European commerce, in the twentieth century as in earlier centuries, stemmed from peculiar problems such as high fixed overheads and top-heavy administrations.[76] Maurel and Prom, ardent proponents of a liberal economy in Senegal during the 1850's, vacillated in their commitment to the idea as circumstances demanded. With other expatriate merchants in Nioro, they petitioned the governor-general around 1900 to restrict competition there. The complaints of these European merchants were probably echoed throughout the Western Sudan.

> The European traders and [their] native agents request that you suppress the sale of European cloth [by independent African traders] at Nioro, as well as at Kayes and Medine.

The competition by small juulas and the Moors helps make all serious and durable trade at Nioro disappear. We transport at great cost our stock of considerable merchandise, and each year we see an increase thanks to our durable commerce. But because we pay the license fees and because of [the overhead cost of] our installation, we can see [a profit margin] of only .10 to .20 francs [per unit] for the duration of our stay, even though we sell 500 to 1,000 francs worth of goods on market days.

[The native traders] rarely sell on the market, are very well informed [about prices], do not stay when it is not useful, and can therefore sell their goods at a low price.[77]

These complaints reflected the frustrations of European merchants in the retail sphere. They resented competition from Africans, especially from small traders who worked close to the margin and close to consumers. Profits for European commerce could be enormous, but unrestrained competition cut deeply into them. Certainly European commercial houses were subject to tighter licensing and they operated at considerable disadvantages in their competition with African merchants who did not have high overheads and large stocks. Often, however, the very operation of European commerce was inefficient. The lieutenant-governor's official report on commerce in the Western Sudan for 1903 is telling in this respect. It also indicates something of the administration's ambivalence to European commerce:

I must begin with a little digression on the manner in which [commercial] studies have been made in the Western Sudan by the agents of the Companies, which are created all the time for the exploitation of different regions of the land.

These young men, who are without any preparation for these countries when they leave the Ecoles Coloniales, are sent by the Companies to travel in the Western Sudan and make studies. They generally stop at Kayes, where they pass one or two months sick from the excesses that they have indulged in, and are sent home without having seen anything and know absolutely nothing about the needs of the land. Their Companies then send to the Western Sudan merchandise not salable in these regions. Others with capital travel along the routes overused [by other merchants] from Kayes to Bamako, Faranah, Kouroussa, Timbo, and Konakry in French Guinea to trade for rubber, and are [thus] obliged to buy [it] at whatever price. The rubber thus bought without consideration of the price ties up capital that was given to them to open new areas. This [practice] resulted, between November 1898 and May 1899, in the rise of the rubber price from 2.5 francs/kilo to 6.75 francs.[78]

Echoing another feature of the Umarian warriors before them, senior administrators often barely disguised their contempt for European merchants' petty efforts to accumulate huge profits.[79] According to the 1903 report, profits themselves were not at risk; only the size of the profits. For example, profits for the three large Bordelais commercial houses that dominated the trade of the Upper Rivers averaged 20 to 50 percent.[80] The Nioro-based firm of Richaud and Schwab, importers of cloth and exporters of gum, ivory, rubber, and ostrich feathers, "calculate their profits at 110 percent, which is not probability, but the exact consequences of serious sales that are both certain and remunerative." Profits from the export of African produce such as gum from Nioro and peanuts from Kayes were possible because of the proximity of these areas to the cheap transport of the Senegal river. Profits could be made from rubber, but the boom ended in 1906 thanks to high producer prices, rapidly declining supply, and poor quality.[81]

Richaud and Schwab, however, did not rely on the import-export market to realize their fortunes. In 1903, they also traded some 100,000 muules of millet, 3,000 bars of salt, and 10,000 sheep, all of which they converted through a series of local exchanges into gold.[82] Many commercial houses, especially those in Bamako before the arrival of the railway and the smaller ones like Richaud and Schwab of Nioro, participated in African trade networks. This was especially true in the growing grain markets in Bamako and Kita. By the beginning of the century, European commercial houses had established a parallel grain supply and marketing operation that both fed and occasionally competed with the administrative services of the state.

Because the grain market was so vital to the operation of the colonial state and to the survival of the urban populations of Bamako and the mining regions to the south, the state reacted forcefully in 1900 to regulate manipulations of the grain market. "Some inhabitants of Bamako," wrote the commandant in October of that year, "buy millet in neighboring villages and sell it on the market at exorbitant prices. . . . It has been selling at .80 francs/kilo." The commandant then recommended that the administration set price controls and standardize weights and measures. He also proposed that merchants who attempted to evade these restrictions by selling their grain from concessions should be liable to fines.[83]

Despite the state's measures to reserve for itself direct control over the grain market, the allure of profits continued to attract European commercial houses. The Niger Soudan Company, for example, opened a workshop to make metal barges for the river transport of grain. Moving grain from the point of production to Bamako was a lucrative business. It often tripled prices. Efficient transport was therefore the cornerstone of the colonial market.[84]

Opportunities in transport attracted Africans. By 1902, the Moors had captured the entire overland movement of grain from Beledugu to Bamako. The Moors could transport grain fairly cheaply during their annual transhumant movement in search of pasture. When the railhead finally reached Bamako in July 1904, the commandant of Sikasso hoped that the Moors would now cross the river and begin moving goods between Sikasso and Bamako.[85] Caravans organized by Moors, probably using donkeys and not camels, were already making the run between the Ivory Coast and Bamako by way of Bouguni. By 1907, Moors were regularly selling goods in the Ivory Coast and supplying the mines of Siguiri. Many of these new routes took the Moors well beyond their regular pastures. Even when the Moors used the opportunity created by their livestock's quest for pasture, it still cost six times more to move a metric ton of grain overland than by water.[86] Water carriage remained basic to the viability of the Bamako grain market.

European merchants were also attracted to the grain market because profits were made on seasonal changes in supply and demand. A futures market in grains, which resembled the precolonial market in salt and kola, was already well established in Bamako by 1903:

> Transactions become slower during the rainy season. Streams are all swollen, the rains torrential, and the routes destroyed or overgrown with vegetation that considerably constrains transportation. This does not permit more than a localized retail trade, that is to say, a very reduced commerce. . . . In fact, the majority of Bamako merchants consider this a dead season in which work is not remunerative enough to

warrant an effort. It does not escape them that they can easily procure good profits from speculating on the variations of cereal costs. One European representative had made these kinds of transactions, and from previous experience, he is sure that *the profits from this area are at least as great as those from the regular commercial season*. . . . It is common for the merchant to make 300 percent profit.[87]

Profits from grain trade and speculation more than compensated European commercial houses for the decline in the rubber trade. Even if grain did not fulfill the expectations of exports to France, the possibilities of sales to neighboring districts and neighboring colonies seemed almost limitless. "Rice from the Niger valley," noted the annual report for 1905, "which appears to have found not only in the colony but also in the neighboring territories a large opening, now begins to reach Senegal, where it is much in demand by the natives because of its price and because the native prefers the taste of this rice to that of [Asian rice]."[88] During the first quarter of 1908, the railway exported 955 metric tons of rice and 580 metric tons of millet. In 1911, over 3,000 metric tons of grains were shipped to markets in Guinea. In the first quarter of 1912, more than 2,000 metric tons of grains were sent from Bamako to Kayes, and 500 metric tons from Bamako to Upper Guinea. The most important markets for grains remained Guinea and Senegal, where the availability of food imports permitted full-time commercial agriculture, rubber gathering, or mining.[89]

Despite the profits available from speculating on changes in the price of local goods, European commercial houses continued to complain about being undercut by African traders. As late as 1912, merchants in Kayes and Bamako echoed the complaints of their Nioro predecessors of 1900. They petitioned the governor for an exclusion of Africans from the trade in European manufactured goods, especially cloth. The administration's position was clear, however. "We cannot do this," wrote the governor, "without restraining the commercial liberty our natives now enjoy."[90]

The administration could flaunt its commitment to free-market forces in the face of the French commercial houses that demanded special privileges, but the commitment sometimes proved difficult. On the one hand, administrators on all levels understood the willingness of African peasants to work in their own interests. The Bamako commandant singled out the grain market as an example of peasant responsiveness. "The cercle," he wrote in 1892, "has been able to furnish grain over the past year to those less-favored regions of the Upper Niger and Milo. Inhabitants who have found profits [in this market] have the intention of cultivating larger fields than they normally do in order to more easily supply the quantities of millet and rice that are in demand."[91] The case of grain, which serviced a market within Africa, posed few problems to the colonial state. Protecting the liberal economy did not interfere with the colonial mission; rather, it supported it. On the other hand, colonial administrators could not ignore the needs of metropolitan producers. If the administration created the Bamako grain market and intervened strategically to make it conform to the needs of the state, its interventions in the cotton market were at once more direct and more frustrating. The world cotton crisis at the end of the century created the first concrete possibility of colonial solutions to raw material needs of metropolitan industries.[92] In 1898, Fossat, a cotton industrialist from Le Havre, came to the Western Sudan to study local cotton. "My intention," wrote Governor Trentinian on Fossat's arrival, "is to proceed with considerable purchases [of cotton] in all the cotton regions of the Western Sudan in order to supply metropolitan industrialists with samples in large quantities to [permit them to] appreciate the exact value of our cottons."[93] Plans for the 1899–1900 harvest were even grander. Commandants were to engage directly in cotton purchases, which were to be shipped to Bamako for ginning and pressing. The single biggest obstacle, Trentinian believed, was transporting bulky raw cotton to the Senegal River. He accordingly ordered ginning machines and presses from France and erected them in Bamako.[94] Enthusiasm for cotton was contagious. In 1899, Captain Charnet, the Bamako commandant, saw the future of the colony in terms of cotton: "Despite everything, native industry without capital or tools will always remain insignificant. The future is in the association of native workers with European tools and capital. And the Frenchman who establishes a textile factory to satisfy the needs of the Western Sudan and uses local cotton and local labor will have a brilliant commercial success."[95] The colonial state had other ideas about cotton, and developing a mechanized local industry was not one of them.[96]

After all, cloth was the leading French manufacture imported into the Western Sudan. The 1899 commercial report from Bamako ranked imports according to consumer preference:

> In order of preference, the most demanded European goods are [cloth, including] guinée, indienne, linieaneas, blanche, percale, bazin, roum, and secreton, [then] sugar in loaves, indigo, guilded beads, small glass ware, sieves, balls of white iron, perfume, soap bars, absinthe, and pipes. Our cloth competes advantageously with similar English products. French industry does not have the same designs, so [our products] have a good market.[97]

Sponsoring the development of a local textile factory, as Charnet proposed, would undermine two important areas of the colonial economy: imports of French manufactures and exports of raw materials suited to the needs of French industry. Colonial policy sought to balance demand for imported cloth with the export of cotton. The policy had its advocates in France too. In March 1901, delegates from the regional cotton syndicates met and formed the Industrie Cotonnière Française under the leadership of Esnault-Peletier. Esnault-Peletier was pivotal in the campaign for such a colonial raw materials policy. By the beginning of 1903, the manufacturer's association had formed a branch designed to encourage cotton production in the colonies. The *Dépêche Coloniale* reported that "following the example of Russia in Turkistan, England in Egypt and the Indies, and Germany in Togo, these men want to encourage cotton production in Africa, notably in the Western Sudan."[98]

The Association Cotonnière Coloniale became the somewhat autonomous colonial arm of the French textile manufacturer's association with a rather ambiguous relationship to both the metropolitan and the colonial state.[99] The Association was not to engage in marketing of cotton, but was invited to aid the diffusion of seed and technology, and to erect and maintain ginneries in order to encourage cotton production for export. In the 1904–5 cotton season, the first in which the Association participated, some 20,000 kilograms of exotic cotton seed, mostly Sea Island and other American long staples, were distributed to village chiefs in designated cotton regions. "Each village," remarked Governor Ponty in his annual report in 1905, "has its fields of cotton." He anticipated that cultivators would "bring their next harvests to the ginning stations, [just] as our peasants bring their wheat to the mill."[100] The French continued to think in extravagant terms: they saw the future bringing 400,000 hectares under American cotton without special projects and with the existing population. At the very least, the agronomist Vuillet expected an annual yield of 60,000 metric tons. This vision of a cotton future persisted despite contradictory results, and it continued to dominate the twentieth-century colonial development policy in the Western Sudan.[101]

The first task of the new *politique cotonnière* was to convince producers to part with the cotton they were already producing. French industrialists were prepared to experiment with local varieties of cotton. The second task was to distribute long staple cotton, which the French spinners preferred, and to encourage more rational farming methods. Village chiefs from Bamako were asked to attend demonstrations of plowing techniques held at the Kati agricultural station.[102] How to compensate cotton producers, however, remained a problem. "Several commandants," wrote the lieutenant-governor to the commandant of Bamako, "have asked me to provide white cloth to pay for their [cotton] purchases. This means of payment is to be encouraged: the administrative procurement service makes a profit, and besides, the native prefers this type of payment because it replaces the cotton that has [been sold]."[103] Some producers might have been happy to exchange their cotton for imported cloth, but not all. Already by February 1899, peasants were complaining about the demands made on them for labor, grain, and now cotton.[104] By August, it was clear that the euphoria about the future of cotton had been misplaced. Local administrators cautioned against pushing the producers too far. "One must expect acts of indiscipline if one requires natives to bring all their cotton to the headquarters of the cercle. This will only risk losing their goodwill."[105]

Cotton was a demanding crop. It needed continuous attention, careful weeding, and proper soil and water conditions, and above all it needed to be rapidly harvested and properly stored before it was damaged by heat, light, and insects.[106] It was a basic part of savanna agriculture, however, and was well suited to the technical operation of local weavers. Local cloth of both ordinary and luxury manufacture was widely produced and widely worn in the Middle Niger valley. Thus, in the absence of direct administrative coercion, against which local administrators warned, the only way to liberate sufficient amounts of cotton was to pay for it. The commandant of Segu in 1903 worried about this particular dilemma. "The price [of cotton] in the Segu market is .30 francs/kilo, clearly a price too high for the export markets. We have lowered this price to .20 and even to .15 francs/kilo. . . . The native retains always a very large part of the harvest. What the native wants most of all is to pay his annual tax and satisfy his desires and fantasies with the product of his labor. If we offer a price that permits this, we shall have large areas cultivated."[107]

Paying the right price was the most important problem to resolve if cotton was to have the future of which colonial administrators and metropolitan industrialists dreamed. Despite the massive imports of European manufactures, the persistence of local cloth industries in the Middle Niger valley created a parallel market for raw cotton. In his study of cotton in French West Africa published in 1904, Yves Henry argued that "if [the native] is a lover of our imported cloths, this is not because of their strength, but because their loud colors are attractive, and they are above all an object of admiration and covetousness by women."[108] Local cloth, however, was more durable, and because it had traditionally catered to luxury consumers in addition to serving ordinary uses, the African textile industry was able to maintain itself throughout the colonial era.

Large and sustained imports of manufactured cloth into the Middle Niger region resulted in changes in the organization of the handicraft industry. Cheaper varieties of local cloth probably gave way to cheap imports.[109] More expensive varieties of local cloth, wraps, robes, and blankets continued to compete favorably with expensive imports. The increase in consumption of both local and imported cloth suggests some of the ways in which income earned by participating in the colonial economy was being spent.

Instead of undermining the local textiles industry, the colonial economy actually encouraged its expansion. In 1901, the commercial reports from Segu were signaling an important future for the local cloth industry:

> The local cloth, which is of simple bands not sewn together, or [sewn together] pagnes, is much in demand by all the black populations, notably those in the Western Sudan, but also those of Senegal and Guinea. This branch of local commerce does not have a unique direction of export; rather, much [cloth] is sold in Siguiri, Bamako, Konakry, Kayes, and Rufisque, and also to the markets of the south. . . . At Rufisque and at Konakary, according to information received from the natives, pagnes sell for as much as 20 francs. . . . Trade in local pagnes greatly increases each day; it goes without saying that cotton and indigo cultivation are also developing.[110]

As the local industry expanded, so too did the demand for cotton. The local market for raw cotton was the nemesis of the colonial export policy; the local industry consistently absorbed a large share of the harvest and paid higher prices. For the export market, prices paid to producers had to be figured in terms of the world market price current in Le Havre, less the cost of shipment, overhead, and profits made by the exporters. The problem, summarized by the Segu administrator in 1938, was one faced by the administration from the turn of the century: "In effect, prices in Europe do not permit an offer of more than .80 francs/kg to the producers, at the same time when the interior market offers 2.50–3 francs/kg. Almost all the harvest is thus absorbed internally."[111]

Expanding output from the local textile industry contributed to the transformation of the industry after 1905. Most of the weavers in the Middle Niger valley were slaves, usually second-generation slaves. The steady decline of slavery, beginning in Banamba in 1905 and continuing throughout the Western Sudan in the following decade, had a profound effect on the organization of the industry. Until the 1900's, the Maraka had a virtual monopoly in the dyed cloth industry, which had been rationalized through the use of slave labor. Since the turn of the century, however, Maraka monopoly over indigo-dyed cloth was being eroded. "Manufactured only last year by the Maraka exclusively," wrote the Segu commandant in 1901, "[the cloths] are being imitated by the Somono and even the Bambara."[112] When the Maraka slaves fled their masters, they took their skills with them, which led to the further dispersion of the industry throughout the Middle Niger valley. That weavers could find gainful employment in the expanding industry certainly contributed to their ability to survive the first few years on their own. By 1909, the number of weavers in the Segu region, the new center of local cloth production, exceeded demand to the point where weavers migrated annually to neighboring districts in search of work.[113]

From 1883 to 1905, the regional economy remained precolonial in the sense that ecological specialization was intrinsic to its orientation, and its expansion followed forms similar to that experienced before the French conquest. The end of slavery and the coincident decline in ethnic monopolies over occupations and economic resources were the twin components of a fundamental social and economic change. 1905 therefore signified a rupture, not necessarily in the form of the economy, but in the social relations and social organization of the economy. The colonial state contributed to the conditions making this transformation possible, but Africans ultimately gave the new economy its character. The next chapter examines the end of slavery and its consequences for the structure and performance of the economy.

FIVE

The End of Slavery, 1905-1914

THE PROSPECT of too hasty a move to dismantle the precolonial economy, with its protected ethnic monopolies over economic resources and with its reliance on unfree labor, was alarming to administrators, metropolitan commercial interests, and indigenous ruling classes alike. But the ideologies of state and society emanating from France demanded changes. Cardinal Lavigerie and National Assembly member Victor Schoelcher helped focus the issues in their campaigns to end slavery in Africa. Their campaigns also crystallized the seemingly antagonistic forces shaping the colonial state. Most local administrators were convinced that the end of slavery would mean economic and political chaos. Ending slavery would change the state's role in reproducing the means and relations of production.

At the beginning of 1905, slaves began a massive exodus from Banamba that marked the beginning of the end of slavery. The French administration responded quickly. In June, it managed to halt the exodus by re-establishing the customary relationship between masters and slaves. In December, Governor-General Roume declared an end to the slave trade and the denial of a person's liberty. When the exodus resumed in the spring of 1906, the slaves again tested the French administration's ideological commitment to a free economy that rested on personal freedom. This time the French did nothing to prevent the slaves from leaving.

The consequences of the social transformation that accompanied the end of slavery were not exactly those anticipated by colonial administrators and traders. It was clear, however, that the end of slavery represented a new phase in the maturation of the colonial state. It was the triumph of a free-market economy in which the state's role was decidedly different from what it had been in the precolonial period. Free markets and free labor also meant freedom to withhold one's goods and labor from the marketplace. The organization of labor and the organization of the economy changed gradually between 1905 and 1914. The deeper structures of production and commerce, however, remained rooted in the interregional dynamics of the West African subcontinental region.

This chapter begins with an overview of the colonial administration's attitude toward slavery in Senegal and the Western Sudan. The colonial administration was profoundly ambivalent about slavery, and despite increasing pressures from France to take a stand on the slavery issue, it was unprepared when the slaves of Banamba seized the initiative in 1905. I conclude the chapter by examining the processes through which slaves ended their enslavement and the consequences this had for the structure and performance of the economy of the Middle Niger valley.

Assault on the Precolonial Foundations of the Colonial State

As governor in 1893, Alfred Grodet was certainly aware of the long and tortuous history of efforts to curtail slavery in Senegal. Faidherbe's governorship, which shaped the patterns of military presence in West Africa, also influenced efforts to abolish slavery. Faidherbe argued that application of the French law of 1848 on the abolition of slavery would have ruinous consequences for the little colony of Senegal. Senegal was not, he argued, the same as the Antilles; Senegal was a colony of commerce, not a colony of production. Any impediments to commerce would destroy the fragile effort of French colonization.

The 1848 law was unambiguous, however. Thanks to the efforts of Victor Schoelcher, then secretary of state for the colonies, there was to be no doubt about the law's intent or where it was to be applied. Article 7 maintained that "the principle that the soil of France liberates the slave who touches it is applied to colonies and possessions of the Republic."[1] The law's initial application in Saint-Louis and Gorée, where slaves were actually freed, frightened masters and merchants. African suppliers of gum and grain cut off trade. Inhabitants of these towns, fearing the loss of both their labor and their commerce, petitioned the governor for a suspension of the law, which he granted. Working with Frederick Carrère, the head of the judiciary in Senegal, Faidherbe further compromised abolition in 1857 when, by restricting its terms, he made its application a political tool in colonial expansion. At Carrère's suggestion, inhabitants of African villages newly annexed by Faidherbe were considered subjects, not citizens. As subjects, they were not bound by abolitionist decree.[2] Faidherbe applied abolition selectively: only slaves of enemies were freed; fugitive slaves of friendly chiefs were expelled from French soil as vagabonds.

The legality of returning fugitive slaves and of the slave trade was tested in 1867 and again in 1878, when a seemingly minor incident forced a change in policy. Under a particularly energetic magistrate, who was less eager than his predecessors to subordinate the rule of law to political expediency, four Africans were accused of procuring slaves and selling them in Saint-Louis. Only one of the cases, against N'Jak N'Diaye, who was also a French citizen, made its way through the appeal courts. He was found guilty of contravening the abolition act but received just the minimum sentence of six months in prison. Obviously, the tensions between the rule of law and the rule of empire in 1878 were not well reconciled.[3]

The abolitionist viewpoint was an intimate part of an aggressive belief in the new industrial economy and society. In Africa, it was coupled with an eagerness to transform different societies into models imported from Western European experience. Abolitionist ideals contrasted sharply, however, with the power of the state to implement them.[4] Newly erected colonial states were fragile entities whose viability depended largely on alliances forged with indigenous elites. Issues regarding fugitive slaves and policies on what was euphemistically called "domestic slavery" had deep ramifications in political, social, and economic spheres. Senegalese colonial authorities were not alone in their ambivalent attitudes toward African slavery. The British in Sierra Leone, Nigeria, and East Africa grappled with similar conflicts.[5] By 1883, public opinion in France, inflamed by the same Victor Schoelcher who was instrumental in the initial abolition of 1848, brought pressure on local authorities to make practice conform to legislation.[6] The principle that French soil liberates could no longer be applied selectively.

Colonial administrators at all levels argued that the French presence was still too weak and their power too poorly established to chance a wholesale application of the principles of 1848. In 1895, Penel, who later became governor of Guinea, put into print what had probably been common discourse:

> No man of good sense having experience of the land will counsel immediate abolition of slavery. That would provoke a general uprising, in which slaves would participate and which would ruin the colony. . . . Commerce, which is progressing, would be paralyzed. Thus we are under an obligation to accommodate ourselves for the time being to the institution of slavery. Previously, and at every occasion, we have formally promised the natives that we will not directly suppress slavery. . . . In all our dealings with the blacks, it is necessary to be loyal and consistent or lose moral credibility in their eyes.[7]

Nonetheless, commandants were instructed to introduce a procedure for liberating fugitive slaves following a three-month waiting period. If during this time the master had not reclaimed his slave or if the slave could prove that he or she had been mistreated, the fugitive was liberated.[8] The burden of proof was thus on the slave, and local commandants retained the power to apply the law as they saw fit. Paris, however, kept demanding closer adherence to its instructions, and by 1884 the three-month delay was abolished and local administrators were instructed to inform masters that they could no longer enforce their rights over their fugitive slaves.[9] Wholesale abolition, however, was still two decades away. In the meantime, conquest created new demands for labor, and fugitive slaves could be put to use within the new colonial state.

The conquest of the Western Sudan depended on successful recruitment of manpower for two different services. First, recruits were needed for the new companies of Tirailleurs Sénégalais established in 1879 on the eve of expansion into the Western Sudan. Serving the French offered African recruits attractive rewards: relatively high and steady pay, regular subsistence, and a share of the booty following successful campaigns. Expansion of colonial conquest created a lively market for those with appropriate military skills or the willingness to learn them.[10] Additional recruits came from the pool of fugitive slaves. Slaves who volunteered were offered their freedom through a variety of different and sometimes complex procedures. In Senegal, they were shielded from their former masters' attempts to reclaim them.[11] Along the Middle Niger, some tirailleurs remained legally bound to their former masters. The following report of January 1898 from Segu describes this practice and indicates a form of accumulation available to recruits:

> The non-free join the tirailleurs searching for a modification in their situation. In some cases, the master can reclaim his non-free. In most of these cases, the non-free pays to his master a small rent. There is also the possibility of redeeming the non-free for use in the auxiliary at between 5,000 and 10,000 cowries.
>
> I want to signal the passage of a large number of tirailleurs libérés coming from Masina with horses. The horses, it seems, were given as payment, their wages having been part in money and part in goods are now all in goods. These tirailleurs want to sell their horses, but not in Segu, where the price is not high, but in Kenedugu.[12]

It is interesting to speculate about the tirailleurs' decision to sell their horses in Kenedugu at that time. Since his coronation in 1894, Babemba had tolerated a minor French presence at Sikasso, but relations were not cordial. In February 1898, Babemba expelled the French mission, and the French began to plan their attack on Sikasso. There is an apparent contradiction in the tirailleurs' supplying Babemba with the means to escalate his struggle against a French army they had fought well and bravely for. But warfare remained primarily a means of accumulation for the tirailleurs, and they did not hesitate to take advantage of all opportunities. The report on the aftermath of Samori's capture is suggestive: "The tirailleurs have profited from the disarray occasioned following the capture of Samori, and his enormous entourage that trailed behind him, to appropriate without authorization captives in excessive numbers. That is how, for example, Moriba Camara and Suie Camara of Bankoumana village managed to send their village 23 captives, after selling three others."[13] Recruitment offered former slaves and fugitives opportunities to amass large numbers of slaves and considerable wealth. Not until the recruitment campaigns of World War I did the tirailleurs lose their central place in the colonial armed forces.[14]

The French also recruited porters, who were needed to haul goods along the route de ravitaillement. From the 1880's until 1904, the demand for manpower to build the Kayes-Bamako railway competed with the demand for porters along the same route. Local administrators made constant demands for food, livestock, and labor on natives unfortunate enough to live close to the supply route. Those who could, fled. Without adequate manpower to meet the demands of the annual military campaign, the success of the conquest was in jeopardy. Reducing the level and incidence of requisitions might have slowed the emigration, but with manpower in short supply at the best of times, this was never seriously considered. Alternatively, the administration could encourage resettlement along the route at strategic points. The only inhabitants amenable to such settlement, however, were those directly dependent on the new state: fugitive slaves.

The concept of freedmen's villages was not invented to serve the needs of the French in the Western Sudan. The colonization of Sierra Leone in the eighteenth century and Liberia and Libreville in the nineteenth century was based on a perceived obligation to minister to the needs of freedmen. *Villages de liberté* became an official feature of the Western Sudanese landscape in 1887, when Gallieni as Commandant Supérieur established the first such settlement at Kayes. The settlements proliferated as conquest proceeded.

Liberty villages offered considerable advantages to a French administration still uneasy about the slavery issue. In the first year of its formal operation, Gallieni settled nearly 6,000 fugitive slaves along the Kayes-Bamako line. But as many as half the fugitives located in liberty villages in the 1890's were eventually returned to their masters, and the slaves formally liberated each year constituted only .015 percent of the estimated total slave population of the Western Sudan.[15] Additional recruits for the liberty villages came from the pool of slaves from enemy territories (both fugitive slaves and slaves captured by the French), slaves of masters who had died intestate and without obvious heirs, and slaves confiscated as punishment for their masters' crimes. One can only guess the number of slaves who escaped both their masters and the French authorities during this period of conquest and pacification.

Inhabitants of the liberty villages worked for the privilege of living there. New recruits were especially liable to the daily call for manpower. They were usually compensated for tasks that took them away from the village for several days, but not for tasks performed locally. All the inhabitants of the liberty villages were seen as labor units that could make up shortfalls from recruitment at the larger district level. In 1901, for example, inhabitants of Nioro and Yelimane liberty villages, well off the main supply route, were sent to work on the railway. Having easy access to a pool of coercible labor led to excesses. Colonel Trentinian warned that "commandants of cercles must carefully avoid falling into abuse and profiting from the proximity and submission of the [inhabitants of] the liberty villages by extracting from them all sorts of corvées for all purposes."[16] Not surprisingly, inhabitants of these villages were considered "the slaves of the commandant."

The appointment of Grodet as governor shook the military's complacency about its relationship to the colonial endeavor in the Western Sudan. Grodet's aversion to the military, which predated his Sudanese administration, was compounded when he read in monthly administrative reports of continued military connivance with certain traditional institutions antithetical to French ideals and political and civic spirit. Nor would Grodet turn a blind eye to the continued evidence of French acquiescence and, indeed, participation in the slave trade. "I cannot admit," Grodet wrote in 1894, "that on territory of the Republic at the headquarters of a cercle, among the articles of purchase and sale are representatives of the human species."[17] He singled out and summarily sentenced Lieutenant Mangin to 30 days' detention for distributing slaves among his servants and interpreters, although many other officers had done the same, including Archinard.[18]

Grodet was clearly repulsed by the continued trade in slaves in areas under direct colonial authority. But he pursued his attack on the trade as a means of weakening the military's control over the new colonial state. Grodet's instructions therefore signaled a departure from the patterns established during the conquest, and threatened to weaken the precolonial underpinnings of the new colonial state.

As a direct consequence of French destruction of the Umarian empire, security of investment and trade in the Middle Niger valley led to a significant increase in the number of slaves purchased. Large numbers of slaves still emanated from Samori and Babemba, the two leading warriors engaged in systematic warfare and enslavement. In 1894, Grodet commissioned from each local administrator in the Western Sudan a report on slavery in his jurisdiction. He also issued several decrees limiting the free circulation of slave caravans. Of these, the levy of a special tax of 20 francs on each slave struck directly at the profit margins of slave traders.[19] Immediately before his departure for France, Grodet issued even stronger decrees. Order 273 required village chiefs, under threat of punishment and fines, to report all slave caravans to the French administrator, who then automatically liberated the slaves and fined the traders.[20] Grodet's measures pushed the slave trade underground. Traders continually devised new subterfuges to maintain their supply of slaves to the markets of the Western Sudan and the desert. Some relied on a loophole in the decree when they designated their slaves porters or salaried workers. Others changed routes to avoid French posts. Slave markets located next to French posts probably disappeared, but others emerged to take their place.[21]

Trentinian, who succeeded Grodet, did not see the issues of slavery in quite the same way. He could not undo Grodet's measures without creating a political scandal, but in a memorandum in July 1895 he cautioned his administrators to follow a more gradualist course: "The orders taken by my predecessor in regard to the subject of the trade and circulation of captives in the interior of the colony seem to have given rise to a certain misunderstanding by those who have applied them with too much rigor. Rigor in the application of these laws may in certain cases be prejudicial to the most serious interests of the colony."[22] Several months later, Trentinian reaffirmed the basic argument of the military establishment when he wrote that "the issue of slavery requires infinite tact and prudence, if one does not wish to turn the land topsy-turvy and result in its complete economic ruin."[23] For a brief moment, the military sealed the cracks in the precolonial foundation of the colonial state.

Thus far, the slaveowners had received ambiguous and contradictory signals from the administration. The Segu commandant tried to reassure local masters that the order suppressing the trade in slaves did not signal an intent to end slavery. The slaveowners, he wrote in 1895, "were happy to learn that this order was not, as they thought, a movement toward the liberation of all captives. They have seen that if captives are mistreated by their masters, they can find protection with us, but if they evade their masters without motive, they will be returned."[24] Slaves, however, understood that conditions were changing. They began to flee their masters in numbers that worried the Bamako commandant. Even the slaves, he argued, had misinterpreted the suppression of slave trade and slave market decrees. (The decrees were posted in Arabic in the central markets of Bamako, Kangaba, Nyamina, Banamba, and Touba.) In July 1895, he reported that the number of escapes had increased significantly in the past year.[25]

In 1899, William Ponty was named governor of what was then called Haut Senegal and Moyen Niger. Ponty oversaw the first sustained period of civilian rule in the Western Sudan. Slavery had to be handled carefully, and in a circular sent to all district administrators in 1901, he defined his administration's policy:

> You are quite aware that we cannot recognize the condition in which people called captives, slaves, or non-free are found. If we are in some cases obliged to support this organization so dear to the blacks, we must be consistent with the traditions of republican France, and little by little take measures destined to make this secular sore disappear.
>
> Above all, we must not forget that to act *ex-abrupto* would suddenly provoke large political disorder. We must thus proceed with prudence but with firmness, without losing sight of the goal we must follow here.[26]

Ponty was clearly afraid of moving too rapidly against institutions and classes that seemed to be the basis of the commercial system of the Western Sudan, just when trade and commerce were reaching levels unmatched earlier in the colonial era. Barat, who after three years of study produced a compendium of indigenous customs to inform policy, did not equivocate on the matter of slavery's contribution to the economy. "The prosperity of the land varies directly with the number of slaves," Barat wrote in 1900. "The captive is also at the base of all commerce."[27] Under Ponty's early administration, the tensions between policy and practice remained unresolved. Ponty also had more concrete tasks before him. He had to ensure that population density along the supply route remained stable while the railway was being built. Labor requisitioned by district officers invariably consisted of slaves sent by their masters.[28]

District reports from Segu and elsewhere supported Ponty's gradualist position. "The principal notables of the cercle," reported the Segu commandant, "consider the emancipation of slaves should operate naturally and completely within a short time without recourse to special measures."[29] This was comforting evidence for the established policy of non-intervention, but events on two fronts made this belief in a natural elimination of slavery illusory.

In 1903, as part of the general reorganization of the judiciary in French West Africa, Secretary-General Martial Merlin sent explicit instructions that "native tribunals cannot be permitted to rule in litigations relative to the state of captivity, which we cannot permit to be juridically recognized. Furthermore, in cases submitted to them, neither native or French courts can any longer take account of the supposed status of the captive."[30] The effect of this decree was to remove the legal mechanisms for returning fugitive slaves to their masters. But the decree also meant much more than that. It abolished the legal underpinnings to slavery and tied the hands of the administration. No longer could the state support the power of the master over his slaves. No longer could a master use the power of the state to secure the return of his property. The political and legal structures that bound slavery to the economic base of society were changed. The 1903 decree was thus a fatal blow to the precolonial foundations of the colonial state.

But the story does not end here. If French policy had delivered the fatal blow to slavery, it was ultimately the slaves themselves who put an end to slavery. For the end of slavery occurred when slaves left their masters. Events in Banamba in 1905 started a massive and spontaneous exodus of slaves that spread throughout the Western Sudan in ever-widening circles over the next ten years.

The End of Slavery in Banamba

The rains were especially heavy in 1904. By the end of March 1905, it was clear that the harvests of a wide band of savanna districts from Kayes through Bamako had been adversely affected by rain and by parasites that thrived in wet environments. The situation was not critical, however. Famine, the annual report for 1904 advised, was not imminent. The harvests would still be sufficient to feed the population.[31] Before the lieutenant-governor dispatched his annual report, events in Banamba, in the heart of Bamako's granary, already signified a disturbing trend. In March 1905, large numbers of slaves belonging to the Maraka of the seven cities of Beledugu started to leave their masters. They were returning to their homes in the cercles of Bouguni, Sikasso, Koutiala, and Bobo Juulasso, and to the territories of the northern Ivory Coast. Not all of them completed their journey. Some stopped along the route and some moved to Bamako. Between the end of 1904 and the end of 1906, Bamako's population increased dramatically, and small towns along the fugitives' route or near the river, like Gouni across the Niger from Koulikoro, absorbed fugitive families.[32]

The commandant of Bamako questioned the fugitives. Their responses were ambiguous. "They had no animosity to their masters," reported the commandant. "They simply wanted to return [home]."[33] Though the slaves did not volunteer their underlying motivations, the commandant was convinced that they were responding to poor treatment by their Maraka masters.

The escapes that occurred in 1905 were not the usual isolated escapes of one or two individuals that had always plagued African slave systems. They were part of a self-conscious social movement. The French called it an exodus, and it threatened the economic foundations of the Maraka commercial system. By April 1905, the situation had become serious. Maraka masters, seeing their capital investment march steadily away, decided to oppose the exodus with armed force. They formed vigilante groups and patrolled the routes leading out of the region. Slaves also armed themselves, and they traveled in compact groups for security. The slaveowners escalated the conflict by confiscating slaves' property and imprisoning their wives and children in the masters' compounds within the walled towns. Far from intimidating the slaves, these actions further incensed them. Many slaves who had wavered now joined the movement. At least one slave was killed on the route from Banamba to Koulikoro.[34]

The Banamba exodus was a serious test of French colonial policy. It was the situation the French had most dreaded; events were taking a course consonant with the administration's purported objective of ending slavery, yet they were proceeding too rapidly. The French learned of the events of Banamba as they happened. As the site of a desert-side customs station, Banamba was already linked to Bamako by telegraph. The administration's response reflected its deep-seated ambivalence toward slavery. As late as the end of April 1905, Governor-General Roume could instruct his district administrators that: "We are not able, in effect, to impose on our subjects the disposition of our French law, which is manifestly incompatible with their social state. But we should not tolerate the continuance, under the shelter of our authority, of certain customs contrary to our principles of humanity and natural right."[35]

Roume's instructions neither clarified colonial policy nor aided action in the field. Events in Banamba demanded clear signals and direct action. Roume's instructions in effect changed nothing: administrators could neither halt the exodus by military means nor declare the slaves free. By mid-May, however, the situation had deteriorated to the point where public order was threatened, and the French no longer hesitated. Roume declared that the emigration of slaves was not authorized and should be halted by "administrative means." Chiefs of neighboring villages were ordered to stop fugitives, and slaves caught leaving without permission were declared vagabonds and subject to civil action.[36] Roume sent a detachment of tirailleurs to Banamba and instructed acting Lieutenant-Governor Fawtier to take direct control of the situation. Fawtier was to "negotiate with the Maraka and their servants to discover if reconciliation by reciprocal concessions is not possible."[37] Roume cautioned that repression might be necessary.[38]

Fawtier arrived in Banamba at the beginning of June to find that the situation remained volatile. Masters claimed that they depended on their slaves for their very existence, and they warned that what was happening in Banamba would happen elsewhere unless action were taken. Slaves, on the other hand, maintained that they had declared themselves free because future reconciliation with their masters was impossible. The detachment of tirailleurs helped reduce the hostilities in Banamba, but did not put an end to the conflict. Slaves were disarmed, the Bamako commandant reported to Kayes, but "masters resist disarming despite injunctions. . . . To disarm masters would make them equal to the servants."[39] Yet this was exactly what was necessary if reconciliation was to succeed. Slaveowners finally allowed themselves to be disarmed only when Fawtier threatened military reprisals.

Fawtier held separate talks with slave representatives and with Maraka masters in an attempt to resolve the immediate crisis and avert the agricultural disaster that would result if the fields were not prepared in time. In his report on the events in Banamba, Fawtier expressed his position on the negotiations:

> Could we authorize an exodus of 4,000–5,000 individuals at a time when the blacks must prepare the planting for the year? This is a vital question for the natives of the region. The exodus would mean ruin and maybe death by starvation for Marakas incapable of cultivating their fields, as well as for the servants, who, at this period of the year, could not hope to prepare other fields, find necessary seeds, and construct houses in the middle of the rainy season. This would mean, finally, the return to bush of this beautiful part of Beledugu and the rich plains of Touba, Kiba, and Banamba. It would also mean the death of a very important center of horse rearing, whose horses are renowned throughout the entire Western Sudan.[40]

Fawtier's position during the negotiations was consistent with the administration's policies. The most important task was to preserve the productive capacity of the region even if this meant also preserving the existing economic system.[41] This the French managed to do, at least temporarily.

Before the end of June, the slaves resumed work in the fields in return for the restoration of their customary rights. The agreement Fawtier secured consisted of three principal elements: (1) slaves would be well treated in the future, their women and children would not be taken from them, and their individual property would be respected; (2) slaves would have the right to cultivate their own fields two days out of seven, and masters would supply the seed grain; and (3) slaves would work for their masters on the five remaining days. Moreover, disagreements would be settled by the local *cadis* without considering the plaintiff's social status.[42] The conditions under which the slaves agreed to continue working were reminiscent of the customary reciprocity of the master-slave relationship as it had developed during the early nineteenth century. By agreeing to return to this relationship, replete with the safeguards against exploitation, both slaves and masters admitted that the reality of their relationship had diverged considerably from its customary practice.

If slaves did not admit to their hatred of their masters, Fawtier was convinced of the masters' disdain for their slaves. He wrote in a report on Banamba that the Maraka profoundly despised their slaves and treated them "with the least concern."[43] In another report he was more specific: "If the Maraka had treated their slaves with less stinginess in their food [ration] and with more humanity in their customary relations, then escapes would have been less frequent."[44] Fawtier's explanation of the escapes echoed the report on Banamba slavery written the previous year. Brevié, the author of the 1904 report, had also talked with slaves, and his report reflects their concerns, especially over the erosion of the basic reciprocity of Maraka slavery:

> Slaves are poorly fed, mistreated, and poorly clothed. Masters rarely give them their two days free [which is theirs] by custom. They prefer to feed them poorly and to be assured of all their labor all the time. . . . Mako Tala, a slave of Touba, belongs to a master who "generously" gives three muules of millet [about six kilograms] for the rations of 25 slaves. . . . Another slave called Hinebahalafe Konati, also of Touba, told us that 20 slaves of his master were given four kilograms a day.[45]

The examples cited by Brevié are examples of extreme underfeeding, especially when compared with the French standard of one kilogram of cereal per person per day.[46] By underfeeding his slaves, the master threatened the very basis of the master-slave relationship. Going without sufficient food was a periodic risk for slaves, especially when the rains failed.[47] But to deny slaves food when the harvest was plentiful, as it was in the years before 1905, was to deny the reciprocity underlying the master-slave relationship. I have described earlier how the master was obliged to provide his slaves with their main meals while they worked for him. At other times, slaves provided their own subsistence. The customary practice of Maraka slavery permitted the master to exploit his slaves' labor more intensely, but only if he compensated them with additional nourishment. To use the slaves' entire working day and to begrudge them adequate food exceeded the customary limits on exploitation. By 1905, slaves no longer had a stake in Maraka slavery.

Why, then, had masters tinkered with a system from which they were obviously benefiting? What opportunities were Maraka masters responding to? We have no direct evidence from Maraka masters about how they justified these changes. We do, however, have some information about Maraka participation in an expanding grain market that provides indirect evidence of how, if not why, the Maraka came to transform the master-slave relationship.

Banamba and the other Maraka cities of Beledugu had become the center of commercial life during the Umarian period. The Maraka invested in a plantation sector to service the desert-side and forest zone trades, which they increasingly controlled. The plantations surrounding these Maraka cities expanded most rapidly in the 1880's and 1890's. The state-building activities of Samori and Tieba provided a steady supply of slaves. As Bamako became the hub of colonial ravitaillement along the Niger, the growing demand for grain provided another outlet for surplus Maraka grain. Slaves provided a sufficiently large pool of labor to increase the scale of production and to overcome the constraints of weeding and threshing, and by 1894 Banamba was one of the main granaries of the Bamako grain market.[48]

Except during unfavorable climatic conditions, grain purchases by Bamako increased steadily from 1891 to 1904. By early 1905, the railway connected Koulikoro to Bamako. The railway established a relatively inexpensive means of moving cereals overland, and the railhead at Koulikoro provided a bulking point for grains moved by riverine transport. The Bamako and Koulikoro railway thus opened a huge potential for grain exports from the Middle Niger region. However, the opportunity to expand production occurred as the supply of slave labor declined.

The fall of Sikasso and the capture of Samori in 1898 ended the careers of the two major suppliers of slaves to the markets of the Western Sudan. Supplies of slaves therefore declined and slave prices rose accordingly. The lack of new labor inputs for the Banamba plantations, coupled with the new openings for grain sales with the arrival of the railway, meant that the only way for masters to increase output was to rationalize the labor of their slaves. The aspects of the master-slave relationship most susceptible to rationalization were the length of the working week and the amount of the food ration, the sources of the slaves' complaints to Breviè and Fawtier. Moreover, with the conquest of Babemba and Samori, the original homelands of most Banamba slaves appeared once again to be safe to inhabit, a fact that may have given slaves a further incentive to leave their masters. The population of these areas increased significantly during the first decade of the twentieth century.

The 1905 slaves' exodus was the culmination of a process of labor rationalization and a change in the relationship between the Maraka economy and the political economy of the region for at least a decade. In 1895, we have the first recorded instance of a slave revolt, albeit on a small scale. In July of that year, the local customs collector of Banamba reported that a slave, Bananfile Jara, led 30 other slaves armed with hoes against their master.[49] In his August report, the customs collector noted that the situation was under control and that Bananfile Jara had been punished.

The reports reveal little about the underlying motivations of either party, but they do record the immediate cause of the revolt. Apparently, Bananfile Jara and the slaves reacted to their master's effort to force a female slave to work in the fields.[50] Perhaps the slaves were protecting the woman; perhaps they were resisting changes in the customary gender division of labor. In any event, the incident captured in the archives hints at a gradual process of labor rationalization. A division of labor by gender was basic to most West African societies. To deny the established division was to deny the reciprocity of male and female labor on which the complementarity of marriage was based.[51] It also dehumanized slaves. The slaves' reactions were significant because they departed from traditional forms of slave resistance in West Africa. Instead of taking flight, these slaves collectively threatened their master. That Banamba slaveowners succeeded in quelling the incident through punishment only indicates the level of violence inherent in the master-slave relationship.

Throughout the decade from 1895 to 1905, the political reports from virtually every district in the Western Sudan refer to the movement of population. Samori's flight to the east opened the western Wasulu region to returning fugitives. Some of them were free men and women who had fled to French-occupied territory on the left bank in the 1880's and 1890's. Slaves could scarcely have been unaware of these changes, and their escapes during this period were consistent with the general gravitation of populations back to their homelands. But this may not have been the only motivation. In 1901, the Segu commandant reported several requests from slaves to cultivate for themselves.[52]

Certainly slave flights were disturbing. Collective slave flights, however, raised the specter of social disorder and economic collapse. In April 1901, a group of 27 slaves under the leadership of their fellow slave Metana Taraore fled Nyamina to the Segu side of the river. As they left, they took firearms and lances. The younger brother of the chief of Nyamina led 215 young Maraka men in pursuit. Surrounding the fugitives near Koulimana, they killed fourteen of them, including Taraore, and seriously wounded several others. Seven Maraka were killed in the battle, among them the chief's brother. Only six slaves returned to Nyamina alive.[53]

The reports on the 1901 incident gave different explanations. The Segu commandant was convinced that the slaves were blindly following their leader. He wrote that "like all naive [people], they were impressed by his counsel and fled with him to the right bank without resources, without motive, and without knowing what to do. They left their masters without motive."[54] William Ponty, lieutenant-governor of the Western Sudan, thought that the slaves had been mistreated.[55] The timing of the collective flight, mid-April, was significant, coinciding as it did with the beginning of the new agricultural season. Metana Taraore and his followers may have decided to leave before the onset of what would probably have been another year of heavy labor demands.

A collective escape like that of 1901 was a direct threat to a society dependent on slave labor. The Maraka were willing to accept casualties because they needed to demonstrate their collective will against such an obvious assault on their authority, their livelihood, and their society. The death of the slaves at Koulimana was a clear statement to other slaves. However, the seven Maraka deaths surely had a chastening effect on the slaveowners, who had probably underestimated the slaves' willingness to resist. The reaction of the slaves is not recorded, but Ponty sensed that the incident itself might represent a significant change in the spirit of the slave population. "This event should be particularly noted," he wrote, "because it is the first time that I record an act of energy on the part of blacks wanting to regain their liberty. Could this be the beginning of a new era in the *morale indigène*?"[56] Ponty's rhetorical question remained unanswered. The significance of the event lay in the yet unresolved tension between the administration's commitment to a new economy and its fear of social and economic disorder resulting from a radical transformation. Ponty, for one, was not ready to authorize the slaves' exodus. By 1905, slaves had taken the initiative away from the administration.

The Expansion of the Exodus

In early spring 1906, Fawtier's truce between masters and slaves in Banamba collapsed. The two parties had reaffirmed the mutual obligations and customary limits on exploitation in Maraka slavery. But the reciprocity underlying this affirmation quickly evaporated, and Maraka slavery could no longer survive without direct state intervention. In 1906, such intervention was no longer possible. Now that Governor Roume's decree of 12 December 1905 had outlawed enslavement and the sale of slaves, the administration could scarcely allow its offices to be used in support of an institution it no longer recognized.

In April, at the first sign that slaves were renewing their exodus from the plantations of Banamba, the Maraka repudiated the terms of their reconciliation by seizing their slaves' children and all their personal goods. Although these actions were consistent with customary practice that permitted slaves usufruct only, they served only to increase the tensions just as they had during the previous year. "These odious measures," wrote the Bamako commandant, "have naturally provoked a heated excitement on the part of the domestics, and grave troubles will surely result unless rapid and energetic action is taken on our part."[57] Ponty did not hesitate to act, but he did not act as he had done in 1905. "Protect the domestics who want to leave their masters," he wrote in May.[58] To demonstrate his administration's commitment, he sent a small detachment of troops to Banamba to reinforce the Resident's authority. At the end of May, the Bamako commandant reported:

> Thanks to the energetic measures taken by the Resident of Banamba . . . the movement was conducted in absolute order. [We note] the passage to Bamako of compact bands of men, women, and children rushing to regain their homelands. Dispossessed of their meager possessions by their masters, they go long days with little or nothing to eat. . . . During this period, the attitude of the Maraka was one of defeat and resignation.[59]

By the end of May, 3,000 slaves had walked away from their masters and the exodus from Banamba was over. When the administration finally assessed the consequences of the exodus, they estimated that 20,000 slaves from the seven Maraka towns had left their masters.[60] Some slaves made it home to the cercles of Bouguni, Sikasso, and northern Ivory Coast. Others wound up in Bamako where, after 1906, they easily found temporary work.[61]

The Maraka responded to the exoduses of 1905 and 1906 quite differently. Both the Bamako commandant and Ponty had expected in 1906 that the Maraka would once again use violence to dissuade their slaves from leaving. Instead, the Maraka resigned themselves to the end of an era and restricted their resistance to "imploring divine protection through interminable prayers."[62] But the Maraka knew that divine intervention would not provide their subsistence in the coming year, and by June many of them were working their own fields. "The Maraka," wrote the Bamako commandant at the end of 1906, "who for a long time have lost the habit of work and constituted unproductive elements, have begun resolutely to take a counter approach, that of replacing their lost manpower [through their own work], and because of the lower returns [expected] of these inexperienced workers, [they] have also lowered their consumption levels."[63] Wives and children formed the bulk of the new labor force, though some Maraka quickly discovered a supply of temporary agricultural workers among Bambara villagers.[64]

The French were inclined to take credit for the events of 1906, and by extension also those of 1905. The annual report of Bamako stated with a certain degree of self-righteousness: "The year 1906 will remain a historic year for the Maraka who form the population of the cantons of Nyamina, Touba, and Banamba. It was during the course of this year that an event [changed] the population that would not have occurred except as an ineluctable and logical consequence of our *pénétration civilisatrice*."[65] The Bamako commandant was right to claim credit for the events that changed the political economy of the Middle Niger valley. He overestimated, however, the role of the new ideology of state power. It was not ideas of individual liberty so central to French bourgeois political economy that transformed social and economic organization. The triumph of the liberal economy and the implantation of capitalist relations of production were a consequence of state policy, but that of a policy that operated indirectly. The state undermined the precolonial political economy because it no longer participated directly in the reproduction of established relations of production. Some of these relations of production, like those on the plantations of the Banamba, could not survive without the direct action of the state.

Maraka masters had warned the French in June 1905 that unless they stopped the slaves' exodus, what was happening in Banamba would happen throughout the Western Sudan. The masters clearly understood the instrumental role of the state in guaranteeing the form of plantation slavery that had emerged in the Middle Niger valley. Just as they predicted, between 1906 and 1911 the events of Banamba were reproduced in hundreds of villages and hamlets throughout the Western Sudan. The consequences of the administration's willingness to affirm slaves' freedom rippled out from Banamba in ever wider circles throughout the savanna and sahel. In each case, slaves chose either to leave their masters or to redefine their relationships. In March 1907, the Segu commandant noted that whereas previously slaves had presented themselves at district headquarters to claim their rights in ones, twos, or threes, they now arrived in large numbers: "What happened last year in Bamako [cercle] is being reproduced here in Segu by hundreds of slaves who daily present themselves to the residence and declare that they do not want to work any more except for themselves."[66] Slaves left most frequently between April and June, just before the beginning of the new agricultural season. In these three months, the Segu commandant counted 5,331 slaves who had officially requested permission to leave.[67] There is no way of estimating how many slaves simply left without informing the authorities. The administration's position was now clear: any slave who paid his taxes was free to go wherever he wished.[68]

The exodus was brief in duration, but it was lasting in its effects. The exodus from Bamako, Segu, Kayes, Kita, Bafoulabe, Sikasso, and Bouguni districts virtually ended in 1908. After the initial one or two years of massive departures, only very small numbers of slaves continued to leave their masters. The 1909 annual report for the colony observed that "from the social point of view, the statistics indicate that the exodus of the slaves to their homelands had been considerably diminished and tends to disappear."[69] Just as the exodus was ending in Segu and Bamako, it spread outward to Masina and into the sahel.

In 1907, the commandant of Bandiagara noted the beginning of an exodus from Masina, and large numbers left in 1908. In Masina, however, the pattern was different, in part because of the peculiar relationship between the nomadic FulBe and their agricultural slaves, in part because of the strategies of the colonial state. Instead of leaving their villages, the slaves refused to pay their customary dues to their masters. Whereas in Bamako, Segu, and the other savanna districts, the state protected the rights of slaves to go where they wished, the Masina case required a different response.

The administration pursued two objectives in Masina. It wanted to protect the strategic role of the region's livestock production, and it was obligated to protect the freedmen. The masters claimed the land, and the freedmen their labor power. A logical solution was to establish large capitalist holdings worked by freedmen under arrangements that guaranteed them long-term tenure and a higher return on their labor.[70] The administration tried reconciliation of the kind it had used in Banamba in 1905.

By December 1908, the administration had reconciled the freedmen and their former masters. The parties agreed to an accord that resurrected the traditional master-slave relationship while reducing the level of exploitation. It also reasserted the rights of the freedman to land without contesting the FulBe's property rights.[71] The Masina accord therefore differed from the administration's general policy. But it also reflected Governor Roume's vision of an established landed estate of property owners whose land was worked by sharecroppers. In 1905, Roume had written:

> The experience [of Banamba], which has been imposed on us by force of circumstances, and was not something we expected, demonstrates that with firm resolve to respect the individual liberty of all natives, one can arrive at a rational decision that conforms to our principles in regard to the delicate question of agricultural workers. These workers would be regulated as well as protected by an equitable division of the product between owners of the land and the cultivators, based on an analogous model of sharecropping in France between owners and peasants. Contracts [are to be] at once respected by the community and guaranteed by the tribunals.[72]

The administrator in charge of resolving the conflict in Masina seems to have been guided by Roume's belief in a mutually understood and respected set of obligations.

In Masina, as in Banamba, the controversy was initiated by the slaves. Commandant Gaubert explained in his report why the slaves acted when they did: "The creation of personal taxes, which the FulBe oblige their slaves to pay; the infiltration, by way of the river banks, of our principles of liberty; and the news of numerous liberations, served to animate the slaves to raise their heads and oppose the customary requirements."[73] The

French, however, were not ready to give their support exclusively to the slaves in this case. They had other considerations. The FulBe owned the largest herds, and livestock was clearly a crucial resource of the colony. "My inquiries," wrote Gaubert in 1908, "revealed that the FulBe were not yet ready for the complete application of our principles. Far from leaving tradition, one cannot find a FulBe who cultivates the soil with his own hands." But, as Gaubert stressed in his report, the soil belonged exclusively to the FulBe. Gaubert's objective in the course of negotiations was to convince the FulBe that a new era had arrived, and if they wanted to retain their labor force, they would be obliged to offer their slaves significant concessions.

Under instructions from the governor, Gaubert proceeded to transform the individual payments that had characterized the slave-master relationship into a form of sharecropping. Article 2 of the 1908 accord specified that the individual annual payment be replaced by a fixed portion of one-sixth of the harvest. Article 3 gave the freedmen perpetual rights to occupy the land in return for fulfillment of the previous article and article 5. Article 5 was "the obligation for the freedwomen to put at the service of their previous masters the eldest of their sons, and to replace him on his marriage with a younger one" if the previous master would renounce his claims to his share of the harvest.[74] Gaubert's reconciliation meant a significant reduction in the customary dues, but it also meant that the freed slaves persisted in providing the FulBe with unfree labor.

The clause requiring a freedwoman to give her eldest son in service to her master was central to the reconciliation, since it avoided the radical transformation of FulBe social and economic organization. It was also the most problematical clause. The acting governor of the Western Sudan saw it as an obvious threat to the state's commitment to personal freedom and reacted quickly. In a telegram to Gaubert, he wrote:

> It is equivalent to a temporary alienation by administrative measure of the liberty of an entire category of population to the profit of the masters of the soil, and therefore has the character of falling under the decree of 12 December 1905, which prohibits acts that reduce individual freedom. [You] should intervene to suppress this clause that is opposed to the goal we pursue and in manifest contradiction to the current legislation.[75]

The state's objective of engineering a sharecropping system under the guise of maintaining customary relations between masters and slaves had obvious shortcomings. Sharecropping could hardly be instituted in an environment where effective control over the land could not be ensured. Some FulBe slaves simply moved away from their masters and established a separate village. Where the former slaves of the FulBe were willing to accept the conditions of the 1908 accord, sharecropping effectively replaced prior practices of unfree labor.[76]

The exodus from the sahelian districts of Sokolo and Gumbu followed the pattern of Banamba and Segu. The exodus began in 1908 and ended with the 1909-10 harvest. By 1910, departures from the sahel had diminished to a trickle.[77] By 1911, Ponty could boast that 500,000 slaves had liberated themselves in French West Africa.[78] The numbers collected from selected districts do not support this assessment, but most slaves who left their masters probably did so without informing the administration. The end of slavery offered freed men and women three choices, with much variation within those choices: they could return to their homelands, declare themselves autonomous without returning home, or redefine relations with their masters.

The speed of the exodus reveals its distinctive character. When the slaves decided to leave, they left quickly. This was often a difficult decision to make, since it occasionally meant leaving family and friends. Once having made the decision, the freed men and women simply moved away.[79] Many went home. Reports from Bouguni district, one of the slaves' stated destinations, suggest a very rapid increase in population. In 1906, more than 4,000 immigrants were reported to have returned to the cantons of Tiondugu, Nieni, and Gonautiedugu; nearly 6,000 returned to the cantons of Foubala, Nonolojana, Yorobabugu, and Ziendugu. The actual numbers, however, were probably much larger. Since the administration sought to collect taxes from each immigrant, a large part of the population movement went underground.[80]

The return of freed men and women was not uniformly welcomed. Many of their families had since dispersed. Reintegration of freedmen without clearly defined lines of kinship, authority, or patronage often led to political and social conflicts. Many arrived too late to begin farming and relied on the goodwill of their neighbors. The commandant of Bouguni described some of the repercussions in October 1906: "The grand conqueror [Samori] destroyed all the villages, and the inhabitants all fled to the region of Banamba. A larger number of these people have come back to the places occupied by their ancestors. This has resulted in numerous confusions and difficult questions for the commandant to resolve. For example, in one village there are two groups, each claiming to owe allegiance to a different canton chief."[81]

Others established new villages that were wholly autonomous. Some settled in established villages. Still others, such as the slaves on the Niarela plantation belonging to the Sukule family of Sinsani, decided to remain where they were, but chose to sever all ties with their former masters.[82] How many freedmen chose a particular option is difficult to determine from the existing evidence. In Segu, for example, 20 percent of the slaves requesting formal permission to leave their masters chose to remain in the district.[83] In 1907, the Bamako commandant reported that "the dislocation of previous [slave] villages and the formation of numerous [new] agricultural villages has augmented the production of the country, especially the production of peanuts, which has given a feeling of security to the natives."[84] The first few years were always the most difficult, but a well-chosen location close to the expanding commodity markets of the colonial economy could ensure survival. In many of the new villages, freed men and women worked side by side to establish their independence. In 1895, slaves at Banamba had rebelled against their masters when they were forced to work with women. But on their own, the ex-slaves themselves disregarded established gender divisions of labor. For several years after establishing their own farms, men and women worked side by side in the fields.[85]

Not all freed slaves, however, left their masters. The proportions are unclear, but those who remembered their origins generally left; those who were second-generation slaves generally remained. More women and children remained than adult males.[86] In all cases, the end of slavery demanded that ex-slaves and ex-master redefine their relationship. The new relationships were clearly more explicitly reciprocal. Some freedmen voluntarily paid what they termed the *zakat* to their masters in recognition of the master's ownership of the land they used. A freedman often acknowledged his master as his protector, provided him with small presents and services, and expected him to help in marrying his daughters. Others worked side by side with their masters and became more fully incorporated in their master's household. But even if masters and freedmen now "ate from the same bowl," subtle distinctions remained. Freedmen did not marry their master's daughters.[87]

The end of slavery also obligated masters to reorganize their households and labor force. Because of their reliance on slave labor, the Maraka had come to associate agricultural work with slavery. Many masters had to learn how to farm for the first time. The French saw this as a positive development since it humbled the Maraka and increased the numbers of agricultural workers. The Bamako commandant noted in 1907 that the modification in Maraka social status had not occurred easily but was certain to have a "salutary effect [owing to] the need to perform manual work."[88] The commandant seemed to have overstated the effects, for the annual report of 1910 contrasted the "prosperous and proper" villages of the freed slaves who remained in the sahelian districts with the "miserable agglomerations where the previous masters still lived."[89] Nor did the end of slavery affect all Maraka family members in the same way. Wives and children became the new captive labor of the Maraka. At least one Baraweli inhabitant, whose slaves had all departed, requested that his children in residence in French schools be returned to aid in agricultural work.[90]

The transformation in the organization of work among the Maraka affected women severely. The plantation economy had given women more leisure time and enabled them to devote themselves to the production of indigo-dyed cloth. With the departure of the slaves, women lost both their leisure time and their effective monopoly over dyed cloth. Almost all the women of Banamba complained of ill-treatment; some asked for divorce. A report from 1907 described their complaints in their own terms: "My husband gives me nothing; my husband forces me to work. My husband does nothing himself, and I, I work continuously."[91]

Maraka household heads tried to control their new labor force by denying their wives divorce and by disinheriting children who refused to work.[92] Yet the new exploitation of family labor occurred within very different social and economic conditions. Heightened exploitation often resulted in the flight of young men and the breakdown of the authority on which household heads relied. Pollet and Winter have argued that the liberation of the slaves weakened the hierarchical principle that organized both the family and society.[93] The departure of the slaves certainly contributed to the weakening of the family, but it was no mere functional relationship. Among the Maraka, the weakening of the family coincided with increased exploitation of family labor by household heads, with the decline in inheritable property, and with the opening of new employment opportunities outside the structure of the family. Maraka fathers could disinherit their sons, but with little to be gained from remaining at home, few sons were intimidated. Sons of slave masters and freedmen often followed the same routes to Upper Guinea, Ivory Coast, and Senegal, where there were new employment opportunities in mining, construction, and temporary agricultural work. In 1910, over 2,000 young men from the Bamako cercle went to the mines of Siguiri or to work on the Ivory Coast railway.[94] Wives and daughters, however, had fewer options. Wives could return to their families, but usually their fathers were increasing the exploitation of familial labor as well. Some undoubtedly became prostitutes, and a few committed suicide.[95]

With the end of slavery, the Maraka lost their distinctive place in the economy and society of the Middle Niger valley. Previously dynamic and wealthy Maraka commercial centers were reduced to depressed communities. A 1909 report noted that a large number of houses in Banamba, Touba, and Keruane were in ruins and that the population had dispersed. Most of the Maraka were forced to move to outlying agricultural hamlets.[96] Paul Marty, the student of West African Islam in the early 1900's, perceptively wrote that the "suppression of slavery has dealt a death blow to Islam; many Bambara and Maraka masters are obliged to devote themselves to work. . . . They do not have much time or enthusiasm for praying."[97]

Coincidentally, the Maraka share of trade in the region declined and their commitment to Islam waned, at least for the moment. The basic attributes of Maraka social boundaries were thus threatened. The Maraka, wrote the Bamako commandant in 1909, "rapidly lose their ethnic character, their language, and their Muslim religious practices and entirely mix with pagan Bambara who encircle them and absorb them."[98] By 1914, the number of Koranic schools in Banamba had also declined.[99] In becoming like their Bambara neighbors, the Maraka clearly indicated how the crumbling of the precolonial foundations of the political economy affected the social history of the region.

By all accounts, the end of slavery portended the decline of the once-flourishing agricultural zone of Beledugu. Governor Clozel's report for 1908, however, signaled the contrary:

> Far from being ruinous for the colony, as certain pessimistic spirits predicted, the liberation of the former servants has created a happy transformation of the conditions of production, which tends at the same time to increase the numerical importance of and the return to labor: the numerical importance from the fact that the former masters must participate in agricultural labor in order to meet their needs, the return as a result of the increase in the work of the former servants that comes from their consciousness of their liberty and the personal nature of their efforts.[100]

The annual report for 1910 claimed that despite the departure of 20,000 slaves, the total area of cultivated land in the Banamba region had not declined.[101] Maraka masters and their families applied themselves to agriculture, but their efforts could hardly compensate for the loss of their slaves. Perhaps the Maraka were now more inclined to adopt new agricultural technologies. However, basic technical innovations such as the plow, fertilizers, and new seeds did not enter the region until the interwar period.[102] How, then, can we explain the apparent maintenance of agricultural production?

The French did not hesitate to see in the exodus and the subsequent patterns of economic growth the development of free-wage labor. Ponty had, since his hesitant response in 1905, rapidly changed his position on slavery. Now that liberation was a reality, he could safely see in it a celebration of a new economy. In 1907, he wrote the Segu commandant a letter criticizing the latter's fears of economic disaster following the massive departures of that year. "The positive factors will be the definitive establishment of the principles of individual liberty. [The end of slavery] forces patrons to work for themselves and creates the need for free workers."[103] The next year, Governor Clozel identified the free worker as the explanation for the continued prosperity of the Banamba region. "It is worth noting the appearance of a new social class which will be called on to develop rapidly: the class of free paid agricultural workers."[104] The annual report of 1910 was most explicit about the triumph of the new economy: "The first economic result of this social transformation has been clearly encouraging. Everywhere, the free worker affirms his superiority and intelligence over the captive."[105] The development of a labor market was indeed the most significant effect of the new colonial economy, and it had emerged rather suddenly.

On the eve of the 1905 Banamba exodus, the Bamako commandant complained about the difficulties of recruiting workers for the railway and other public works. It was only through the operation of administrative compulsion that any labor was forthcoming. By the end of the year, he worried about the rapid growth of the Bamako population. He noted that there were now workers and porters unsuccessfully looking for work, and that unless the influx was stopped, Bamako would face even more severe unemployment.[106] A similar situation prevailed in the agricultural sector. As late as 1903, a Bamako agricultural report noted that "agricultural workers rarely consent to work the fields of another. Only those natives whose own fields were destroyed by bad luck consent to work for others. Hiring of this nature is short-term, never longer than one month; young men in particular—who want to buy a *bubu* [Bambara: traditional robe] or other small object—work three or four days."[107]

Despite the propensity of freed slaves for establishing themselves as independent farmers, the end of slavery brought a fundamental change to the labor market. Labor shortfalls could be alleviated by hiring freedmen, young men who had escaped their households in search of an independent source of revenue, and even previous masters. The very demand for labor probably encouraged dissatisfied sons to desert their fathers. By securing an independent source of income, sons could bypass the traditional sanctions on independence and thus accumulate enough capital to marry and start their own farms. The archival reports clearly indicate that Bambara made up the bulk of these agricultural workers, although the term Bambara in the reports may refer to the generic category of pagan peasant producers and thus include freedmen of varied origins. In 1909, the Maraka regularly hired Bambara agricultural workers and paid them 320 cowries a day plus food and lodging.[108] Somewhat more notable is the development of labor gangs and the emergence of entrepreneurs of temporary labor: according to a 1908 report, "daily agricultural wages vary according to the cercles, between 30 and 50 centimes; often work contracts are conducted between a proprietor and a large team head who engages 70–80 workers."[109] It is possible that this large team consisted of members of the Bambara young men's association, which already provided labor within its community. Engaging in work outside the community would have been a departure from the association's traditional role in Bambara society. Several Maraka informants said that they had often hired such Bambara labor groups.[110]

The Maraka did not rely solely on the labor market to overcome their labor shortages. They also used two forms of cooperative labor. The first, *dama* (Bambara: number), was an agreement between two or more cultivators who each worked a fixed number of days on the others' field or fields.[111] The other form was called *sirquatu*, derived from the classical Arabic legal term *sharikah*, which means "company" or "partnership." For the Maraka it was a straight cooperative venture in which producers held shares of the harvest. Two parties pooled their labor and resources and shared the product evenly. Both forms of cooperative labor had precolonial roots, but were new alternatives for the Maraka, who had lost their unfree labor.[112]

The new political economy saw in the Western Sudan its fullest expression in the end of slavery and in the consequent establishment of free workers. The development of a free market coincided with the expansion of free labor, but it owed its origins to the erosion of ethnic boundaries surrounding economic resources. The reorganization of access to economic resources was probably the most revolutionary shift during the early colonial period, but it is also the most difficult to trace. Sometimes the changes were dramatic; most often they were gradual. Always they had profound long-term effects on economic and social history.

The erosion of the old system began in the early years of the twentieth century. Conflicts over access to economic resources predated the end of slavery, but the movement of freed slaves into all sectors of the economy accelerated the change. Despite the colonial state's efforts in 1890 to preserve at least some of the ethnic economic monopolies, those monopolies came increasingly under attack with the expansion of commodity production and trade. The first visible signs occurred early in the new century. In 1901, Somono and Bambara began to invade the Maraka monopoly of indigo-dyed cloth. By the end of 1905, the French recognized a significant change in occupational distribution in the Middle Niger valley.

> Trade, agriculture, and herding, monopolies long recognized [as belonging] to this or that race, are today contested by all. Today, more common are the natives of all origins who during the dry season follow the juulas of profession, who go by new routes to Bamako, San, and Tonge, and who bring to the markets of the west and the south livestock, products of local industries, salt, and a small assortment of European goods.[113]

Commerce opened first. It had never been juridically exclusive. Trading long distances on a regular basis involved technical problems that were best solved through ethnic and religious ties. But the conquest of the southern savannas made travel safer, and the railway made travel easier. Some (though not all) of the technical problems that had favored ethnicity thus melted away. Access to trade goods was also facilitated by a general expansion of production and an increase in demand for ecologically specialized African products and imported manufactures. The increased availability of goods on the market, along with easier access to capital, even a small amount of which could now be transformed into an assortment of trade goods, thus eliminated the need for the kind of long-term investment in production the Maraka had engaged in.

Moreover, the French conquest had subtly altered the conditions under which production now expanded. First, the state did not enter directly in the reproduction of the conditions of production as the precolonial state had done. Second, the colonial state was committed to individual freedom, and although it was reluctant to implement policy on these lines, it celebrated acts of personal liberty when they occurred. And third, the state did not recognize the immutability of precolonial ethnic restrictions on occupations and resources. In this sense, Africans could now turn to the French legal system in the expectation of receiving impartial judgments in accordance with the new political economy. The expansion of production in the early 20th century occurred at the expense of previously restricted economic resources. The commandant of Jenne wrote at the end of 1907 that the difficulties he had faced that year were conflicts over land and between ethnic groups. "They are all due," he wrote, "to the working of new fields or rivalries between races. The natives see their needs increase every day, and they can barely procure their resources except by the sale of the products of the soil and industry."[114] How well the Somono fared in the new economy is indicative of the new conditions of production.

Once the river was liberated from the political restrictions of Umarian rule, the Somono's control over transportation put them in an excellent position to reap benefits from a revived commerce. The expansion of the Bamako grain market fitted exactly the specialized skills of the Somono. The transport of grain by water was crucial to this market, and was handled almost exclusively by the Somono. Some entrepreneurial Somono moved into grain trading and by 1907, the rice market of Segu was virtually controlled by the Somono.[115] As the grain market expanded, however, European commercial houses moved into the transport business. They now hired sailors.[116] The Europeans' incursions into the riverine transport business and their demand for sailors weakened the Somono monopoly over the river. Now that the Somono no longer controlled the supply of labor, wages, and canoes, their sense of corporate character was threatened. The Somono were also quick to diversify into all areas of commodity production they saw as lucrative. In addition to their customary occupations, they entered the weaving industry, grew tobacco, and traded and speculated in grains. These increased activities occurred at a time when the state no longer provided the Somono with slaves as new recruits. In 1908, Deherme described the consequences of Somono diversification under these new conditions of production and reproduction. "The Somono were previously strictly specialized in this profession [fishing]. Today, they farm, trade, act as bankers, weave. . . . The Somono are a caste in the process of dissolution."[117]

The end of slavery was a vital part of this erosion of ethnic monopolies over resources. Many freed men and women moved into occupations whose skills they had learned as slaves. I have already mentioned the case of the textile industry, but it is safe to assume that freed slaves also entered other occupations, including commerce and transportation. As the end of slavery gave freed slaves new opportunities to earn their livelihood, it also transformed established forms of capital accumulation. Slaves had been both units of labor and units of value. This point is basic to Dubois' 1911 discussion:

> In Western Sudanese society, the slave or the captive corresponded precisely to a serf in our society. He corresponded as well to an institution of our modern society—the savings bank. Agricultural and commercial profits were quickly invested in slaves. . . . At the present time, the suppression of domestic slavery is a problem that has been resolved in all its forms. . . . New economies are constituted. And available funds no longer go into purchases of slaves; the owner is very judiciously advised to place them . . . in livestock.[118]

Livestock was one of the principal Western Sudanese exports to neighboring colonies. As capital was steadily invested in livestock, ownership of cattle, sheep, and goats was diversified among all ethnic groups. Indeed, investment in herds was one of the primary forms of capital accumulation during the early colonial period.[119] With the opening of the livestock market in the Ivory Coast and the Gold Coast and the coincident change in ownership patterns, the monopolies of the FulBe and the Moors were effectively broken.[120]

In its first quarter-century, the colonial political economy was characterized by two phases. In the first, the colonial state rested on precolonial economic and social foundations. During this period, metropolitan commerce made very little impact on the deeper structures of the region's history. The second phase, which occurred at the beginning of the new century, was unrelated to any clear political demarcations. It led, however, to a fundamental transformation in the social and economic organization of the Middle Niger valley. This transformation was based on twin revolutions: the emergence of free labor and an end to ethnic restrictions over resources. The end to ethnic restrictions seems to have preceded the end of slavery, but both were intimately related. As slaves left their masters, many moved into previously restricted occupations and therefore gave substance to the gradual erosion of ethnic monopolies over resources. The new economy was therefore made by the actions of Africans, but it was fashioned of institutions made flexible by the operation of the colonial state.

SIX

Conclusion

IN HIS ANNUAL REPORT of 1911, Governor Clozel reflected on the development of commerce in the colony:

> The prodigious development of commerce in agricultural products and in livestock with the neighboring colonies contributes more and more to a general movement of exchanges. It is thanks to the returns taken from this movement that our natives of the Western Sudan have conserved and indeed augmented their capacity to purchase, despite the considerable diminution of receipts derived from the sale of rubber and European commerce.
>
> It is important to remark that, because of its geographical position and its long distance from the Atlantic, Haut-Sénégal-Niger's exports overseas are limited only to those products whose value is sufficiently elevated to support transport costs.
>
> It is natural that the Western Sudanese producer must look beyond European trade for openings for the surplus of his production. Happily, these openings are around him, especially to the colonies of the south, Ivory Coast and the Gold Coast.[1]

This was a sobering assessment of the impact of nearly 30 years of colonial rule on the economy of the Western Sudan. In effect, Clozel argued that the French had not been able to direct production to fit their needs, but had encouraged the patterns of production and consumption that predated colonial conquest.

Clozel's comments are even more significant insofar as they coincided with the end of slavery and the erosion of ethnic monopolies over economic resources. These twin revolutions transformed the social organization of production in key sectors of the economy. Far from bringing forth new ways of working, these transformations had only deepened the precolonial orientation of the economy along lines of ecological specialization for the subcontinental market of West Africa. Only the year before, Clozel had celebrated the end of slavery as the triumph of a new economic system in which both former slaves and masters worked and sold their goods in the marketplace. Instead, the end of slavery gave freed men and women the freedom to assert their autonomy from their old masters and the new colonial rulers alike. Freed men and women shaped the regional economy in the light of their needs and their efforts to control their labor processes. The colonial state, like the Umarian state before it, had failed to control the social transformations it engendered.

In this study I have argued that the state and the economy were integrally connected and that the forms of intervention in the economy, which ensued from the patterns of social reproduction of warriors and their control over the state, were the most telling sign of that integration. The state and the economy were not identical, however. The sum of the state's economic roles and the varieties of its intervention in the economy did not constitute the economy. None of the three states I examined was sufficiently powerful either to shape the economy in its own image or to destroy the economy outright. No matter how the state intervened, producers were not deprived of access to land or to the resources of the river. Producers, even slaves, never entirely lost control over their production processes. Producers could and did resist changes in the forms of state intervention in the economy, sometimes by withdrawing from the marketplace altogether, as so many did during the Umarian period, and sometimes by violent means, which the Maraka used. Slaves resisted changes in the work patterns their masters introduced. These forms of resistance fundamentally weakened the ability of the state and the ruling classes to direct production. Although the state could only rarely control production, it did contribute to the conditions in which the economy operated. What needs to be explained, therefore, is why the economy expanded when it did and why it took the forms it did.

The Umarian period, 1861–90, is the central analytical puzzle in the economic and social history of the Middle Niger valley. During this period, the articulated regional economy that had developed under the Bambara state disintegrated. As I examined the history of this period, it became increasingly clear that the state had a central part to play in the structure and performance of the economy. The Umarian experiment and its influence on the economy was related to the contradictions internal to the endeavor itself. Failure to extract sufficient resources through systematic taxation or investment and failure to control warriors limited the Umarian leadership's ability to substitute state policy for the petty predations of subject peoples that came to characterize the period. The Umarian experiment reminds us that the performance of the economy reflected the form and nature of state intervention in the economy and that economic performance in turn shaped the form of the state and the expression of its power.

Of the three states examined in this study, only the French colonial state monopolized warfare. Instead of reinforcing the French military's control over the colonial state, the monopoly of warfare eventually cost the military its strategic location within the state. Despite differences in weapons, tactics, military command, strategies, forms of warfare, and ideologies of state power, the French colonial state, the Segu Bambara state, and the Umarian state were warrior states. In each case, however, warfare had different consequences for the economy and political history.

Since the states were warrior states, the reproduction of warriors and their capacity for making war were paramount to each state's survival. In each case, the patterns through which warriors reproduced their domination over the state affected the structure of both the state and the economy. The Segu Bambara state differed from the other two because it emerged, at the beginning of the eighteenth century, out of a set of local conditions. The state retained elements of the ideology and institutions of the bachelors' association that lay at the core of the state-building process. The retention of these elements shaped the structure of state power and revealed itself in tensions between the slave warriors and the king. The king intervened in the economy to maintain the state's capacity to launch full military campaigns and thus sustain warriors' dependence on the state. The state thus fostered the development of a specialized group of fishermen, the Somono. The state also established conditions that led to the emergence of the Maraka plantation economy. Both these groups relied on the state, directly or indirectly, to ensure the conditions for the reproduction of their own relations of production.

The Umarians were conquerors and they too relied on warfare for their survival. After 1865, when warriors no longer participated in full-scale state-sponsored campaigns, the social relations between warriors and the state and between warriors and the conquered peoples changed. The Umarians engaged almost exclusively in razzia, which were conducted by loose-knit warrior bands ostensibly under the direction of a military commander and thus tenuously linked to the state. Usually, however, the Umarians were indistinguishable from brigands and from Bambara rebels. Failure to control the processes of social reproduction of warriors led to a serious weakening of state power and to conditions antithetical to the security of commercial and productive investment.

The French also came as conquerors. Until the turn of the twentieth century, warfare remained the most important means of reproducing the state and expanding its domain. Continued warfare provided French officers with avenues for advancement and it provided their African auxiliaries with booty. Except in 1893–95, when the state had a civilian governor, the French military was the colonial state. After 1898, as warfare became less significant to the survival of the state, French warriors lost their control over the state.

Even the French colonial state, which was the most powerful warrior state in the Middle Niger valley and the Western Sudan, failed to control the forces of social change it had unleashed. Paradoxically, the very success of the French colonial warrior state led to its collapse. The monopoly of war after 1898 meant that the state no longer depended on warfare or on the local community for its direct survival. Only at this time did the state withdraw its support of the precolonial relations of production. In doing so, it weakened the state's role in guaranteeing the precolonial forms of production and reproduction.

To account for the integrity of the state and the economy and for the process of social change after 1905, I have applied a broad concept of the state to the history of the Middle Niger valley. I argued that the state should be considered a "field of force," within which the forces and social relations of production, appropriation, and exploitation were articulated and defended. Even in the context of a weak state, the field of force may extend well beyond the effective power of the state. When applied to the Umarian case, the concept helps explain why the economy reacted as it did. The state neither participated in the reproduction of the relations of production, as the Bambara state had done, nor left the communities sufficient independence to generate their own dynamic. Instead, the state intervened by extracting surplus without encouraging the conditions necessary to sustain or expand production. Widespread popular revolts further constrained the Umarians' capacity to establish the state institutions that would have controlled the forces of disruption and violence and thereby fostered conditions for economic growth. Mere power, however, did not assure the state capacity to control and direct production, as the experience of the French colonial state proves.

The forces for economic growth that led the Maraka to develop a production and exchange complex in which plantation slavery was a central feature during the era of the Bambara were not eliminated by the failure of the Umarian state system or the success of the French in monopolizing war. The ecological diversity of the West African interior fostered markets that catered to the production, movement, and distribution of products not generally available locally. It also encouraged producers to increase the production of commodities that had no significant local demand. When conditions permitted, certain producers became specialized, as the Maraka plantation owner and the Somono transporter did. Even the end of warfare and the decline of the warrior state did not alter the dynamics of the regional economy of the Middle Niger valley. The regional economy remained an African one.

In the years after 1905, the French celebrated the beginning of a new freedom and a new political economy as the slaves throughout the Middle Niger valley and the Western Sudan left their masters or redefined their relations with their ex-masters. The transformation of society and the social relations of production occurred within a relatively short period. In some places, the old order died hard; in others, the transition to new forms of dependency and labor occurred smoothly. In all cases, the period from 1905 to 1914 was one of adjustment and change. The colonial state had created the conditions that made this transformation possible, but it was Africans who determined the pace and direction of change.

Reference Matter

Notes

Complete authors' names, dates, and publication data may be found in the Bibliography, pp. 250–77.

Chapter One

1. Raffenel, *Nouveau voyage*, 2: 208.
2. Caillié, *Journal*, 2: 214–15.
3. Gallais, *Le delta*; Meniaud, *Haut Sénégal Niger*, 1: 62.
4. Bird, "Development of Mandekan"; Bird and Kendall, "Mande Hero"; Welmers, "Mande Languages"; Long, "Northern Mande Languages"; Galtier, "Correspondances."
5. Gallais, "Signification du groupe ethnique," pp. 106–29; Grayzel, "Ecology"; J. V. D. Lewis, "Descendants and Crops"; L'équip, ed., *Pastoral Production*; Docteur Collomb, Notice sur le cercle de Bamako, 1885, Bamako, ANM 1 D 33, no. 1D2.
6. Notice sur le royaume et le cercle de Segou: Notice géographique, 1896, ANM 1 D 55, no. 1D1; Notice historique du royaume et du cercle de Segou, 1896, ANM 1 D 55, no. 2; Delafosse, *Haut Sénégal Niger*, 2: 282; Monteil, *Les Bambara*, pp. 7, 11.
7. Gallais, *Le delta*, 1: 83; J. Bazin, "Notes," p. 404; H. Bazin, *Dictionnaire*. Also interviews with Ismaila Fane, 15 Mar. 1977, Tesserela; Almamy Malik Yattara, 26 Nov. 1976, Bamako. On Soninke traditions of Ancient Ghana, see Delafosse, *Haut Sénégal Niger*, vol. 1; Levtzion, *Ancient Ghana and Mali*.
8. Kati, *Tarikh el-Fettach*; Africanus, *Description de l'Afrique*; Monteil, *Une cité soudanaise*; McIntosh, "Reconsideration of Wangara/Palolus"; Monteil, *Les Bambara*, p. 11, n. 1. See also Quinton, "Etude ethnologique," p. 305; Tauxier, *Histoire des Bambara*, p. 56; Ly-Tall, "Decline of the Mali Empire" and *Contribution à l'histoire*; Niane, *Le Soudan occidental*; Abitbol, *Tombouctou et les Arma*; J. R. Willis, "Western Sudan"; Brown, "Caliphate of Hamdullahi."

9. Friedman and Rowlands, eds., *Evolution of Systems*; R. Cohen and E. Service, eds., *Origin of the State*; G. A. Cohen, *Marx's Theory of History*; Anderson, *Lineages*; Tilly, ed., *Formation of National States*; R. Willis, *State in the Making*; Wilks, *Asante in the Nineteenth Century*; Godelier, "La notion" and "Concept"; Crummey and Stewart, eds., *Modes of Production*; Wittfogel, *Oriental Despotism*; Bailey, "Renewed Discussions"; Claessen and Skalnik, eds., *Early State*.

10. For example, Goody, *Technology, Tradition*; Smaldone, *Warfare*; Law, *Oyo Empire*; Akinjobin, *Dahomey*; Adeleye, *Power and Diplomacy*; Azarya, "Trade and the Center."

11. Gilbert, ed., *Essays of Otto Hintze*, pp. 181, 183; J. Bazin and E. Terray, eds., *Guerres*. For additional African definitions see, Nadel, "Nupe State and Community," pp. 315–17; Fried, *Evolution of Political Society*, pp. 229–40; Balandier, *Anthropologie politique*, pp. 153–73.

12. Lonsdale, "States and Social Processes," p. 156.

13. Marx, *Capital III*, p. 791; Poulantzas, *State, Power, Socialism*; Anderson, *Passages*, p. 22. For the effort to locate class conflict in domestic African societies, see for example Meillassoux, *Femmes, greniers et capitaux*; Dupre and Rey, "Reflections"; Rey, *Les alliances de classes*. Frederick Cooper ("Africa and the World Economy") also stresses class conflict. On the debate concerning the relative autonomy of the state and state institutions, see Miliband, *The State*; Poulantzas, *State, Power, Socialism*; Skocpol, *States and Social Revolutions*. On the structuralist approach to the state and its limitations, see Balibar, "Basic Concepts"; Wolpe, ed., *Modes of Production*; Thompson, *Poverty of Theory*; Kahn and Llobera, "Towards a New Marxism"; Lonsdale and Berman, "Contradictions."

14. Poulantzas, *State, Power, Socialism*. I find intriguing but not helpful, Philip Corrigan's notion of the state as a relation of production (Corrigan, *Capitalism*).

15. Braudel *The Mediterranean*.

16. Marx, *Capital I*, p. 531.

17. Cooper, "The Problem of Slavery"; Roberts, "Women's Work"; Alpers, "State, Capital, Gender."

18. Rapport général de fin d'année sur la situation politique du cercle, Bamako, 1903, ANM 1 E 19.

19. Hopkins, *Economic History*, confuses luxuries with social class and purchasing power.

20. A. Cohen, "Cultural Strategies"; Curtin, *Economic Change*, ch. 2, and *Cross Cultural Trade*; Lovejoy, "Kambarin Beriberi"; Baier, *Economic History*; Amselle, *Les négociants*; Coquery-Vidrovitch and Forest, eds., *Entreprises et entrepreneurs*.

21. Curtin, *Economic Change*, pp. 278–86; Lovejoy, *Caravans of Kola*, pp. 91–92, 122; Lovejoy and Coquery, eds., *Porters and Canoemen*; Baillaud, *Sur les routes*.

22. Hopkins, *Economic History*, p. 5.

23. Allen, *African Husbandman*; Barker, "Stability and Stagnation"; Barker, ed., *Politics of Agriculture*. See also Scott, *Moral Economy*, and Watts, *Silent Violence*; Hyden, *Beyond Ujaama*; Marx, *Capital III*, pp. 444, 449; Freund, *Labour and Capital*.

24. Dumett, "Precolonial Gold"; Terray, "Gold Production."

25. F. Barth, ed., *Ethnic Groups*.

26. Park, *Travels*, p. 433.

27. For recent summaries see Cooper, "Africa and the World Economy"; Lovejoy, *Transformations*; Manning, "Contours of Slavery"; Inikori, ed., *Forced Migration*. On the trans-Saharan trade see Austen, "Trans-Saharan Slave Trade."

28. Curtin, *Atlantic Slave Trade*; Lovejoy, "Volume of the Atlantic Slave Trade," pp. 485, 490.

29. Curtin, *Economic Change*, ch. 4; Roberts, "Production and Reproduction."

30. Slave warriors disdained all work except war. When they did not work, warriors probably survived from the labor of their wives in the fields. Compare Curtin, "Abolition," p. 89.

31. J. Bazin, "Guerre et servitude," p. 142. Warriors, like artisans, owned their means of production. On the armament of Bambara warriors see Monteil, *Les Bambara*, p. 313. On the process of enslavement and insertion in slave-holding societies, see Miers and Kopytoff, eds., *Slavery in Africa*.

32. Park, *Travels*, p. 433.

33. For example, Duby, *Early Growth*; Anderson, *Lineages*, p. 31. Milward, *German Economy at War*, argues that the structure of German industry in the 1930's and 1940's was such that it could not sustain more than the blitzkrieg tactics favored by the German high command in the early years of World War II. Once the German armies were engaged in long campaigns, German industry could no longer provide sufficient matériel, and the German military collapsed.

Chapter Two

1. Cissoko, "Famines," p. 819; Lovejoy and Baier, "Desert Side Economy"; Nicholson, "Methodology"; Watts, *Silent Violence*, pp. 94–104.

2. It took five to seven good harvests to replenish grain stocks in Katsina. Watts, *Silent Violence*, p. 548.

3. Manning, *Slavery, Colonialism, and Economic Growth*, pp. 27–36, 49, and "Enslavement"; Meillassoux, "Plans d'anciennes fortifications"; Smaldone, *Warfare*, pp. 62–86; Bah, "Les forts français."

4. Carrère and Holle, *De la Sénégambie*, pp. 186–87; Raffenel, *Nouveau voyage*, 2: 131–32. Merchants were keenly aware of the avarice of certain princes and avoided areas where the risks to their person and property were too high. Mungo Park, who was both observer and victim, was very clear on this issue (*Travels*).

5. There may be a high correlation between ethnic identity and regional control over certain aspects of trade. For examples see Curtin, *Economic Change*, ch. 2; Lovejoy, *Caravans of Kola* and "Kambarin Beriberi"; Wright, "Darbo Juula."

6. Mage, *Voyage*, pp. 106–7; Newbury, "Prices," p. 104; Swindell, "Serrawollies."

7. La Roy Ladurie, "Histoire et climat," pp. 3–34; Clarence-Smith, "For Braudel," pp. 275–84. Changes in the organization and performance of the agricultural sector can only be traced from the advent of French statistics on climate and economic conditions. For a beginning, see Roberts, "Emergence." The quantifiable sources are found in ANM 1 Q and 1 R series.

8. Manning, *Slavery, Colonialism, and Economic Growth*, pp. 6, 88, 115.

9. Leynaud, "Fraternités"; W. I. Jones, "Food Economy"; Holas, *Les Senoufo*; Brasseur, *Les établissements humains*; Capron, *Anthropologie économique*; Gallais, *Le delta*, pp. 84, 109–10; J. V. D. Lewis, "Descendants and Crops."

10. Notices historiques et géographiques du cercle de Bamako, 1903, ANM 1 D 33, no. 1; Jaime, *De Koulikoro à Tombouctou*, p. 123; Grayzel, "Ethnic-Class Identity."

11. Besides birth, the only means of entry into an artisanal group in West Africa was sexual contact, which obviously suggests a degree of volition. For discussion see Vaughan, "Caste Systems"; Richter, "Further Considerations on Caste."

12. N'Diaye, *Les castes*, pp. 66–75; Curtin, *Economic Change*, pp. 31–32; Markiarius, "Observations," pp. 622–40.

13. Lonsdale, "States and Social Processes," pp. 139–225; R. Willis, *State in the Making*; Reefe, *Rainbow and the Kings*; Vansina, *Children of Woot*; Miller, *Kings and Kinsmen*.

14. For example, Lévi-Strauss, *Structural Anthropology* and *Myth and Meaning*; Feierman, *The Shambaa Kingdom*; Miller, ed., *African Past Speaks*; de Heusch, *Drunken King*.

15. Kesteloot and Dumestre, *La geste de Ségou*; Kesteloot, "Le mythe et l'histoire" and "Acteurs et valeurs"; J. Bazin, "Production d'un récit,"

pp. 435–83; Bird and Kendall, "Mande Hero"; Cashion, "Hunters." A more complete historical analysis of the variants of the Mamari Kulubali cycle awaits the publication of Lilyan Kesteloot's study of ten versions that she has collected over the past two decades, and David Conrad's forthcoming study "Bambara Segu in the Eighteenth and Nineteenth Centuries: Tayiru Banbera's Traditional History."

16. Meillassoux, "Histoire et institutions du *kafo*," p. 215; Curtin, *Economic Change*, pp. 143, 181; Tauxier, *Histoire des Bambara*, ch. 4. Jean Bazin ("Etat guerrier") is equivocal on this point, although he does suggest that as leader of the bachelors' association Mamari subordinated the hunters. On Malinke hunters see Cisse, "Notes sur les sociétés"; Sidibe, "Nouvelles notes."

17. Monteil, *Les Bambara*, pp. 25–26.

18. Meillassoux, "Essai d'interprétation"; *Femmes, greniers et capitaux*; "Recherche"; "From Reproduction to Production"; "Social Organisation." Meillassoux, however, does not draw these conclusions about the internal rupture in Bambara society.

19. Goody, ed., *Development Cycle*.

20. Paques, *Les Bambara*, pp. 47, 56; J. V. D. Lewis, "Descendants and Crops."

21. Monteil, *Les Bambara*, pp. 291–92.

22. Ibid., pp. 28–38, 292–96; Kesteloot, *Da Monzon*, 1: 4; Levtzion, "Northwest Africa," 4: 175. Also interview with Yusufu Traore, 13 Dec. 1976, Segu-Koro.

23. Monteil, *Les Bambara*, pp. 31, 47; Tauxier, *Histoire des Bambara*, p. 71; Delafosse, *Haut Sénégal Niger*, 2: 284; J. Bazin, "Etat guerrier."

24. Fisher and Fisher, *Slavery*; Cooper, "Problem of Slavery"; Meyers, "Class, Ethnicity, and Slavery"; Crone, *Slaves on Horses*; Lovejoy, "Slavery in the Sokoto Caliphate"; Anderson, *Lineages*.

25. Traditions suggest that the Segu Bambara were exposed to firearms by the army of Kong in the 1740's, although the Arma had used firearms since the end of the sixteenth century. On Kong see Green, "The Foundation of Kong."

26. Monteil, *Les Bambara*, p. 69; also J. Bazin, "Guerre et servitude," p. 158.

27. A full-scale military offensive would hardly be directed against a small village, where the gains would not have been worth the social and economic costs. Oral traditions, however, consistently explain events in personal terms such as revenge, humiliation, and courage. For a discussion of the differences between political and economic motivations for warfare, see Curtin, *Economic Change*, ch. 4.

28. Kesteloot, *Da Monzon*, 1: 10; Tauxier, *Histoire des Bambara*, p. 83;

Ba and Daget, *L'empire peul*, p. 135; Monteil, *Les Bambara*, pp. 310–18; J. Bazin, "Etat guerrier," pp. 342–43.

29. The sofa was a slave warrior, or, according to Mage, a slave employed to care for horses who accompanied his master into war. Mage, *Voyage*, p. 13.

30. Park referred to jado by a word of Arabic derivation, *tekere*, which means to steal (*Travels*, p. 436). See also J. Bazin, "Guerre et servitude"; Curtin, *Economic Change*, p. 181, and "Abolition"; Meillassoux, "Histoire et institutions de *kafo*." Also interview with Ismaila Fane, 15 Mar. 1977, Tesserela.

31. Coste, Coutumiers juridiques, cercle de Segou, 1 Apr. 1897, ANS-AOF 1 G 229. Ironworkers were enslaved, but probably they were not sold, although one Sinsani merchant had a slave village composed solely of ironworkers. Interview with Sidi Yaya Kone, 1 Feb. 1977, Sinsani.

32. Park, *Travels*, pp. 382–84; Monteil, *Les Bambara*, p. 47. Also Conrad, "Slavery." Also interviews with Binke Baba Kuma (session 2), 21 Mar. 1977, Sinsani; Baba Kuma (sessions 1 and 2), 28 Dec. 1976 and 13 Mar. 1977, Segu; Cemoko Ture, 5 Mar. 1977, Segu; Dahou Traore, 11 Feb. 1977, Sibila.

33. Compare Wilks, *Asante in the 19th Century*, p. 270; Terray, "Contribution à une étude"; Smaldone, *Warfare*, pp. 132–37.

34. Kesteloot, *Da Monzon*, 1: 10–11.

35. Notice historique du royaume et du cercle de Segou, 1896, Segu, ANM 1 D 55, no. 2.

36. Kesteloot, "Le mythe et l'histoire," p. 597.

37. Interviews with Cemoko Ture, 5 Mar. 1977, Segu; Ismaila Fane, 15 Mar. 1977, Tesserela; Fama Keita, 18 Jan. 1977, Segu; Baba Sako, 9 Jan. 1977, Segu; Mama Traore, 10 Feb. 1977, Niaro; Monteil, *Les Bambara*, p. 29; Kesteloot, *Da Monzon*, 1: 11.

38. Interviews with Ismaila Fane, 15 Mar. 1977, Tesserela; Cekoro Dembele, 12 Dec. 1976, Banakoro; Kesteloot, "Le mythe et l'histoire," p. 597; Capitaine Briquelot, résident of Segu, letter to commandant supérieur, 18 Aug. 1891, Segu, ANM 1 E 219.

39. Marty, trans., "Chroniques de Oualata," pp. 568–69; Brown, "Caliphate," p. 40; Person, "Ngolo Jara," p. 291; Monteil, *Les Bambara*; Raffenel, *Nouveau voyage*; Abitbol, *Tombouctou et les Arma*; D. Robinson, *Holy War*.

40. On the drought see Marty, trans., "Chroniques de Oualata," p. 565; Cissoko, "Famines"; Nicholson, "Methodology"; Curtin, *Economic Change*, vol. 2; Lovejoy and Baier, "Desert-Side Economy"; Watts, *Silent Violence*.

41. Monteil, *Les Bambara*, pp. 44, 64; Person, "Ngolo Jara," p. 291.

42. Park, *Travels*, pp. 338–39.

43. Brown, "Caliphate," p. 40; Delafosse, *Haut Sénégal Niger*, 2: 289; Notice sur le cercle de Sokolo, 31 Dec. 1903, Sokolo, ANS-AOF 1 G 323; Rapport politique, région du Sahel, 25 June 1898, ANM 1 E 11; Marty, *Etudes sur l'Islam*, 4: 95–96; Tauxier, *Histoire des Bambara*, pp. 90–95; Izard, *Introduction à l'histoire*, 2: 320; Bime, *Ségou*, p. 26; Person, "Ngolo Jara," pp. 300–301.

44. Delafosse, *Haut Sénégal Niger*, 2: 289–90; Raffenel, "Deuxième voyage," p. 229; Capitaine Perignon, Généralités sur Haut Sénégal et Moyen Niger, 1900, ANS-AOF 1 G 248; Capitaine Bellat, Renseignements historiques sur le pays de Sansanding et du Macina, 1893, ANS-AOF 1 G 184; Brown, "Caliphate," pp. 43–45. Also interviews with Cekoro Kulubali, 26 Feb. 1977, Segu; Ismaila Fane, 15 Mar. 1977, Tesserela; Baba Kuma (session 1), 28 Dec. 1976, Segu; Binke Baba Kuma (session 2), 21 Mar. 1977, Sinsani. Cekoro Kulubali, 26 Feb. 1977, Segu, lists two other sons of Ngolo, Tankane and Sery.

45. Park, *Travels*, pp. 130, 142, 144, 343, 431–32; Notice historique du royaume de Segou, 1896, ANM 1 D 55, no. 2; Delafosse, *Haut Sénégal Niger*, 2: 291; Bime, *Ségou*, p. 29.

46. Park, *Mission*, p. 210.

47. Park, *Travels*, pp. 359–60, 390–91, 436–38.

48. Delafosse, *Haut Sénégal Niger*, 1: 247.

49. Ba and Daget, *L'empire peul*, p. 85; Brown, "Caliphate," p. 43.

50. Park, *Travels*, p. 299, and *Mission*, pp. 196–97.

51. Rapport politique sur l'organisation du pays de Segou, 1890, ANS-AOF 15 G 172, quoted in Brown, "Caliphate," p. 53; J. Bazin, "Production d'un récit," p. 476. Compare Wilks, *Asante Policy*, pp. 477–97, and *Political Bipolarity*.

52. Curtin, *Economic Change*, p. 22; Bernus, "Le contrôle," pp. 68–74.

53. Baier, "Trans-Saharan Trade," p. 53, and *Economic History*, pp. 25–26.

54. For parallel trends in what Lovejoy calls "the frontiers of Islam," see *Transformations*, chs. 2 and 9.

55. Mage, *Voyage*, p. 276.

56. McDougall, "Idjil Salt Industry" and "View from Awdaghust"; Meillassoux, "Commerce précolonial," p. 189; A. Cohen, "Cultural Strategies," pp. 266–78; Lovejoy, "Kambarin Beriberi"; Hill, "Landlord and Broker"; interview with Binke Sukule, 21 Mar. 1977, Sinsani.

57. Capitaine Lartigue, Notice sur la région du Sahel, Appendix 2, 1896, ANM 1 D 9; Roberts, "Long Distance Trade." Also interviews with Mulaye Sise (sessions 1 and 3) 22 Dec. 1976, Sinsani, and 8 Mar. 1977, Sinsani; Almamy Jawara, 23 Feb. 1977, Segu; Binke Sukule, 21 Mar.

1977, Sinsani; Dahou Traore, 11 Feb. 1977, Sibila; Mama Traore, 10 Feb. 1977, Niaro.

58. Mauny, *Tableau géographique*, p. 358; Curtin, *Economic Change*, p. 226; Capitaine Lartigue, Notice historique, 1896, ANM 1 D 9; McDougall, "Idjil Salt Industry"; Lovejoy, "Borno Salt" and *Salt of the Desert Sun*. Also interview with Mulaye Sise (session 1), 22 Dec. 1976, Sinsani. Another Bambara term for black salt is *kogo fin*.

59. Caillié, *Journal*, 2: 376.

60. H. Barth, *Travels and Discoveries*, 5: 26.

61. Roberts, "Women's Work."

62. J. V. D. Lewis, "Descendants and Crops"; J. Bazin, "Guerre et servitude."

63. Park, *Mission*, pp. 210–23.

64. This was also the case elsewhere in West Africa. See Hill, "Hidden Trade" and *Rural Hausa*, pp. 138–39, 268–69.

65. Johnson, "Cowrie Currencies"; Lovejoy, "Interregional Monetary Flows."

66. Park, *Mission*, pp. 214–16.

67. Ibid., p. 216.

68. Mage, *Voyage*, pp. 187–91.

69. H. Barth, *Travels and Discoveries*, 5: 19. For similar views see Baillaud, *Sur les routes*, p. 247, and Dubois, *Tombouctou*, p. 195; Hopkins, *Economic History*, pp. 106–12; Lovejoy, "Polyani's 'Ports of Trade,'" pp. 270–75.

70. Meillassoux, ed., *Development of Indigenous Trade*, pp. 55, 63–67, and "Rôles de l'esclavage."

71. See Lovejoy and Hogendorn, "Slave Marketing"; Curtin, "Abolition"; Johnson, "Atlantic Slave Trade"; Curtin, *Economic Change*, pp. 68–80; Wilks, "Mossi and Akan States," 1: 378. Also interviews with Mulaye Sise (session 3), 8 Mar. 1977, Sinsani; Koke Keita, 2 Feb. 1977, Sinsani; Binke Baba Kuma (sessions 1 and 2), 19 Dec. 1976 and 13 Mar. 1977, Segu; Bakary Dukure, 30 Jan. 1977, Segu; Amadu Sanago, 8 Jan. 1977, Sinsani.

72. Raffenel, letter to king of Segu, 18 Feb. 1848, Bakel, ANS-AOF 1 G 18; Curtin, *Economic Change*, pp. 140–41.

73. The economics of transport is brilliantly discussed in Curtin, *Economic Change*, pp. 278–95.

74. Caillié, *Journal*, 2: 87–88; Howard, "Relevance of Spatial Analysis" and "Big Men, Traders, and Chiefs." Also interviews with Bakary Dukure, 30 Jan. 1977, Segu; Baba Kuma (session 2), 13 Mar. 1977, Segu; Binke Baba Kuma (session 2), 21 Mar. 1977, Sinsani; Amadu Sanago, 8 Jan. 1977, Sinsani; Binke Sukule, 21 Mar. 1977, Sinsani.

75. Interviews with Baba Kuma (session 2), 13 Mar. 1977, Segu; Musa Kouyate, 26 Jan. 1977, Segu; Binke Sukule, 21 Mar. 1977, Sinsani. Also Rapport sur l'esclavage, Circonscription de San, 1904, San, ANS-AOF K 19; M. Klein, "Slavery, Forced Labor and French Colonial Rule."

76. Commandant, cercle of Bamako, letter, 3 Sept. 1892, ANM 1 E 18.

77. Park, *Travels*, p. 354.

78. Caillié, *Journal*, 2: 103, 115–16; Curtin, *Economic Change*, p. 272; Lovejoy, *Caravans of Kola*, pp. 101–2; Hopkins, *Economic History*, p. 63.

79. Caillié, *Journal*, 2: 68–69. An interesting study of time, labor, and distance in caravan trade could be made by examining accounts of travelers who were equipped with watches, for example, Soleillet, *Voyage à Ségou*.

80. For a discussion of the costs and benefits of the various forms of animal carriage, see Curtin, *Economic Change*, pp. 279–80; Roberts, "Long Distance Trade," pp. 178–79.

81. Bulletin commercial et agricole, Bamako, 1890–91, ANM 1 R 31.

82. Interviews with Bakary Dukure, 30 Jan. 1977, Segu; Yahaya Haidara, 30 Mar. 1977, Sinsani; Baba Sako, 9 Jan. 1977, Segu; Demba Suragassi, 18 Feb. 1977, Segu.

83. Caillié, *Journal*, 1: 425.

84. Interviews with Malamine Kone, 7 Feb. 1977, Segu; Baba Sako, 9 Jan. 1977, Segu; Yahaya Haidara, 30 Mar. 1977, Sinsani; Binke Baba Kuma (session 1), 19 Dec. 1976, Sinsani; Cemoko Ture, 5 Mar. 1977, Segu.

85. Interview with Malamine Kone, 7 Feb. 1977, Segu; Demba Suragassi, 18 Feb. 1977, Segu. See also A. Cohen, "Cultural Strategies," pp. 266–78; Curtin, *Economic Change*, pp. 81, 84, 274.

86. A. Cohen, "Cultural Strategies," pp. 267, 271–72, and *Custom and Politics*; Lovejoy, "Kambarin Beriberi."

87. Curtin, *Economic Change*, pp. 74, 83; Lovejoy, *Caravans of Kola*, p. 128. Also interview with Binke Baba Kuma (session 2), 21 Mar. 1977, Sinsani; Mulaye Sise (session 3), 8 Mar. 1977, Sinsani; Yahaya Haidara, 30 Mar. 1977, Sinsani; Binke Sukule, 21 Mar. 1977, Sinsani; Demba Suragassi, 18 Feb. 1977, Segu.

88. Interviews with Mulaye Sise (session 3), 8 Mar. 1977, Sinsani; Binke Baba Kuma (session 1), 19 Dec. 1976, Sinsani; Cemoko Ture, 5 Mar. 1977, Segu; Yahaya Haidara, 30 Mar. 1977, Sinsani; Curtin, *Economic Change*, p. 298.

89. Caillié, *Journal*, 1: 466, 2: 5–6, 16–18; interview with Sanussi Danyogo, 1 Feb. 1977, Sinsani. Commandant, fort of Bamako, letter, 1 July 1885, ANM 1 E 18, and Commandant, cercle of Bamako, letter, 1 May

1886, ANM 1 E 18, are examples from the archives. Also interviews with Yahaya Haidara, 30 Mar. 1977, Sinsani; Cemoko Ture, 5 Mar. 1977, Segu; Musa Kouyate, 26 Jan. 1977, Segu.

90. Mollien, *Travels*, p. 308; Lovejoy, *Caravans of Kola*, pp. 128–29; Curtin, *Economic Change*, p. 140. Also interviews with Mulaye Sise (session 1), 22 Dec. 1976, Sinsani; Yahaya Haidara, 30 Mar. 1977, Sinsani; Demba Suragassi, 18 Feb. 1977, Segu.

91. Interview with Mulaye Sise (session 1), 22 Dec. 1976, Sinsani; Demba Suragassi, 18 Feb. 1977, Segu; Amadu Sanago, 8 Jan. 1977, Sinsani; Cemoko Ture, 5 Mar. 1977, Segu. Also Penel, "Coutumes soudanaises," 1: 116; Wilks, "Mossi and Akan States"; Terray, "Long Distance Exchange"; Lovejoy, *Caravans of Kola*. See also the report of Capitaine Payne, Oussourou, 1906, ANM 1 D 288 for detail on merchants avoiding French frontier customs stations; Curtin, *Economic Change*, p. 290, and "Precolonial Trading Networks," p. 237; Caillié, *Journal* 1: 70; Johnson, "Economic Foundations."

92. Levtzion, "Seventeenth Century Chronicle."

93. The term may derive from the term *komo* (Bambara: to fish the streams), which the Sorko use to mean *captifs de pêche*. Gallais claims that the komo were the boatmen of ancient Mali, but I have not seen supporting evidence for this contention. See Ligers, *Sorko*, 2: 121; Gallais, *Le delta*, 1: 67.

94. Kati, *Tarikh el-Fettach*, p. 179; Perron, "Traditions claniques," pp. 441, 451–52; Ligers, *Sorko*, 5: iv, xii; Tymowski, "La pêche," pp. 17–20; Villien-Rossi, "Bamako," p. 264.

95. Mage, *Voyage*, pp. 373–74.

96. Ibid., p. 374; Delafosse, *Haut Sénégal Niger*, 2: 285; Soleillet, *Voyage à Ségou*, p. 308; Bime, *Ségou*, p. 21; Sundstrom, *Ecology and Symbiosis*, p. 160. Also interviews with Cekoro Kulubali, 26 Feb. 1977, Segu; Birama Kamite, 17 Dec. 1976, Kokou; Karamoko Kane (session 2), 6 Jan. 1977, Segu; Mady and BaIssa Kone, 11 Dec. 1976, Segu.

97. Sundstrom, *Ecology and Symbiosis*, pp. 18–27; Daget, "La pêche"; Jacquemond, "Les pêcheries"; Perron, "Pêcheries et sécheries"; Deherme, *L'Afrique Occidentale française*, p. 289. Also interviews with Mady and BaIssa Kone, 11 Dec. 1976, Segu.

98. Park, *Mission*, p. 200.

99. Gallais, *Le delta*, 2: 430. Also interviews with Cekoro Dembele, 12 Dec. 1976, Banankoro; Karamoko Kane, 6 Jan. 1977, Segu; BaSidiki Kamite, 20 Dec. 1976, Markaduguba; Mady and BaIssa Kone, 11 Dec. 1976, Segu. See also Perignon, Généralités sur Haut-Sénégal et Moyen Niger, 1900, ANS-AOF 1 G 248.

100. Gallais, *Le delta*, 1: 108.

101. Mage, *Voyage*, pp. 202–3.

102. Park, *Travels*, p. 293; Correnson, De l'organisation de la justice chez les populations de la région de Segou, 1910, ANS-AOF 1 G 336; Binger, *Du Niger au golfe de Guinée*, 1: 12–13; Robin, Réponse au questionnaire sur les coutumes indigènes, cercle de Bamako, 1909, ANM 1 D 186; Passage du Niger, n.d. (probably 1915), ANM 1 E 20; Commandant, Rapport politique, Nyamina, Mar. 1913, ANM 1 E 20.

103. Africanus, *Description de l'Afrique*, p. 465; Park, *Mission*, p. 224.

104. Dubois, *Tombouctou*, p. 191.

105. Jaime, *De Koulikoro à Tombouctou*, p. 218.

106. Binger, *Du Niger au golfe de Guinée*, 1: 10; Park, *Travels*, p. 293.

107. Caillié, *Journal*, 2: 241–45; Dubois, *Tombouctou*, p. 190; Jaime, *De Koulikoro à Tombouctou*, pp. 178–79.

108. Jaime, *De Koulikoro à Tombouctou*, pp. 188, 221; Dubois, *Tombouctou*, p. 191; Caillié, *Journal*, 2: 240–41.

109. Jaime, *De Koulikoro à Tombouctou*, p. 223; Soleillet, *Voyage à Ségou*, p. 308.

110. Dubois, *Tombouctou*, p. 192. Compare Meniaud, *Haut Sénégal Niger*, 1: 89, who estimates that freight rates for goods were .03 francs per metric ton per kilometer, and .01 francs per passenger per kilometer. See also Jaime, *De Koulikoro à Tombouctou*, p. 221.

111. Johnson, "Economic Foundations," p. 492.

Chapter Three

1. For background on Umar and the Umarian experiment, see Abun-Nasr, *The Tijaniyya*; D. Robinson, *Holy War*, especially chs. 2 and 3; Jah, "Sufism"; J. R. Willis, "Writings"; Marquet, "Des *Ikhwan al-Safa*"; Martin, "Notes sur l'origine"; Salenc, "La vie d'Al Hadj ʿOmar. See also Hiskett, *Sword of Truth* and "Nineteenth Century Jihads."

2. J. R. Willis, "Writings," p. 178; D. Robinson, *Holy War*, pp. 112–27.

3. J. R. Willis, "Jihad fi sabil-Allah"; Jah, "Sufism," pp. 192–93, 201, 206–7.

4. J. R. Willis, "Writings," p. 180; Smaldone, *Warfare*, pp. 24–37; Oloruntimehin, *Segu Tukulor Empire*, p. 55; Tyam, *La vie d'el hadj Omar*, p. 158.

5. D. Robinson, *Holy War*, pp. 165–72, 204–41.

6. Interview with Mamuru Fomba et al., 21 July 1981, Sinzena; D. Robinson, *Holy War*, p. 250. The Umarians skirmished with Segu's forces at Damfa before the battle of Ngano.

7. Mamadu Racine, commandant, cercle of Nyamina, letter, Sept. 1889, ANM 1 E 18.

8. Interview, Musa Kouyate, 26 Jan. 1977, Segu; Oloruntimehin, *Segu*

Tukulor Empire, p. 124; Monteil, *Les Bambara*, p. 324; Quinton, "Souvenirs d'un voyage," 1: 530. This was, after all, the hungry period.

9. Kamara, "La vie d'el hadj Omar," p. 91; Mage, *Voyage*, p. 257.

10. Mage, *Voyage*, p. 257; Kamara, "La vie d'el hadj Omar," p. 91; Oloruntimehin, *Segu Tukulor Empire*, p. 124–25.

11. Triaud and Mahibou have recently translated and annotated Umar's *Bayân mâ Waqaʿa*, which was composed on the eve of the Umarian-Masina conflict. It is a major work justifying the Umarian jihad and refuting Amadu III's arguments, which form part of the *Bayân*. Triaud and Mahibou, *Voilà ce qui est arrivé*. See also Zebadia, "Career"; D. Robinson, *Holy War*, pp. 262–64.

12. Bellat, Renseignements, 1893, ANS-AOF 1 G 184; Underberg, Notes sur l'histoire de Macina, Mar. 1892, ANS-AOF 1 G 122; Jah, "Sufism," pp. 209–16; Oloruntimehin, *Segu Tukulor Empire*, pp. 127–28; Saint-Martin, *L'empire toucouleur*, p. 62.

13. Underberg, Notes sur l'histoire de Macina, Mar. 1892, ANS-AOF 1 G 122.

14. Bellat, Renseignements, 1893, ANS-AOF 1 G 184; Underberg, Notes sur l'histoire du Macina, Mar. 1892, ANS-AOF 1 G 122; Mage, *Voyage*, pp. 259–60; Delafosse, *Haut Sénégal Niger*, 2: 316–17; Saint-Martin, *L'empire toucouleur*, p. 62; Kamara, "La vie d'el hadj Omar," pp. 92–93. Also interviews with Ismaila Fane, 15 Mar. 1977, Tesserela; Seydu Jane (session 1), 4 Jan. 1977, Sinsani; Musa Keita (session 2), 30 Dec. 1976, Sinsani; al hajj Ibrahima Magane, 4 Jan. 1977, Sinsani.

15. Lieutenant Mage, letter to governor, 5 Mar. 1864, Segu Sikoro, ANS-AOF 1 G 32. Informants in Sinzena claimed that the Somono had stolen much of the Jara treasure during this fluid time, and that Umarian relations with the Somono were thereafter influenced by their desire to recapture the Jara gold. Interview, Mamuru Fomba et al., 21 July 1981, Sinzena.

16. Mage, *Voyage*, p. 269; Bellat, Renseignements, 1893, ANS-AOF 1 G 184; Jah, "Sufism," p. 224. Also interview with Ismaila Fane, 15 Mar. 1977, Tesserela.

17. See D. Robinson, *Holy War*, ch. 1, for a critical assessment of internal and external sources on the jihad.

18. Oloruntimehin, *Segu Tukulor Empire*, p. 127.

19. Mage, *Voyage*, pp. 525–26. Also interviews with Ismaila Fane, 15 Mar. 1977, Tesserela; Almamy Kone et al., 23 July 1981, Nyamina.

20. Bellat, Renseignements, 1893, ANS-AOF 1 G 184. Also interview with Ismaila Fane, 15 Mar. 1977, Tesserela.

21. Interview, Soumana Oulale et al., 22 July 1981, Nyamina. This tradition suggests that Sumana plied the Niger-Milo trade route, in

which case Nyamina was a logical place to reopen his business. Lassana Sako, "Traditions de Nyamina," typewritten manuscript, 1949; "Petite histoire."

22. Sako, "Traditions de Nyamina"; Delafosse, *Haut Sénégal Niger*, 2: 316. Also interviews with Soumana Oulale et al., 22 July 1981, Nyamina; Musa Keita (session 2), 30 Dec. 1976, Sinsani; Binke Baba Kuma (session 1), 19 Dec. 1976, Sinsani; al hajj Ibrahima Magane, 4 Jan. 1977, Sinsani. Also Bellat, Renseignements, 1893, ANS-AOF 1 G 184. Copies of these letters have never been located.

23. Interview with Basidiki Sako et al., 22 July 1981, Nyamina; Sako, "Traditions de Nyamina"; "Petite histoire."

24. Tyam, *La vie d'el hadj Omar*, verse 873.

25. Bellat, Renseignements, 1893, ANS-AOF 1 G 184; Quinton, "Souvenirs d'un voyage," p. 531.

26. Mage, *Voyage*, p. 258. This is also the view of Fama Mademba's son and biographer, Mademba, *Au Sénégal*, p. 69.

27. Rodinson, *Islam and Capitalism*, pp. 14, 72–75. On Northern Nigeria, see for example, Lovejoy, *Caravans of Kola*; Shea, "Development"; Adamu, *The Hausa Factor*; Watts, *Silent Violence*, ch. 2; Lubeck, *Islam and Urban Labor*. On Hamdullahi, see Johnson, "Economic Foundations"; Lieutenant Sargolis, Notice sur l'administration, 1895, ANM 1 D 17; Brown, "Caliphate," pp. 61, 72, 96. On Futanke rule in Masina, Monteil, *Une cité soudanaise*, p. 118, writes that they left "only memories of bandits who lived in pillage."

28. Quinton, "Souvenirs d'un voyage," p. 531.

29. The term "juula revolution" comes from Person, *Samori*, which explores how Samori sought to regenerate Malinke society and integrate the Dyula, who had hitherto been excluded from political power. See also M. Klein, "Dyula Revolution"; Green, "Foundation."

30. Kamara, "La vie d'el hadj Omar," pp. 390–91.

31. Khadduri, *War and Peace*, p. 168. This notion of international relations assumes, however, the existence of a central caliphate, and disregards, for example, the many examples of Muslim-Christian alliances.

32. Smaldone, *Warfare*, pp. 91–92; Ruxton, *Maliki Law*, p. 80; Khadduri, *War and Peace*, p. 123.

33. Meniaud, *Pionniers*, 1: 131; Jaime, *De Koulikoro à Tombouctou*, p. 150, n. 1; Gallieni, *Mission*, pp. 354, 382; Kanya-Forstner, "Mali-Tukulor," p. 57; D. Robinson, *Holy War*, pp. 185, 258, 267.

34. Soleillet, *Voyage à Ségou*, p. 393; Saint-Martin, *L'empire toucouleur*, p. 184.

35. Jah, "Sufism," p. 203; Kanya-Forstner, "Mali-Tukulor," p. 57; Meniaud, *Pionniers*, 1: 132; Saint-Martin, *L'empire toucouleur*, p. 185.

36. Soleillet, *Voyage à Ségou*, p. 258–59; Saint-Martin, *L'empire toucouleur*, p. 187; D. Robinson, *Holy War*, pp. 129–30, 331–32.

37. See the special issue of the *Journal of African History*, 12, nos. 2 and 4 (1971); Inikori, "Import of Firearms," pp. 339–68.

38. Soleillet, *Voyage à Ségou*, p. 394.

39. Quinton, "Souvenirs d'un voyage," p. 542; Gallieni, *Mission*, p. 354; Saint-Martin, *L'empire toucouleur*, p. 185.

40. Holle was an eyewitness and Carrère his collaborator in Carrère, "Siège de Medine"; Ruxton, *Maliki Law*, p. 77, n.1.

41. Mage, *Voyage*, p. 296; Notice sur le cercle de Segou, 1904, ANS-AOF 1 G 320; Oloruntimehin, *Segu Tukulor Empire*, p. 82.

42. D. Robinson, *Chiefs and Clerics*, pp. 112, 167; Kanya-Forstner, "Mali-Tukulor," pp. 48, 61; Jaime, *De Koulikoro à Tombouctou*, pp. 152, 154.

43. Johnson, "Economic Foundations," pp. 486–88; Monteil, *Une cité soudanaise*, pp. 106–10; Mage, *Voyage*, p. 447. Mage refers to razzia as *bame*, which is defined as the action of pounding grain with mortar. The analogy is very appropriate, since razzia came to be the basic source of Futanke subsistence.

44. Mage, *Voyage*, pp. 437–38.

45. Ibid., p. 493.

46. Ibid., pp. 335, 406.

47. Jaime, *De Koulikoro à Tombouctou*, p. 150, n. 1. They apparently did not want to leave Segu. Bellat, Renseignements, 1893, ANS-AOF 1 G 184. On the ethnic composition of Umar's army in 1869, see D. Robinson, *Holy War*, p. 258.

48. Sargolis, Notice sur l'administration, Segu, 1895, ANM 1 D 17; Saint-Martin, *L'empire toucouleur*, pp. 84–85; Oloruntimehin, *Segu Tukulor Empire*, p. 71; Kanya-Forstner, "Mali-Tukulor," p. 61.

49. Capitaine Briquelot, résident at Segu, letter to Lieutenant Colonel, commandant supérieur, 27 Apr. 1891, Segu, ANM 1 E 219.

50. In this I disagree with Oloruntimehin, "Resistance Movements," p. 126, who argues that the achievements of Bambara resistance were by 1864 still meager.

51. Briquelot, Rapport sur la situation politique des territoires dépendants de la Résidence de Segou, 15 Sept. 1891, Segu, ANM 1 E 71.

52. Mage, *Voyage*, pp. 272–73.

53. Barker, "Stability and Stagnation." See also M. Klein, ed., *Peasants in Africa*, pp. 30–32; Gallieni, *Mission*, pp. 386–87.

54. Kamara, "La vie d'el hadj Omar," p. 397.

55. Notice sur le royaume bambara de Segou, 1889, ANM 1 D 55, no. 5; Saint-Martin, *L'empire toucouleur*, p. 99.

56. Mage, *Voyage*, pp. 464, 577; Bellat, Renseignements, 1893, ANS-

AOF 1 G 184. Also interviews with Seydu Jane (session 1), 4 Jan. 1977, Sinsani; Ismaila Fane, 15 Mar. 1977, Tesserela; Musa Keita (session 1), 12 Dec. 1976, Sinsani; Baba Kuma (session 1), 28 Dec. 1976, Segu; al hajj Ibrahima Magane, 4 Jan. 1977, Sinsani; Mamadu Tunkura, 19 Feb. 1977, Sinsani; Basidiki Sako et al., 22 July 1981, Nyamina.

57. Bellat, Renseignements, 1893, ANS-AOF 1 G 184; Oloruntimehin, "Resistance Movements."

58. Mage, *Voyage*, pp. 513–15. That Amadu should require the tax in cloth is consistent with the Senegambian roots of empire. Senegambia had a localized cloth currency, while the Middle Niger used a cowrie currency.

59. Saint-Martin, *L'empire toucouleur*, p. 100; Bellat, Renseignements, 1893, ANS-AOF 1 G 184; Lieutenant Marchand, letter, 10 Sept. 1889, Nyamina, Mission Marchand, ANS-AOF 1 G 115; Monteil, *Les Bambara*, p. 101.

60. Lieutenant Mage, letter to governor, n.d. (probably June 1865), Segu Sikoro, ANS-AOF 1 G 32; Quinton, "Souvenirs d'un voyage," p. 544. Brown notes that "few social crimes were more reprehensible in the Islamic social order than brigandage. . . ." That such brigandage should stem from the Islamic state was even more disquieting. Brown, "Caliphate," p. 112.

61. Mage, *Voyage*, pp. 306, 464–72, 483; Sako, "Traditions de Nyamina," pp. 9–19; Kamara, "La vie d'el hadj Omar," pp. 391–92. Also interview with Basidiki Sako et al., 22 July 1981, Nyamina.

62. Ancelle, *Les explorateurs*, p. 311; Mage, *Voyage*, pp. 498–508.

63. Lieutenant Mage, letter to governor, 23 Oct. 1865, Segu Sikoro, ANS-AOF 1 G 32. Musa Keita (session 1), 12 Dec. 1976, Sinsani, stated that the letter came from Amadu's mother in Segu. Almamy Jawara, 23 Feb. 1977, Segu, supports Mage's version.

64. Notice sur le royaume bambara de Segou, 1889, ANM 1 D 55, no. 5.

65. Caron, *De Saint Louis*, p. 330; Kone and Roberts, "Résistance bambara."

66. Gallieni, letter, Nango, 14 Nov. 1880, ANF-SOM, Sénégal et dépendances III 10 bis; Gallieni, *Mission*, pp. 5–6.

67. Mage, *Voyage*, p. 229; Gallieni, letter to governor, 10 Sept. 1880, Nango, ANS-AOF 1 G 50; Saint-Martin, *L'empire toucouleur*, pp. 172, 254; Hargreaves, *Prelude*, p. 259.

68. Gallieni, letter to governor, 3 July 1880, Nango, ANS-AOF 1 G 50.

69. Gallieni, letter to governor, 25 Oct. 1880, Nango, reprinted in *Moniteur du Sénégal et dépendances—journal officiel*, 28 Dec. 1880.

70. Soleillet, *Voyage à Ségou*, p. 300.

71. Ibid., pp. 273, 277. Soleillet thought the escort service was merely a ruse to extract a tax from merchants. He found the route secure and traveled to Banamba safely with only one companion.

72. Mage, *Voyage*, p. 385.

73. Ibid., p. 108.

74. Soleillet, *Voyage à Ségou*, pp. 96–97.

75. Gallieni, *Mission*, pp. 349, 351, 356.

76. Interview with Mamuru Fomba et al., 21 July 1981, Sinzena.

77. Meniaud, *Pionniers*, 1: 133.

78. Pietri, *Les Français*, p. 217. Both Meniaud and Pietri were staunchly anti-Umarian, and their evidence should be viewed skeptically. However, my informants, mostly Bambara and Maraka, almost unanimously supported the Meniaud-Pietri perspective. Interviews with Ismaila Fane, 30 July 1981, Tesserela; Basidiki Sako et al., 22 July 1981, Nyamina; Almamy Kone, 23 July 1981, Nyamina; Ahmadu Traore, 1 Aug. 1981, Segukoro; Baye Fofana, 20 July 1981, Banamba.

79. Interview with Soumana Oulale et al., 22 July 1981, Nyamina.

80. Mage, *Voyage*, p. 374.

81. Ibid., pp. 373–74, 377, 408. Also interview with Mady and BaIssa Kone, 11 Dec. 1976, Segu.

82. Interview with Mady and BaIssa Kone, 11 Dec. 1976, Segu.

83. Mage, *Voyage*, p. 373.

84. Ibid., p. 513.

85. Pietri, *Les Français*, p. 227; Soleillet, *Voyage à Ségou*, p. 310.

86. Soleillet, *Voyage à Ségou*, p. 310.

87. Jaime, *De Koulikoro à Tombouctou*, pp. 155–56, 159; Pietri, *Les Français*, p. 281.

88. Baillaud, *Sur les routes*, presents an aerial view of commercial routes in the Western Sudan. Banamba reached its preeminent position at the time Baillaud mapped these routes.

89. Interviews with Mustafa Simpara et al., 18 July 1981, Banamba; Baye Fofana, 20 July 1981, Banamba; Sadya Sylla et al., 20 July 1981, Touba; Mamuru Fomba et al., 21 July 1981, Sinzena; Tijani Sylla et al., 3 Aug. 1981, Baraweli; McDougall, "Idjil Salt Industry," pp. 263–64.

90. Beledugu did not have a monopoly on horse rearing, however. Even if they did not thrive, horses did fairly well in the area from Gumbu to Banamba. Here the indigenous strains were replenished by horses supplied by the Moors. Notices historiques et géographiques du cercle de Bamako, n.d. (probably 1890), ANM 1 D 33, no. 1; Meniaud, *Haut Sénégal Niger*, 2: 93–163; Meillassoux, "Esclavage à Gumbu," p. 187; Law, *The Horse*. Because he could not replenish his supply of horses normally provided by the Maraka caravans, Samori abandoned his attack on Kan-

kore. Commandant of Bamako fort, letter, 28 Feb. 1885, ANM 1 E 18. Also Rapport politique, cercle de Bamako, 1 July 1898, ANM 1 E 18.

91. Mage, *Voyage*, p. 168; Soleillet, *Voyage à Ségou*, p. 238, 468; Besancon, Commandant of Bamako, Rapport sur la tournée, 1897, Bamako, ANM 1 D 18; Baillaud, *Sur les routes*, p. 294.

92. Interview with Mustafa Simpara et al., 18 July 1981, Banamba.

93. McDougall, "Desert."

94. Person, *Samori*; Meillassoux, "Introduction," in *Development of Indigenous Trade*.

95. Interview with Mamuru Fomba et al., 21 July 1981, Sinzena.

96. In 1828, horses were part of the goods exported to the south from Jenne. The horse trade was restricted at the time of the Umarian conquest. Tijani in Masina permitted horse trading only in Bandiagara, the capital. Unauthorized horse dealing, however, was a serious offense. Caillié, *Journal*, 2: 140; Caron, *De Saint Louis*, p. 174. On Sikasso's Mossi horse connection, see Holmes, "Tieba Traore," pp. 193–94, 223, 233. The Fofana family of Banamba provided horses to Keme Birama, Samori's younger brother. These horses were so valued that the offspring of one mare fetched ten and twelve slaves. Interview with Baye Fofana, 20 July 1981, Banamba.

97. Interview with Mamuru Fomba et al., 21 July 1981, Sinzena.

98. On kola see Lovejoy, "Kola."

99. Interviews with Mamuru Fomba et al., 21 July 1981, Sinzena; Sadya Sylla et al., 20 July 1981, Touba.

100. Capitaine Delmotte, letter, commandant cercle de Bouguni, 1 Aug. 1894, ANM 1 Q 7.

101. Capitaine Didio, letter to lieutenant governor, 20 Jan. 1899, Bamako, ANM 1 Q 44.

102. Zimmermann, "L'avenir économique," pp. 23–24.

103. Notice d'ensemble sur le Soudan, ch. 3, 1895, ANM 1 D 3.

104. Rapport du Capitaine MacLeod, Tournée faite dans le Marcadougou, 1 Oct. 1894, Bamako, ANS-AOF 1 G 189. For more information, see chs. 4 and 5.

105. Interview with Tijani Sylla et al., 3 Aug. 1981, Baraweli. See also Meniaud, *Haut Sénégal Niger*, 2: 110.

106. Interview with Tijani Sylla et al., 3 Aug. 1981, Baraweli.

107. Gallieni, *Mission*, p. 358; interview with Amadu Gaku, 3 Aug. 1981, Baraweli.

108. Interview with Tijani Sylla et al., 3 Aug. 1981, Baraweli.

109. The place of indigo in the Maraka economy reflects the complex operation of the Maraka household over the course of the nineteenth century. For more detail see Roberts, "Women's Work."

110. Lovejoy, "Characteristics of Plantations," pp. 1271–74; Mandle, *Roots*, pp. 3–15.

111. Park, *Travels*, pp. 382–83; Binger, letter, 29 July 1887, Wolossebugu, Mission Binger, ANS-AOF 1 G 199; Gallieni, letter, 3 July 1880, Nango, ANS-AOF 1 G 50; Vallière, "Explorations," p. 321; Legassick, "Firearms"; Person, *Samori*, 2: 925–29.

112. Gallieni, letter, 14 Oct. 1880, Nango, ANM 1 G 50.

113. Vallière, "Explorations," p. 320.

114. Bechet, *Cinq ans de séjour*, p. 37; Pietri, *Les Français*, pp. 302–27; Etude sur la captivité, Bamako, 1894, ANS-AOF K 14; Le secrétaire général du gouvernement, Rapport sur le conflit Markas, 26 June 1905, ANS-AOF 15 G 170.

115. Jaime, *De Koulikoro à Tombouctou*, p. 59; Vallière, "Explorations," pp. 321–22. See also Balde, "L'esclavage," pp. 193, 285; Howard, "Big Men, Traders, and Chiefs."

116. Curtin, *Economic Change*, p. 155.

117. A. N. Klein, "Two Asantes." See also A. N. Klein, "Inequality"; Boutillier, "Les trois esclaves de Bouna," pp. 263, 272–73; Muhammad, "Samorian Occupation," pp. 242–57; Handloff, "Trade and Politics."

118. Bayol, "Voyage au pays de Bamako," 2: 59; Carrère and Holle, *De la Sénégambie*, p. 182; Curtin, *Economic Change*, pp. 68–83 and ch. 4. Data on slave markets are drawn from the two series of studies on slavery in the Western Sudan conducted in 1894 and 1904, particularly the reports from Bamako, Segu, Sokolo, and San, ANS-AOF K 14 and K 19, respectively. See also Rapport sur la suppression de la traite, Sokolo, 1 June 1895, ANM 1 E 156. Also interviews with Binke Baba Kuma (session 1) 19 Dec. 1976, Sinsani; Mama Traore, 10 Feb. 1977, Niaro.

119. Interview with Yahaya Haidara, 30 Mar. 1976, Sinsani.

120. Curtin, *Economic Change*, p. 154.

121. Interviews with Mama Traore, 10 Feb. 1977, Niaro; Dahou Traore, 11 Feb. 1977, Sibila.

122. Interview with Dahou Traore, 11 Feb. 1977, Sibila. Robertson and M. Klein, "Women's Importance." See also Thornton, "Sexual Demography"; Meillassoux, "Female Slavery," and the response by M. Klein, "Women in Slavery." Price data are contained in interviews with Dahou Traore, 11 Feb. 1977, Sibila; Almamy Jawara, 23 Feb. 1977, Segu; Binke Sukule, 21 Mar. 1977, Sinsani; Jaime, *De Koulikoro à Tombouctou*, p. 59.

123. Douglas, "Matriliny and Pawnship"; Miller, "The Imbangala," p. 214; MacGaffey, "The Kongo" and "Lineage Structure." For a perspective on the literature of slavery in Africa, see Cooper, "Problem of Slavery."

124. Albert Grodet, Etude sur la captivité au Soudan, 1894, ANM 1 D 2. See also M. Klein, "Demography of Slavery."

125. Brevié, Rapport sur l'esclavage, cercle de Bamako, 1904, ANS-AOF K 19.

126. Brevié, Rapport sur l'esclavage, cercle de Bamako, 1904 ANS-AOF K 19.

127. Etude sur la captivité, Segu, 1894, ANS-AOF K 14; Rapport sur la captivité, Segu, 1904, ANS-AOF K 19; Rapport sur la captivité, Segu, 1904, ANM 1 E 156; Deherme, *L'Afrique Occidentale française*, p. 384; Service géographique, Population du Soudan d'après renseignements reçus, 1 Apr. 1899, ANM 1 D 21.

128. The notion of a self-eliminating slave population was basic to Lugard's premise when he abolished slavery in Northern Nigeria. See Hill, "From Slavery to Freedom"; Lennihan, "Rights."

129. Etude sur la captivité, Sokolo, 1894, ANS-AOF K 14; Etude sur la captivité, Sokolo, 1904, ANS-AOF K 19; Fama Mademba, letter, 17 Mar. 1904, Sinsani, ANM 1 E 220; Rapport sur la captivité, Segu, 1904, ANS-AOF K 19.

130. Brevié, Rapport sur l'esclavage, Bamako, 1904, ANS-AOF K 19.

131. Etude sur la captivité, Segu, 1894, ANS-AOF K 14; Rapport sur la captivité, Segu, 1904, ANM 1 E 156. I have estimated a roughly equal share of male and female children in captivity to arrive at these proportions. Fama Mademba, letter, 17 Mar. 1904, Sinsani, ANM 1 E 220; Etude sur la captivité, Sokolo, 1894, ANS-AOF K 19.

132. Thompson, "Moral Economy" and "Patrician Society"; Scott, *Moral Economy*.

133. African slavery is often defined in terms of domestic units to draw a sharp distinction between it and the form of slavery practiced in the New World. See for instance Kopytoff and Miers, "African 'Slavery'"; Cooper, "Problem of Slavery"; M. Klein, "Study of Slavery"; Grace, *Domestic Slavery*; Le Barbier, *Etudes sur les populations Bambaras*; Conrad, "Slavery Among the Bambara of Segu."

134. Brevié, Rapport sur l'esclavage, Bamako, 1904 ANS-AOF K 19.

135. M. Klein, "Women in Slavery," p. 87; Raffenel, *Nouveau voyage*, 1: 422; Monteil, *Les Bambara*, p. 191; Labouret, "Le servage," p. 151.

136. Interview with Binke Baba Kuma (session 1), 19 Dec. 1976, Sinsani; Kopytoff and Miers, "African 'Slavery,'" pp. 14–34.

137. Penel, "Coutumes soudanaises," 1: 81.

138. Interview with Karamoko Sumare, 6 Jan. 1977, Segu.

139. Interviews with Binke Baba Kuma (session 1), 19 Dec. 1976, Sinsani; Binke Sukule, 21 Mar. 1977, Sinsani; al hajj Moktar Magane, 19 Feb. 1977, Sinsani; Baba Sako, 9 Jan. 1977, Segu; Amadu Sanago, 8 Jan.

1977, Sinsani; Musa Kouyate, 26 Jan. 1977, Segu. Also Etude sur l'esclavage, Segu, 1894, ANS-AOF K 14; Rapport sur l'esclavage, Segu, 1904 ANS-AOF K 19; Coste, Coutoumiers juridiques, Segu, 1897, ANS-AOF 1 G 229; Brevié, Rapport sur l'esclavage, Bamako, 1904, ANS-AOF K 19.

140. Meillassoux, "Esclavage à Gumbu," p. 231; Commandant of Bamako, Rapport du commandant de cercle sur l'affaire de Nyamina, 22 May 1901, Bamako, ANM 1 E 19; Penel, "Coutumes soudanaises," 1: 92–93.

141. Baillaud, *Sur les routes*, p. 295.

142. Cooper, *Plantation Slavery*, pp. 258–68. Also interviews with Binke Sukule, 21 Mar. 1977, Sinsani; Baba Kuma (session 2), 13 Mar. 1977, Segu. See also Roberts, "Ideology."

143. Interview with Mamuru Fomba et al., 21 July 1981, Sinzena. Also Guyer, "Food."

144. Barat, Recueilles des coutumes juridiques du Soudan, 1897–1900, 1900, Nioro, ANS-AOF 1 G 229; Poulet, Rapport sur la captivité, 1905, ANS-AOF K 17; Brevié, Rapport sur l'esclavage, Bamako, 1904, ANS-AOF K 19. Also interviews with Binke Baba Kuma (session 1), 19 Dec. 1976, Sinsani; Binke Sukule, 21 Mar. 1977, Sinsani; al hajj Moktar Magane, 19 Feb. 1977, Sinsani; Baba Sako, 9 Jan. 1977, Segu; Amadu Sanago, 8 Jan. 1977, Sinsani; Musa Kouyate, 26 Jan. 1977, Segu; Mamuru Fomba et al., 21 July 1981, Sinzena.

145. Interviews with Baba Kuma (session 2), 13 Mar. 1977, Segu; Amadu Sanago, 8 Jan. 1977, Sinsani; Demba Suragassi, 18 Feb. 1977, Segu; Yahaya Haidara, 30 Mar. 1977, Sinsani; Malamine Kone, 7 Feb. 1977, Segu; Sidi Yaya Kone, 1 Feb. 1977, Sinsani; al hajj Ibrahima Magane, 4 Jan. 1977, Sinsani; Karamoko Sumare, 6 Jan. 1977, Segu; Meillassoux, "Esclavage à Gumbu," p. 200.

146. Interviews with Amadu Sanago, 8 Jan. 1977, Sinsani; al hajj Moktar Magane, 19 Feb. 1977. Also J. Bazin, "Guerre et servitude," pp. 156–57.

147. Brevié, Rapport sur l'esclavage, Bamako, 1904, ANS-AOF K 19; Marty, trans., "Chroniques de Oualata."

148. Rapport sur la captivité, San, 1904, ANS-AOF K 19; Poulet, Rapport sur la captivité, 1905, ANS-AOF K 17; Penel, "Coutumes soudanaises," 1: 96.

149. For a brilliant overview, see Davis, *Problem of Slavery*.

150. Barat, Recueilles des coutumes juridiques du Soudan, 1897–1900, 1900, Nioro, ANS-AOF 1 G 229; see also the special issue of clientage in *Cahiers d'études africaines*, ed. Balandier, "Relations de dépendance."

151. Mage, *Voyage*, pp. 580–81.

152. Interviews with Amadu Sise, 1 Feb. 1977, Sinsani; Baba Kuma (session 2), 13 Mar. 1977, Segu; Baba Sako, 9 Jan. 1977, Segu; Amadu Sanago, 8 Jan. 1977, Sinsani; Demba Suragassi, 18 Feb. 1977, Segu; Tamba Tigana, 24 Feb. 1977, Segu; Babaje Traore (session 2), 19 Feb. 1977, Sinsani; Mama Traore, 10 Feb. 1977, Niaro.

153. Meillassoux, "Esclavage à Gumbu," p. 240; Boutillier, "Les trois esclaves de Bouna," p. 278.

154. Genovese, *Roll, Jordan, Roll*, pp. 406–7.

155. Caron, letter to commandant supérieur, Manamabugu, 31 Oct. 1887, Mission Caron au Tombouctou, ANS-AOF 1 G 83; Mamadu Racine, commandant of Nyamina, letter, Sept. 1889, Nyamina, ANM 1 E 18.

156. Mage, *Voyage*, p. 86.

157. Saint-Martin, "Un fils d'el hadj Omar."

158. Saint-Martin, *L'empire toucouleur*, pp. 176–77; D. Robinson, *Holy War*, pp. 334–42.

159. Archinard, letter to Capitaine Blanchère, commandant de cercle de Bandiagara, 15 May 1893, ANM B 150; Archinard, letter to Capitaine Blanchère, 15 Apr. 1893, ANM B 150.

160. Johnson, "Economic Foundations," p. 489; Kodjo, "Contribution à l'étude"; Tymowski, "Les domaines"; interview with Cekoro Dembele, 12 Dec. 1976, Banankoro. See also the debate on the term *serf* between Johnson, "Economic Foundations," pp. 488–89, and Lovejoy, "Slavery in the Sokoto Caliphate."

161. Saint-Martin, *L'empire toucouleur*, p. 183.

162. Soleillet, *Voyage à Ségou*, p. 301.

163. The French were ambivalent about African slavery, and by the end of the century they may not have liberated Maki's slaves, but they certainly would not have tolerated his moving them to Bamako. For more on French attitudes toward slavery, see ch. 5.

164. Interview with Ismaila Fane, 30 July 1981, Tesserela.

165. Meillassoux makes this distinction in his discussion of peasants and gatherers in "Social Organisation."

166. Interviews with Basidiki Sako et al., 22 July 1981, Nyamina; Almamy Kone et al., 22 July 1981, Nyamina; Ahmadu Traore, 1 Aug. 1981, Segukoro. Paradoxically, one of the lasting contributions of the Umarian era was the proliferation of Muslim courts of law throughout the realm, since cadis were part of the administration. Cadis and talaba often existed side by side in isolated garrisons, but each approached the law differently.

167. Soleillet, *Voyage à Ségou*, p. 279.

168. Caron, *De Saint Louis*, p. 120.

169. Kami Kuma, letter to Archinard, n.d. (probably 1890), Correspondance indigène, ANS-AOF 15 G 82.

Chapter Four

1. Curtin, *Economic Change*, pp. 215–18; Barrows, "Merchants," pp. 240–42.

2. See Zeldin, *France*, vol. 1; Kuisel, *Capitalism*, pp. 8–20. In the 1880's and 1890's, the debates surrounding the Meline tariff came to embody the complex role the state was willing to take in relationship to the national economy. For details, see Golob, *Meline Tariff*, chs. 4 and 5; Elwitt, *Third Republic*, pp. 230–56.

3. For a discussion of the ideological underpinnings associated with the new order, see R. Robinson and J. Gallagher, "Imperialism"; Temperley, "Capitalism," pp. 94–118; Cooper, *From Slaves to Squatters*, pp. 25–68.

4. M. Klein, *Islam*, pp. 44, 174–89; Brooks, "Peanuts and Colonialism," pp. 51–52; Pelissier, *Les paysans*; Swindell, "SeraWoollies," pp. 100–104.

5. Kanya-Forstner, *Conquest*, p. 87; Hargreaves, *Prelude*, pp. 261–63.

6. Brunschwig, "French Exploration," pp. 149–50; Kanya-Forstner, *Conquest*, p. 87.

7. Kanya-Forstner, *Conquest*, pp. 31–33, 90–94.

8. A three-day trip from Bamako to Wossobugu or from Sinsani to Bamako added 1,240 cowries to the price of a bar of salt, or approximately 5 percent. Dr. Collomb, Notice sur le cercle de Bamako, 1885, ANM 1 D 33, no. 1D2; Gallieni, letter to governor, 7 July 1880, Nango, ANF-SOM Sénégal et dépendances III 10 bis; Meniaud, *Pionniers*, 1: 205–6.

9. Park, *Travels*, pp. 354–56; Park, *Mission*, pp. 191–92.

10. Gallieni, letter to governor, 3 July 1880, Nango, ANS-AOF 1 G 50.

11. Bayol, "Voyages au pays de Bamako," pp. 147–48; Pietri, *Les Français*, p. 391; Gallieni, letter to governor, 3 July 1880, Nango, ANS-AOF 1 G 50.

12. Gallieni, letter to governor, 3 July 1880, Nango, ANS-AOF 1 G 50. Caillié, who had never been to Bamako, argued on the basis of its reputation for the establishment of a French residency there. W. Cohen, "Imperial Mirage," p. 430.

13. Minister of the Marine and Colonies, Projet d'instruction pour Lieutenant Colonel, commandant supérieur du Haut Sénégal, 2 Oct. 1882, Paris, ANM B 165.

14. Borgnis-Desbordes, "Le Général Borgnis-Desbordes," pp. 270–72.

15. Gallieni, letter to governor, 3 July 1880, Nango, ANS-AOF 1 G 50.

16. Person, *Samori*, 1: 396–410; Person, "Guinea-Samori," pp. 127–28.

17. Bayol, unfinished report, n.d., ANS-AOF 1 G 142. These executions, although not the first demonstration of French assertion of judicial superiority in Africa, touch on the interesting issue of the place of law in complex colonial settings. In the Western Sudan in particular, conquest established an implicit hierarchy among systems of law containing several varieties of French metropolitan legal traditions (military justice, civil law, and administrative law), Muslim law, and African customary law. How these systems of laws interacted and were modified by the operation of colonialism is an interesting question.

18. Minister of the Marine and Colonies, Projet d'instruction pour Lieutenant-Colonel, commandant supérieur du Haut Sénégal, 2 Oct. 1882, Paris, ANM B 165.

19. Ruault, letter to commandant supérieur du Haut Sénégal, 1 Sept. 1883, Bamako, ANM 1 E 188.

20. Roberts, "Emergence," p. 43.

21. Raffenel, *Nouveau voyage*, 2: 203; Bulletin agricole et commercial, Segu, Feb. 1893, ANM 1 R 69; Barrows, "Merchants," p. 275; Barrows, "General Faidherbe" (diss.), p. 294.

22. Gallieni, *Mission*, p. 384.

23. Direction des Colonies, Minister of Marine to governor of Sénégal et dépendances, 19 Mar. 1884, ANM B 165.

24. Bouche, *Les villages*, pp. 87–89.

25. Captain Loyer, commandant of Bamako, to commandant supérieur, 5 May 1886, Bamako, ANM 2 D 72. For the rate of compensation, which seems rather high, see Bechet, *Cinq ans de séjour*, pp. 193–95.

26. Monographie du cercle de Mopti, 1920, ANM 1 D 49, no. 1D2, which contains the best data on transport costs.

27. Meniaud, *Pionniers*, 1: 113; Person, *Samori*, 1: 371.

28. Baillaud, *Sur les routes*, pp. 48–49.

29. Minister of Marine to governor of Sénégal et dépendances, 5 Nov. 1883, Paris, ANM B 165.

30. Commandant of Bamako, letter, 1 Aug. 1885, Bamako, ANM 1 E 18. This report contains a detailed list of tariffs; commandant of Bamako, letter, 1 Nov. 1885, Bamako, ANM 1 E 18.

31. Commandant of Bamako, letter, 31 Dec. 1885, Bamako, ANM 1 E 18.

32. Commandant of Bamako, letter, 1 July 1885, Bamako, ANM 1 E 18.

33. Rapport commercial, cercle de Bamako, Jan. 1886, ANM 1 Q 44.

This action was based on the instruction sent by Colonel Frey to the Bamako commandant on 27 Nov. 1885, ANM B 67. The French were fully aware how a constrained supply of horses affected Samori's military strategy. He abandoned his attack on Kankore early in 1885 because of the lack of new mounts. Commandant of Bamako fort, letter, 28 Feb. 1885, Bamako, ANM 1 E 18.

34. Captain Loyer, letter to commandant supérieur, 1 May 1887, Bamako, ANM 1 Q 44.

35. Bulletin commercial et agricole, Bamako, Oct. 1887, ANM 1 R 31.

36. Rousseau, Minister of Marine, to governor of Sénégal et dépendances, 4 July 1885, Paris, ANM B 165.

37. Vice Admiral Peyron, Minister of Marine, to governor of Sénégal et dépendances, 19 Apr. 1884, Paris, ANM B 165.

38. Archinard, letter to governor of Sénégal et dépendances, 9 Jan. 1890, Kayes, ANM B 83.

39. Bulletin commercial et agricole, Dec. 1889 and Jan. 1890, Bamako, ANM 1 R 31.

40. Bulletin commercial et agricole, Feb. 1890, Bamako, ANM 1 R 31.

41. Peroz, *Au Soudan*, pp. 161–62.

42. Rapport sur la situation économique, agricole, et commerciale des territoires du Haut Sénégal et Moyen Niger, 16 Feb. 1900, Kayes, ANS-AOF 2 G 1–23.

43. Rapport commercial, Bamako, 3d quarter 1903, ANM 1 Q 44.

44. Meniaud, *Pionniers*, 1: 459; Ward, "Bambara-French Relationship"; Lieutenant Marchand, Mission Marchand, 1889, ANS-AOF 1 G 115.

45. Meniaud, *Pionniers*, 1: 450–51, for a detailed breakdown of the numbers involved.

46. As quoted, ibid., 1: 455; also Lieutenant Mage, letter to governor, 5 Mar. 1864, Segu-Sikoro, ANS-AOF 1 G 32.

47. Archinard, Rapport militaire, Campagne 1889–1890, ANS-AOF 1 D 105.

48. Caron, letter to commandant supérieur, 31 Oct. 1887, ANS-AOF 1 G 83; Caron *De Saint Louis*, pp. 330–31.

49. Meniaud, *Pionniers*, 2: 278–79; Kanya-Forstner, *Conquest*, pp. 186–89.

50. Kanya-Forstner, *Conquest*, ch. 8.

51. Archinard, "Rapport de campagne"; Kanya-Forstner, *Conquest*, pp. 196–201.

52. For more detail see Ward, "Bambara-French Relationship."

53. Archinard, palabre of 11 Apr. 1890 with Mari Jara, dated 19 Apr. 1890, Nyamina, ANS-AOF 15 G 172; Meniaud, *Pionniers*, 1: 517–19.

54. See note 53 for sources.

55. Archinard, letter to governor of Sénégal et dépendances, 9 Jan. 1890, Kayes, ANM B 83.

56. Perignon, *Haut-Sénégal*, p. 167.

57. Archinard, letter to Under Secretary of State for Colonies, 9 Jan. 1891, Nioro, ANF-SOM Soudan I 1 a.

58. Lettre de investiture de M. Mademba, in Perignon, Généralités sur Haut Sénégal Moyen Niger, 1900, ANS-AOF 1 G 248.

59. Mademba warrants a more detailed discussion than is possible here. In particular, the administrative hearing regarding Mademba's alleged malfeasance raises a series of issues about the rule of law in complex colonial settings. For a preliminary discussion see Roberts, "Rule of Law"; Capitaine Bonnier, Mission dans la région de Segou, compte rendu, 20 July 1892, ANM 1 D 221; Bonnier, *Mission*.

60. Meniaud, *Pionniers*, 2: 365.

61. Ibid., 2: 431.

62. I do not want to imply that Archinard was a monarchist, although the Third Republic was wracked by the quasi-monarchist and putchist actions of General Boulanger. See Levillain, *Boulanger*, and Harding, *Astonishing Adventure*. The colonial conquest also opened avenues for the new rulers of the land to act in ways that would have been unacceptable at home. See for example, Delavignette, *Freedom and Authority*, and W. Cohen, *Rulers*.

63. Telegram, Archinard, 5 May 1893, ANF-SOM Soudan I 2 bis; Mademba, *Au Sénégal*, pp. 87–89.

64. Humbert, letter to Briquelot, résident of Segu, 24 Oct. 1891, Kayes, ANM B 150.

65. Archinard, palabre of 11 Apr. 1890 with Mari Jara, dated 19 Apr. 1890, Nyamina, ANS-AOF 15 G 172.

66. Archinard, Instructions particulières pour le résident de Segou, 16 Apr. 1890, Nyamina, ANS-AOF 15 G 172.

67. For example, the treaty with Ousman Taroare, 20 Sept. 1890, Saro, ANM 1 E 5.

68. Rapport sur la situation politique des territoires dépendant de la résidence de Segou, 15 Sept. 1891, Segu, ANM 1 E 71.

69. Letter, notables of Sansanding to Archinard, n.d. [probably 1890], ANS-AOF 15 G 82.

70. Rapport sur la politique du cercle en 1907, Bamako, ANM 1 E 20.

71. Baillaud, *Sur les routes*, p. 63.

72. Bulletin commercial et agricole, Bamako, Aug. 1891, ANM 1 R 31.

73. Rapport commercial et agricole, Bamako, 4th quarter 1900, ANM

1 R 31; Rapport commercial, Bamako, 1st quarter 1903, ANM 1 Q 44; administrator of Segu, letter to résident of Sansanding, 26 Sept. 1906, ANM 2 D 102.

74. Rapport sur la situation économique de l'année 1904, 15 Apr. 1905, Kayes, ANM 1 Q 40.

75. Rapport commercial, Bamako, 1st quarter 1908, ANM 1 Q 44.

76. Curtin, *Economic Change*, p. 104.

77. Petition, signed by Maurel and Prom and the merchants of Nioro, n.d. [probably 1900], Nioro, ANM 1 Q 4. There is a similar petition by European merchants contained in the letter, Commandant Bamako to délégué du gouverneur général, July 1902, Bamako, ANM 1 Q 4.

78. Rapport sur la commerce du Soudan, 1903, ANM 1 Q 40.

79. The senior administration's contempt for French commercial interests in the Western Sudan was most pronounced in the inter-war years, although it had its roots in the nineteenth-century metropolitan political and social divisions between fonctionnaires and merchants. The long governorship of Terrasson in the Sudan is especially indicative of this; see, for example, Rapport à la Direction des Affaires Economiques, Kouluba, 13 Apr. 1928, ANM 1 R 305.

80. Rapport sur le commerce du Soudan, 1903, ANM 1 Q 40.

81. Rapport commercial, Bamako, 4th quarter 1906, ANM 1 Q 44.

82. Rapport de M. Brun, rédacteur commercial sur l'état de la situation commercial du Poste de Nioro, 1903, ANM 1 Q 40.

83. Commandant of Bamako, letter to délégué du gouverneur général, 6 Oct. 1900, Bamako, ANM 1 Q 4.

84. Bulletin commercial et agricole, Bamako, 2d quarter 1902, ANM 1 R 31; William Ponty, Rapport commercial et agricole, Haut-Sénégal-Niger, 31 Mar. 1900, Kayes, ANS-AOF 2 G 1–23.

85. Rapport commercial, Sikasso, 3d quarter 1904, ANM 1 Q 84.

86. Rapport commercial, Bouguni, 4th quarter 1903, ANM 1 Q 47; Rapport commercial, Bamako, 3d quarter 1907, ANM 1 Q 44; commandant of Bamako, letter, 3 Sept. 1892, Bamako, ANM 1 E 18.

87. Rapport commercial, Bamako, 3d quarter 1903, ANM 1 Q 44, emphasis added. See also Lieutenant Guillaume, Etude sur le marché de Nioro, 1902, ANM 1 D 102.

88. Situation commerciale, année 1905, ANM 1 Q 40.

89. Rapport sur la situation économique du Haut-Sénégal-Niger pendant l'année 1911, ANM 1 Q 40; Rapport sur la situation économique du Haut-Sénégal-Niger, 1st quarter 1912, ANM 1 Q 40; Rapport commercial, Bamako, 1st quarter 1908, ANM 1 Q 44; Rapport commercial, Bamako, 3d quarter 1909, ANM 1 Q 44.

90. Rapport sur la situation économique du Haut-Sénégal-Niger, 1st quarter 1904, ANM 1 Q 40.

91. Bulletin agricole et commercial, Bamako, May 1892, ANM 1 R 31.

92. British cotton industries seemed already to be aware of the crisis pending as a result of the American crop shortfalls and the decade of price increases after 1848. Ratcliffe, "Cotton Imperialism," p. 90.

93. Lieutenant-Governor Trentinian, letter to commandants of Kayes, Kati, Bamako, Segu, Sumpi, Goundam, Jenne, San, and Bandiagara, and the faama of Sansani, 21 Dec. 1898, ANM B 77.

94. Lieutenant-Governor Trentinian, letter to commandant, cercle of Bamako, 11 Aug. 1899, ANM B 77.

95. Captain Charnet, Rapport commercial et agricole, Bamako, 2d quarter 1899, ANM 1 R 31.

96. Indeed, the first tentative request to establish a textile factory in Bamako, made by Louis Colombier and Company in 1941, was rejected by the administration, ANM 1 Q 1909.

97. Rapport commercial, Bamako, 2d quarter 1899, ANM 1 R 31.

98. "La culture du coton," *Dépêche coloniale*, 7 Jan. 1903; Andrews et al., "Le mouvement colonial français."

99. The relationship between the Association Cotonnière Coloniale and the colonial state was fraught with tensions over the terms of their agreements and the amount of the state's contribution to Association activities. After 1927, the metropolitan state placed a surcharge of one franc per hundred kilograms of raw cotton imported into France, and funneled most of this capital into Association activities. Robert, *La culture du coton*, pp. vii–ix.

100. William Ponty, Note sur la colonie du Haut-Sénégal-Niger, 25 June 1905, Paris, ANF-SOM Soudan I ii bis.

101. Vuillet, Régions cotonnières du Soudan, 18 Aug. 1904, ANM 1 R 79. The history of French politique cotonnière and its implications for the well-established local textile handicraft industry in Mali is the basis of my current research.

102. Commandant of Bamako, letter to lieutenant-governor, 3 Jan. 1898, Bamako, ANM 1 R 81.

103. Lieutenant-governor, letter to commandant of Bamako, 19 Sept. 1899, Kayes, ANM B 74.

104. Bulletin politique, Bamako, Mar. 1899, ANM 1 E 18.

105. Capitaine Charnet, letter to lieutenant-governor, 18 Aug. 1899, Bamako, ANM 1 R 81.

106. Fossat, letter to commandant of Bamako, 17 Jan. 1899, Bamako, ANM 1 R 81.

107. Notice accompagné 400 kg du coton destiné à un éssai d'égrenage, commandant of Segu, 20 Dec. 1903, Segu, ANM 1 R 95.

108. Henry, *Le coton*, p. 55.

109. Lenz, *Timbuktu*, 2: 150–51; Johnson, "Cotton Imperialism," pp. 185–86.

110. Rapport commercial et agricole, Segu, 1st quarter 1901, ANM 1 R 69.

111. Rapport économique, Segu, 1st quarter 1939, ANM 1 Q 358.

112. Rapport commercial et agricole, Segu, 1st quarter 1901, ANM 1 R 69.

113. Rapport annuel sur la politique, Segu, 1909, ANM 1 E 72.

Chapter Five

1. Quoted in Renault, *Abolition*, p. 7.

2. Ibid., pp. 10–11.

3. Pasquier, "A propos de l'émancipation," pp. 188–208.

4. Cooper, *From Slaves to Squatters*, pp. 69–124; Miers and Roberts, eds., *End of Slavery*.

5. For example, Miers, *Britain*; Grace, *Domestic Slavery*; McSheffrey, "Slavery"; Dumett and Johnson, "Suppression of Slavery"; Igbafe, "Slavery and Emancipation"; Oroge, "Fugitive Slave Question"; Twaddle, "Ending of Slavery."

6. Schoelcher, *L'esclavage au Sénégal*, deals with the Senate debate of 1 Mar. 1880. Schoelcher kept up pressure well into 1882. See for example Schoelcher, *Polémique coloniale*, 2: 189–91.

7. Penel, "Coutumes soudanaises," 1: 97–100.

8. Bouche, *Les villages*, pp. 102–4.

9. M. Klein, "Slavery and the Conquest of the French Soudan."

10. Echenberg, "Paying the Blood Tax," p. 176.

11. Bouche, *Les villages*, p. 104.

12. Rapport politique, Segu, Jan. 1898, ANM 1 E 71.

13. Rapport semestriel du commandant du cercle de Bamako, 2d quarter 1898, ANM 1 E 18.

14. Echenberg, "Paying the Blood Tax"; Michel, *Appel à l'Afrique*.

15. Bouche, *Les villages*, pp. 98, 106.

16. "Instructions à la usage . . . ," Bulletin du Comité de l'Afrique fr. 1900, quoted in Bouche, *Les villages*, p. 147.

17. Grodet to commandant of région sud, 12 Sept. 1894, ANF-SOM Soudan IV 1.

18. Kanya-Forstner, *Conquest*, p. 228; Jaime, *De Koulikoro à Tombouctou*, pp. 240–41.

19. Etude sur la captivité, Segu, 1894, ANS-AOF K 14.
20. Grodet, Circulaire, 17 May 1895, Kayes, ANS-AOF K 19.
21. Rapport sur la captivité, Sokolo, 1904, ANS-AOF K 19; Rapport politique, Segu, Apr. 1904, ANM 1 E 71.
22. Trentinian, circulaire to administrators, 22 July 1895, ANS-AOF K 19; also Trentinian, letter, 22 July 1895, ANM 1 E 156.
23. No signature [but Trentinian], 16 Nov. 1895, ANS-AOF K 19.
24. Rapport général sur la situation politique du cercle de Segou, 15 Oct. 1895, Segu, ANM 1 E 71.
25. Rapport sur la répression de la traite des captives, 1 July 1895, Bamako, ANM 1 E 156.
26. Rapport sur la situation politique des cercles du Haut-Sénégal-Moyen Niger, 1 Apr. 1901, Kayes, ANS-AOF 2 G 1–14.
27. Barat, Coutumes, 1900, ANS-AOF 1 G 229.
28. M. Klein, "Slavery, Forced Labour and French Colonial Rule."
29. Rapport sur la captivité, Segu, 1904, ANM 1 E 156.
30. Instructions accompanying decree of 10 Nov. 1903, ANS-AOF K 16.
31. Rapport sur la situation économique, année 1904, 15 Apr. 1905, Kayes, ANM 1 Q 40.
32. Interview with Koke Jara et al., 29 Jan. 1984, Gouni.
33. Rapport politique, Bamako, Apr. 1905, ANM 1 E 19.
34. Rapport politique, Bamako, May 1905, ANM 1 E 19; Rapport politique d'ensemble du Soudan, 1905, ANM 1 E 12.
35. Governor Roume, instructions to administrators, 25 Apr. 1905, ANS-AOF K 25, quoted in Renault, *Abolition*, p. 58.
36. Roume, telegram to (lieutenant) governor at Kayes, 26 May 1905, Gorée, ANS-AOF 15 G 170; telegram, 28 May 1905, ANM 1 E 118; Rapport politique, Bamako, May 1905, ANM 1 E 19.
37. Roume, telegram, 26 May 1905, ANM 1 E 118. Roume did not use the term *slave*, but *serviteur*, because the term *slave* could no longer be used after the passing of the 1903 legal code.
38. Roume, telegram 26 May 1903, Gorée, ANS-AOF 15 G 170; telegram, 23 May 1905, ANM 1 E 118.
39. Fawtier, telegram, 29 May 1905, Kayes, ANS-AOF 15 G 170; also telegram, 29 May 1905, ANM 1 E 118.
40. Fawtier, Rapport, 26 June 1905, Kayes, ANS-AOF 15 G 170.
41. This point was bluntly made in a telegram, Bamako commandant to governor, 8 June 1905, Kayes, ANM 1 E 118.
42. Fawtier, Rapport, 26 June 1905, Kayes, ANS-AOF 15 G 170. This was consistent with the 1903 legal code.

43. Fawtier, Rapport, 26 June 1905, Kayes, ANS-AOF 15 G 170.

44. Rapport sur la captivité, 10 June 1905, ANS-AOF K 16, no signature, but probably Fawtier.

45. Brevié, Rapport sur l'esclavage, Bamako, 1904, ANS-AOF K 19.

46. Cited in Brevié, Rapport sur l'esclavage, Bamako, 1904, ANS-AOF K 19.

47. See for example, Marty, trans., "Chroniques de Oualata," and Peroz, *Au Soudan*, pp. 189–90, for a justification of slaves' rights to the product of their own labor on their days off.

48. Bulletin commercial et agricole, Bamako, July 1894, ANM 1 R 31.

49. Rapport politique et militaire, Bamako, July 1895, ANM 1 E 18.

50. Rapport politique et militaire, Bamako, Aug. 1895, ANM 1 E 18.

51. Interview with Mamuru Fomba et al., 21 July 1981, Sinzena; see also Pollet and Winter, *Société Soninké*, p. 244; Guyer, "Food"; Roberts, "Women's Work."

52. Rapport politique, Segu, 1901, ANS-AOF 2 G 1–14; also commandant of Bamako, letter, 1 Mar. 1890, ANM 1 E 18; Rapport politique et militaire, Bamako, Jan. 1895, ANM 1 E 18; Ponty, Rapport politique, Haut-Sénégal-Niger, Feb. 1901, ANS-AOF 2 G 1–14.

53. Rapport du commandant de cercle sur l'affaire de Nyamina, 22 May 1901, ANM 1 E 19; Rapport politique, Segu, Apr. 1901, ANM 1 E 71. Also interviews with Cemoko Ture, 5 Mar. 1977, Segu; Almamy Kone et al., 23 July 1981, Nyamina.

54. Rapport du commandant de cercle sur l'affaire de Nyamina, 22 May 1901, ANM 1 E 19.

55. Rapport politique, Haut-Sénégal-Niger, Apr. 1901, ANS-AOF 2 G 1–14.

56. William Ponty, Rapport politique, Haut-Sénégal-Niger, Apr. 1901, ANS-AOF 2 G 1–14.

57. Rapport politique, Bamako, Apr. 1906, ANM 1 E 19.

58. Ponty, letter to commandant of Bamako, 7 May 1906, Dakar, ANM 1 E 19.

59. Rapport politique, Bamako, May 1906, ANM 1 E 19.

60. Rapport politique, Bamako, May 1906, ANM 1 E 19; Ponty, Rapport politique, Haut-Sénégal-Niger, May 1906, ANS-AOF 2 G 6–6; Rapport politique d'ensemble du Soudan, 1910, ANM 1 E 12.

61. Rapport sur la situation politique du cercle de Bamako pendant 1906, Bamako, ANM 1 E 19.

62. Ponty, Rapport politique, Haut-Sénégal-Niger, May 1906, ANS-AOF 2 G 6–6.

63. Rapport général sur la situation politique du cercle de Bamako pendant l'année 1906, Bamako, ANM 1 E 19.

64. Rapport politique, Bamako, June 1906, ANM 1 E 19; Rapport politique, Haut-Sénégal-Niger, 2d quarter 1906, ANS-AOF 2 G 6–2.

65. Rapport général sur la situation politique du cercle de Bamako pendant l'année 1906, Bamako, ANM 1 E 19.

66. Rapport politique, Segu, Mar. 1907, ANM 1 E 72.

67. Rapport politique, Segu, June 1907, ANM 1 E 72; Rapport politique, Haut-Sénégal-Niger, 3d quarter 1907, ANS-AOF 2 G 7–3.

68. Ponty, letter to commandant Segu, 18 April 1907, Kayes, ANM 1 E 177; governor-general, letter to minister of colonies, 22 June 1908, Dakar, ANS-SOM Soudan I 11. I would like to thank Martin Klein for these references.

69. Rapport politique, Haut-Sénégal-Niger, 2d quarter 1909, ANS-AOF 2 G 9–12.

70. For a comparison with Northern Nigeria, see Shenton, *Development of Capitalism*, and Lennihan, "Rights," pp. 111–39.

71. Gaubert, Rapport sur l'arrangement passé en Macina entre les peuls et rimaibes au sujet du remplacement de toutes redévances anciennes par la régime de la location des terres, 24 Dec. 1908, Jenne, ANM 1 E 192.

72. Governor Roume to Minister of Colonies, 11 July 1905, Dakar, ANS-AOF 15 G 170.

73. Gaubert here clearly identifies ideas as the cause of the slaves' actions in Masina. Gaubert, like many administrative sources, is inclined to credit the state and its ideological policies with responsibility for the revolution in social organization.

74. Gaubert, Rapport sur l'arrangement passé en Macina . . . ANM 1 E 192.

75. Secrétaire général (du gouverneur) per interim, telegram, 6 Feb. 1909, Timbuktu, ANM 1 E 192.

76. Interview with Mamuru Fomba et al., 21 July 1981, Sinzena; Rapport politique d'ensemble du Soudan, 1910, ANM 1 E 12.

77. Rapports politiques, Gumbu, Jan.-Dec. 1910, ANM 1 E 39; Rapports politiques, Sokolo, June and Nov. 1910, ANM 1 E 76.

78. Gouverneur général to consul général d'Angleterre, 22 Feb. 1911, ANS-AOF K 26.

79. Interview with Santa Kulubali, 21 Mar. 1977, Sinsani.

80. Rapports politiques, Bouguni, Nov. and Dec. 1906, ANM 1 E 28. See also detailed village census conducted by Saillard, Rapport sur la tournée de rencensement, 20 Dec. 1907, ANM 1 E 28; Rapports politiques, Bouguni, May and June 1907, ANM 1 E 28.

81. Rapport politique, Bouguni, Oct. 1906, ANM 1 E 28; Deherme, L'esclavage en Afrique Occidentale française, 1906, ANS-AOF K 25.

82. Interview with Binke Sukule, 21 Mar. 1977, Sinsani.

83. Rapport politique, Haut-Sénégal-Niger, 3d quarter 1907, ANS-AOF 2 G 7–3.

84. Rapport sur la politique du cercle en 1907, Bamako, ANM 1 E 19.

85. Interviews with Mamuru Fomba et al., 21 July 1981, Sinzena.

86. Rapport sur les coutumes et institutions juridiques, cercle de Segou, 1909, Segu, ANM 1 D 206.

87. Rougier, Enquête sur l'Islam, Banamba, 1914, ANM 1 D 30, no. 3. Also interviews with Binke Sukule, 21 Mar. 1977, Sinsani; Santa Kubali, 21 Mar. 1977, Sinsani; Baba Kuma (session 1), 28 Dec. 1976, Segu; Binke Baba Kuma (session 1), 19 Dec. 1976, Sinsani; Sidi Yaya Kone, 1 Feb. 1977, Sinsani; Meillassoux, "Esclavage à Gumbu," pp. 246–47.

88. Rapport politique, Bamako, Apr. 1907, ANM 1 E 19.

89. Rapport politique d'ensemble du Soudan, 1910, ANM 1 E 12.

90. Rapport politique, Segu, May 1907, ANM 1 E 72.

91. Rapport politique, Bamako, May 1907, ANM 1 E 19.

92. Barbier, *Etude*, p. 36.

93. Pollet and Winter, *Société soninke*, pp. 371, 394.

94. Rapport politique d'ensemble du Soudan, 1910, ANM 1 E 12; Rapport politique, Bamako, Nov. 1911, ANM 1 E 19.

95. Interview with Cemoko Ture, 5 Mar. 1977, Segu.

96. Rapport politique, Bamako, May 1909, ANM 1 E 19; Rapport politique, Haut-Sénégal-Niger, 2d quarter 1909, ANS-AOF 2 G 9–12. The railway, of course, contributed to the decline of Banamba as the commercial center of the Western Sudan.

97. Marty, *Etude sur Islam*, 4: 178.

98. Rapport politique, Bamako, May 1909, ANM 1 E 19.

99. Rougier, Enquête sur l'Islam, Banamba, 1914, ANM 1 D 33, no. 3.

100. Rapport politique, Haut-Sénégal-Niger, 1st quarter 1908, ANS-AOF 2 G 8–1.

101. Rapport politique d'ensemble du Soudan, 1910, ANM 1 E 12.

102. Interviews with Dahou Traore, 11 Feb. 1977, Sibila; al hajj Moktar Magane, 19 Feb. 1977, Sinsani.

103. Ponty, letter to Segu commandant, 25 May 1907, Kayes, ANS-AOF 2 G 7.

104. Rapport politique, Haut-Sénégal-Niger, 1st quarter 1908, ANS-AOF 2 G 8–1.

105. Rapport politique d'ensemble du Soudan, 1910, ANM 1 E 12.

106. Rapport politique, Bamako, Apr. 1905, ANM 1 E 19; Rapport général sur la situation politique du cercle de Bamako pendant 1906, ANM 1 E 19; for a general discussion see Mercier, *Le travail*.

107. Notices historiques et géographiques du cercle de Bamako, 1880–1900, 1903, ANM 1 D 33, no. 1D1.

108. Robin, Réponse au questionnaire sur les coutumes indigènes, cercle de Bamako, résidence de Banamba, 1909, ANM 1 D 186.

109. Rapport politique, Haut-Sénégal-Niger, 1st quarter 1908, ANS-AOF 2 G 8–1.

110. Interviews with Binke Baba Kuma (session 2), 21 Mar. 1977, Sinsani; Amadu Sanago, 8 Jan. 1977, Sinsani.

111. Interviews with Binke Baba Kuma (session 2), 21 Mar. 1977, Sinsani; Bakary Dukure, 30 Jan. 1977, Segu; Amadu Sanago, 8 Jan. 1977, Sinsani.

112.. Penel, "Coutumes soudanaises," 2: 364–65.

113. Rapport général sur la politique du cercle pendant l'année 1905, Segu, ANM 1 E 177.

114. Rapport général sur la politique du cercle de Djenne, 21 Dec. 1907, ANM 1 E 29.

115. Rapport commercial, Segu, 3d quarter 1907, ANM 1 Q 83.

116. Monographie du cercle de Djenne, 20 Nov. 1909, ANM 1 D 38, no. 3; Meniaud, *Haut Sénégal Niger*, 1: 89; Deherme, *L'Afrique Occidentale française*, p. 194.

117. Deherme, *L'Afrique Occidentale française*, p. 289.

118. Dubois, *Beau Niger*, pp. 135–36.

119. Interviews with Tijani Sylla, 3 Aug. 1981, Baraweli; Batene Kale, 31 July 1981, Segu.

120. FulBe were hired as herders, with distinct contracts; see for example, Notices historiques et géographiques du cercle de Bamako, 1903, ANM 1 D 33, no. 1D1.

Chapter Six

1. Clozel, Rapport d'ensemble sur la situation économique du Haut-Sénégal-Niger pendant l'année 1911, ANM 1 Q 40.

Bibliography

Archival Sources

Archives Nationales, République du Mali, Kouluba, Mali (*ANM*):

ANM B 67. Administrative correspondence, commandant supérieur and Bamako.

ANM B 74. Administrative correspondence, Bamako to lieutenant governor.

ANM B 77. Circulair, Trentinian to commandants, 1898.

ANM B 83. Administrative correspondence, commandant supérieur and gouverneur Sénégal.

ANM B 150. Administrative correspondence, Segu and commandant supérieur.

ANM B 165. Administrative correspondence, arriving at Kayes.

ANM 1 D 2. Albert Grodet, Etude sur la captivité au Soudan, 1894.

ANM 1 D 3. Notice d'ensemble sur le Soudan, 1895.

ANM 1 D 9. Capitaine Lartique, Notice sur la région du Sahel, 1896.

ANM 1 D 17. Lieutenant Sargolis, Notice sur l'administration, 1895, Segu.

ANM 1 D 21. Population du Soudan d'après renseignements reçus, 1 Apr. 1899.

ANM 1 D 22. Notice sur la formation historique et la constitution administrative sur la colonie Haut-Sénégal-Niger, 1905.

ANM 1 D 33, no. 1D1. Notices historiques et géographiques du cercle de Bamako, n.d. (probably 1890).

ANM 1 D 33, no. 1D2. Docteur Collomb, Notice sur le cercle de Bamako, 1885.

ANM 1 D 33, no. 3. Rougier, Enquête sur l'Islam dans le cercle de Bamako, région de Banamba, May 1914.

ANM 1 D 38, no. 3. Monograph du cercle de Djenne, 20 Nov. 1909.

ANM 1 D 49, no. 1D2. Monograph du cercle de Mopti, 1920.

ANM 1 D 55, no. 1D1. Notice sur le royaume et cercle de Segou, 1st part: Notice géographique, 1896.
ANM 1 D 55, no. 2. Notice historique de royaume et du cercle de Segou, 1896.
ANM 1 D 55, no. 5. Notice sur le royaume Bambara de Segou, 1899.
ANM 1 D 57, no. 1D1. Notice géographique sur le cercle de Sokolo, 1895.
ANM 1 D 76. Note sur l'organisation de la famille en pays Bambara, coutume Bambara musulman, n.d.
ANM 1 D 102. Lieutenant Guillaume, Etude sur le marché de Nioro, 1902.
ANM 1 D 156. Rapport sur la répression de la traite, 1895.
ANM 1 D 186. Robin, Réponse au questionnaire sur les coutumes indigènes Bamako, 1909.
ANM 1 D 189. Coutume Bambara du cercle de Bougouni, 1932.
ANM 1 D 206. Rapport sur les coutumes et institutions juridiques, Segu, 1909.
ANM 1 D 210. Coutumes locales, Section Yelimane, 1910.
ANM 1 D 221. Capitaine Bonnier, Mission dans la région de Segou, compte rendu, 20 July 1892.
ANM 1 D 222. Mission Delanneau, 1885.
ANM 1 D 288. Capitaine Payne, Oussourou, Droits de pacage. Mission Capitaine Payne, 1906.
ANM 2 D 72. Commandant of Bamako, letter, 12 Dec. 1891, Bamako.
ANM 2 D 102. Capitaine Underberg, letter, 23 Feb. 1891, Segu; administrator of Segu to résident of Sansanding, 1906.
ANM 5 D 43. Rencensement des Territoires de Sansanding, 1904.
ANM 1 E 4. Traité entre le Colonel Archinard et les gens de Sansanding, 10 Apr. 1890.
ANM 1 E 5. Traité entre le Colonel Archinard et les gens de Sarro, 20 Sept. 1890.
ANM 1 E 11. Rapport politique, région du Sahel, 25 June 1896.
ANM 1 E 12. Rapport politique d'ensemble du Soudan, 1910.
ANM 1 E 18, E 19, E 20. Rapports politiques, Bamako.
ANM 1 E 28. Rapports politiques, Bouguni.
ANM 1 E 29. Rapports politiques, Jenne.
ANM 1 E 39. Rapports politiques, Gumbu.
ANM 1 E 71, E 72. Rapports politiques, Segu.
ANM 1 E 76. Rapports politiques, Sokolo.
ANM 1 E 118. Roume [to lieutenant governor], telegram, 28 May 1905, [Gorée].

ANM 1 E 150. Mademba, letter to Segu administrator, 27 Aug. 1909, Sinsani.

ANM 1 E 156. Rapports sur l'esclavage, La suppression de la traite, 1894–95, 1904.

ANM 1 E 177. Secrétaire général, Haut-Sénégal-Niger, confidential letter, 20 Dec. 1905.

ANM 1 E 177. Ponty, letter to commandant Segu, 18 Apr. 1907, Kayes.

ANM 1 E 188. Correspondence, Bamako cercle.

ANM 1 E 192. Gaubert, Rapport sur l'arrangement passée en Macina entre les peuls et rimaibes au sujet du remplacement de toutes redévances anciennes par la régime de la location des terres, 24 Dec. 1908, Jenne.

ANM 1 E 219. Capitaine Briquelot, résident Segu, to Commandant supérieur, Segu, 27 Apr., Aug., 1891.

ANM 1 E 220. Mademba correspondance, 1891–1918.

ANM 2 E 67. Notes et fiches de renseignements sur les chefs et notables, cercle de Segou, 1897.

ANM 1 Q 4. Commercial correspondance to délégué du gouverneur, including pétition Maurel et Prom, et al., Nioro, [1900].

ANM 1 Q 7. Rapports commerciaux, Bouguni.

ANM 1 Q 37. Rapports agricoles et commerciaux, Soudan français.

ANM 1 Q 40. Rapport sur la situation économique en 1904.

ANM 1 Q 44. Rapports commerciaux, Bamako.

ANM 1 Q 47. Rapports commerciaux, Bouguni.

ANM 1 Q 83. Rapports commerciaux, Segu and Sansanding.

ANM 1 Q 84. Rapports commerciaux, Sikasso.

ANM 1 Q 358. Rapport économique, Segu, 1939.

ANM 1 Q 1909. Correspondence concerning establishment of a textile factory in Bamako, 1941.

ANM 1 R 31. Bulletins commerciaux et agricoles, Bamako; Vuillet, Note sur le coton du Soudan, 10 Mar. 1902, Koulikoro.

ANM 1 R 67, R 69. Bulletins agricoles et commerciaux, Segu.

ANM 1 R 79. Produits exposés par le colonie Haut-Sénégal-Niger, Exposition des Londres, 1913; Vuillet, Régions cotonnières du Soudan, 18 Aug. 1904.

ANM 1 R 81. Correspondence concerning economic and commercial matters between Bamako and governor.

ANM 1 R 95. Notice accompagné 400 kg du coton destiné à un éssai d'égrenage, Segu, 1903.

ANM 1 R 305. Terrasson, Rapport à la Direction des Affaires Economiques, Kouluba, 1928.

Archives Nationales République de Sénégal, Section Afrique Occidentale française, Dakar, Sénégal (*ANS-AOF*):

ANS-AOF 1 D 105. Archinard, Rapport militaire, Campagne 1889–90.
ANS-AOF 1 G 18. Dossier Raffenel, 1848.
ANS-AOF 1 G 32. Mission Mage, 1863–66.
ANS-AOF 1 G 46. Mission Soleillet, 1878–79.
ANS-AOF 1 G 50. Mission Gallieni, 1880.
ANS-AOF 1 G 52. Docteur Bayol, Rapport sur le voyage au pays de Bamako.
ANS-AOF 1 G 83. Mission Caron au Tombouctou, 1887.
ANS-AOF 1 G 99. Dossier Morin, 1888.
ANS-AOF 1 G 115. Mission Marchand, 1889.
ANS-AOF 1 G 122. Capitaine Underberg, Notes sur l'histoire du Macina, Mar. 1892.
ANS-AOF 1 G 142. Mission Bayol au pays de Bélédougou et de Mourdia, 1883.
ANS-AOF 1 G 184. Capitaine Bellat, Renseignements historiques sur le pays de Sansanding et du Macina, 1893.
ANS-AOF 1 G 189. Capitaine McLeod, Tournée fait dans le Marcadougou, 1894.
ANS-AOF 1 G 199. Mission Binger.
ANS-AOF 1 G 224. Notice sur les Maures du Sénégal et du Soudan, 1897.
ANS-AOF 1 G 229. Coste, Coutumiers juridiques, Segu, 1897; Barat, Recueil des coutumes juridique du Soudan, Nioro, 1897–1900.
ANS-AOF 1 G 248. Capitaine Perignon, Généralités sur Haut Sénégal et Moyen Niger, 1900.
ANS-AOF 1 G 320. Notice sur le cercle de Segou, 1904.
ANS-AOF 1 G 323. Notice sur le cercle de Sokolo, 31 Dec. 1903.
ANS-AOF 1 G 336. Correnson, De l'organisation de la justice chez les populations de la région de Segou, 1910.
ANS-AOF 2 G 1–14. William Ponty, Rapport politique, Haut-Sénégal-Niger, Apr. 1901.
ANS-AOF 2 G 1–23. William Ponty, Rapport sur la situation économique, agricole, et commerciale des territoires du Haut-Sénégal-Niger, 16 Feb. 1900.
ANS-AOF 2 G 6–2. Rapport politique, Haut-Sénégal-Niger, 2d quarter, 1906.
ANS-AOF 2 G 6–6. William Ponty, Rapport politique, Haut-Sénégal-Niger, Apr. 1906; Rapport politique, Haut Sénégal Niger, May 1906.
ANS-AOF 2 G 7. William Ponty, letter, 25 May 1907.

ANS-AOF 2 G 7–3. Rapport politique, Haut-Sénégal-Niger, 3d quarter 1907.
ANS-AOF 2 G 8–1. Rapport politique, 1st quarter 1908, Haut-Sénégal-Niger; Vuillet, chef de service agricole.
ANS-AOF 2 G 8–2. Rapport agricole, Haut-Sénégal-Niger, 1st quarter 1908.
ANS-AOF 2 G 9–12. Rapport politique, Haut-Sénégal-Niger, 2d quarter 1909.
ANS-AOF 15 G 82. Correspondances indigènes.
ANS-AOF 15 G 170. Rapport sur le conflict markas, 26 June 1905.
ANS-AOF 15 G 172. Archinard, Palabre avec Mari Jara, 19 Apr. 1890.
ANS-AOF K 14. Etudes sur la captivité, 1894.
ANS-AOF K 16. Etude sur la captivité, 10 June 1905.
ANS-AOF K 17. Poulet, Rapport sur la captivité, 18 Mar. 1905, Dakar.
ANS-AOF K 19. Etudes sur la captivité, 1904.
ANS-AOF K 25. Deherme, L'esclavage en Afrique Occidentale française, 1906.
ANS-AOF K 26. Gouverneur général to consul général d'Angleterre, 22 Feb. 1911.

Archives Nationales de France, Section Outre-Mer, Paris, France (*ANF-SOM*):

ANF-SOM Afrique III 1. Al hajj Boubakar, Itineraire de Seno Palel, ville de Fouta, à la Mecque, 1820.
ANF-SOM Sénégal de dépendances III 10 bis. Gallieni, Nango letters, 1880.
ANF-SOM Soudan I 1. Archinard, 1890 Campagne.
ANF-SOM Soudan I 2 bis. Archinard telegram, 5 May 1893.
ANF-SOM Soudan I ii bis. William Ponty, Note sur la colonie du Haut-Sénégal-Niger, 25 June 1905.
ANF-SOM Soudan I 10 a. Lieutenant Colonel Humbert, Situation du Soudan français, 27 Aug. 1890.
ANF-SOM Soudan I 11. Gouverneur général, letter to Minister of Colonies, 22 June 1908, Dakar.
ANF-SOM Soudan IV 1. Grodet to commandant of région sud, 12 Sept. 1894.
ANF-SOM Soudan V 1 a. Archinard, Renseignements sur la situation des colonies, Campagne, 1890–91.

Books, Articles, and Manuscripts

Abitbol, Michel. *Tombouctou et les Arma*. Paris, 1975.
Abun-Nasr, Jamil M. *The Tijaniyya: A Sufi Order in the Modern World*. London, 1965.

Adamu, Mahdi. *The Hausa Factor in Nigerian History*. Zaria, 1978.
Adeleye, R. A. *Power and Diplomacy in Northern Nigeria, 1804–1906*. New York, 1971.
Africanus, Leo. *Description de l'Afrique*. Trans. A. Epallard. Paris, 1956.
Alagoa, E. J. "The Niger Delta States and Their Neighbours, 1600–1800," in *History of West Africa*, ed. A. Ajayi and M. Crowder. New York, 1972.
Allen, William. *The African Husbandman*. Edinburgh, 1965.
Al Naqar. *The Pilgrimage Route in West Africa: An Historical Study with Special Reference to the Nineteenth Century*. Khartoum, 1972.
Alpers, Edward. "State, Merchant Capital, and Gender Relations in Southern Mozambique to the End of the 19th Century: Some Tentative Hypotheses," *African Economic History*, 13 (1984).
Amin, Samir. "Underdevelopment and Dependence in Black Africa: Origins and Contemporary Forms," *Journal of Modern African Studies*, 10, no. 4 (1972).
Amselle, Jean-Loup. *Les négociants de la savanne: histoire et organisation sociale des Kooroko, Mali*. Paris, 1977.
Ancelle, Capitaine J. *Les explorateurs au Sénégal et dans les contrées voisines de l'antiquité jusqu'à nos jours*. Paris, 1886.
Anderson, Perry. *Lineages of the Absolutist State*. London, 1974.
———. *Passages from Antiquity to Feudalism*. London, 1974.
André, Pierre-Raden. *L'Islam noire: contribution à l'étude des confréries religieuses islamiques en Afrique Occidentale*. Paris, 1924.
Andrews, C. M., P. Grupp, and A. S. Kanya-Forstner. "Le mouvement colonial français et ses principales personalités (1890–1914)," *Revue française de l'histoire d'Outre Mer*, 42, no. 4 (1975).
Archinard, Louis. "Rapport de campagne 1890–91," *Journal officiel*, 18 Oct. 1891.
Austen, Ralph. "The Trans-Saharan Slave Trade: A Tentative Census," in *The Uncommon Market: Essays in the Economic History of the Atlantic Slave Trade*, ed. Henry Gemery and Jan. S. Hogendorn. New York, 1979.
Azarya, Victor. "Traders and the Center in Massina, Kong, and Samori's State," *International Journal of African Historical Studies*, 13, no. 3 (1980).
Ba, Hampte, and J. Daget. *L'empire peul de Masina*, vol. 1. Paris and the Hague, 1972.
Bah, Thierno Mouctar. "Les forts français et le contrôle de l'espace dans le Haut-Sénégal-Niger, 1855–98," in *Le sol, la parole, et l'écrit: 2000 ans d'histoire africaine*, ed. Jean Devisse. Paris, 1981.
Baier, Stephen. *An Economic History of the Central Sudan*. Oxford, 1980.
———. "Trans-Saharan Trade and the Sahel, Damergu, 1870–1930." *Journal of African History*, 18, no. 1 (1977).

Bailey, Anne. "The Renewed Discussions on the Concept of the Asiatic Mode of Production," in *The Anthropology of Pre-Capitalist Societies*, ed. Joel Kahn and Josep Llobera. London, 1981.

Baillaud, Emile. *Sur les routes du Soudan*. Toulouse, 1902.

Balandier, Georges. *Anthropologie politique*. Paris, 1967.

Balde, Mamadou Saliou. "L'esclavage et la guerre sainte au Fouta Jalon," in *Esclavage en Afrique précoloniale*, ed. Claude Meillassoux. Paris, 1975.

Balibar, Etienne. "The Basic Concepts of Historical Materialism," in *Reading Capital*, ed. Louis Althusser and Etienne Balibar. London, 1972.

Barker, Jonathan. "Stability and Stagnation: The State in Senegal," *Canadian Journal of African Studies*, 11, no. 1 (1977).

Barker, Jonathan, ed. *The Politics of Agriculture in Tropical Africa*. Beverly Hills, Calif., 1984.

Barrows, Leland. "General Faidherbe, the Maurel and Prom Company, and French Expansion in Senegal." Ph.D. diss., UCLA, 1975.

———. "The Merchants and General Faidherbe," *Revue française de l'histoire d'Outre Mer*, 61, no. 2 (1974).

Barry, Boubakar. *Le royaume de Waalo: Sénégal avant la conquêté*. Paris, 1972.

Barth, Fredrik. "Economic Spheres in Dafur," in *Themes in Economic Anthropology*, ed. Raymond Firth. London, 1967.

Barth, Fredrik, ed. *Ethnic Groups and Boundaries*. Boston, 1969.

Barth, Heinrich. *Travels and Discoveries in North and Central Africa*, 5 vols. London, 1857–58.

Batran, A. A. "The Kunta, sidi al Mukhtar al Kunti and the Office of Shaykh al-Qadiriyya," in *Studies in West African Islamic History*, ed. J. R. Willis. London, 1979.

Bayol, Jean. *Voyage en Sénégambie, Haut Niger, Bambouck, Fouta Djallon et Bélédougou, 1880–1885*. Paris, 1888.

———. "Voyages au pays de Bamako," *Bulletin de la Société de Géographie de Paris*, 2 (1881).

Bazin, H[ippolyte]. *Dictionnaire bambara-française*. Paris, 1905; repr. London, 1965.

Bazin, Jean. "Commerce et prédation: l'état bambara de Segou et ses communautés marka." Paper presented at Conference on Manding Studies, School of Oriental and African Studies, London, 1972.

———. "Guerre et servitude à Segou," in *Esclavage en Afrique précoloniale*, ed. Claude Meillassoux. Paris, 1975.

———. "Etat guerrier et guerres d'état," in *Guerres de lignages et guerres d'états en Afrique*, ed. Jean Bazin and Emmanuel Terray. Paris, 1982.

———. "Notes," in *Les Bambara de Ségou et Kaarta*, by Charles Monteil. Repr. Paris, 1977.

———. "Production d'un récit historique," *Cahiers d'études africaines*, 19, nos. 73–76 (1979).
Bazin, Jean, and Emmanuel Terray, eds. *Guerres des lignages et guerres d'état*. Paris, 1982.
Bechet, Eugene. *Cinq ans de séjour au Soudan français*. Paris, 1889.
Bernstein, Henry, and Jacques Delpechin. "The Object of African History: A Materialist Perspective," *History in Africa*, 5 (1978) and 6 (1979).
Bernus, Edmond. "Le contrôle du milieu naturel et du tropeau par les éleveurs touregs," in *Pastoral Production and Society*. Cambridge, Eng., and Paris, 1979.
Bime, André. *Ségou, vieille capitale*. Angoulême, France, 1952.
Binger, Louis. *Du Niger au golfe de Guinée par le pays du Kong et de Mossi, 1887–1889*. Paris, 1892. 2 vols.
———. "Les routes commerciales du Soudan Occidental." *La gazette géographique*, 2, nos. 1–2 (1886).
Bird, Charles S. "The Development of Mandekan (Manding): A Study of the Role of Extra-Linguistic Factors in Linguistic Change," in *Language and History in Africa*, ed. David Dalby. New York, 1970.
Bird, Charles S., and Martha Kendall. "The Mande Hero," in *Explorations in African Systems of Thought*, ed. Ivan Karp and Charles Bird. Bloomington, Ind., 1980.
Boisboissel, Y. de. "Contribution à la connaissance de l'histoire militaire de l'Afrique Occidentale française," *Revue internationale de l'historie militaire*, 4 (1956).
Bonnier, Chef d'Escadron. *Mission au pays de Ségou: campagne dans le Gueniekalary et le Sansanding en 1892*. Paris, 1897.
Borgnis-Desbordes. "Le Général Borgnis-Desbordes," *Bulletin du comité d'Afrique française*, Aug. 1900.
Bouche, Denise. *Les villages de liberté en Afrique noir française, 1887–1910*. Paris, 1968.
Bourdier, Jean-Paul. *African Spaces: Designs for Living in Upper Volta*. New York, 1984.
Boutillier, Jean Louis. "Les trois esclaves de Bouna," in *Esclavage en Afrique précoloniale*, ed. Claude Meillassoux. Paris, 1975.
Bovill, E. W. *Golden Trade of the Moors*. Repr. London, 1968.
Bradbury, R. E. *Benin Studies*, ed. Peter Morton-Williams. London, 1973.
Brasseur, Gerard. *Les établissements humains au Mali*. Dakar, 1968.
Braudel, Fernand. *The Mediterranean and the Mediterranean World of Philip the Second*, trans. Sian Reynolds. New York, 1972–73.
Brenner, Louis. "Muhammad al Kanimi and Religion and Politics in Borno," in *Studies in West African Islamic History*, ed. J. R. Willis. London, 1979.

———. *The Shehus of Kukawa: A History of the al-Kanemi Dynasty of Bornu.* Oxford, 1973.
Brenner, Robert. "The Origins of Capitalist Development: A Critique of Neo-Smithian Marxism," *New Left Review*, 104 (1977).
Brooks, George. "Peanuts and Colonialism: Consequences of the Commercialization of Peanuts in West Africa, 1830–70," *Journal of African History*, 16, no. 1 (1975).
Brown, William Allen. "The Caliphate of Hamdullahi, ca. 1816–1864: A Study in African History and Tradition." Ph.D. diss., Univ. of Wisconsin, 1972.
Brunschwig, Henri. "French Exploration and Conquest in Tropical Africa from 1865 to 1898," in *Colonialism in Africa I*, ed. Peter Duignan and Louis Gann. Cambridge, Eng., 1969.
Caillié, René. *Journal d'un voyage à Tomboctou et à Jenne*. Paris, 1830. 3 vols.
Caldwell, John, J. E. Inikori, and Patrick Manning. "Two Comments on Manning, 'The Enslavement of Africans: A Demographic Model,'" and "A Response," *Canadian Journal of African Studies*, 16, no. 1 (1982).
Capron, Jean. *Anthropologie économique des populations Bwa, Mali, Haute Volta: introduction a l'étude des communautés villegoises*. Paris, 1965.
Carneiro, Robert. "A Theory of the Origin of the State," *Science*, 179 (1970).
Caron, E. *De Saint Louis au Port de Tombouctou: voyage d'une canonnière*. Paris, 1892.
Carrère, Frederic. "Siège de Medine," *Revue coloniale*, 19 (1857).
Carrère, Frederic, and Paul Holle. *De la Sénégambie française*. Paris, 1855.
Cashion, Gerald. "Hunters of the Mande." Ph.D. diss., Indiana Univ., 1984.
Chantilly, Marcel. *Histoire de l'Afrique Occidentale française, 1638–1959*. Paris, 1965.
Cisse, Youseff. "Notes sur les sociétés des chasseurs Malinké," *Journal de Société des Africainists*, 24 (1964).
Cissoko, Mody Skekene. "Famines et épidémies à Tombouctou et dans la Boucle du Niger, XVI au XVIII ième siècle," *Bulletin d'IFAN*, ser. B, 30 (1968).
Claessen, Henri, and Peter Skalnik, eds. *The Early State*. The Hague, 1978.
Claessen, Henri, and Peter Skalnik, eds. *The Study of the State*. The Hague, 1981.
Clarence-Smith, W. "For Braudel: A Note on the Ecole des Annales and the Historiography of Africa," *History in Africa*, 4 (1977).
Cohen, Abner. "Cultural Strategies in the Organization of Trading Diasporas," in *The Development of Indigenous Trade and Markets in West Africa*, ed. Claude Meillassoux. London, 1971.

———. *Custom and Politics in Urban Africa: A Study of Hausa Migrants in Yoruba Towns*. London, 1969.

Cohen, G. A. *Karl Marx's Theory of History: A Defence*. Princeton, N.J., 1978.

Cohen, Ronald, and Louis Brenner. "Borno in the Nineteenth Century," in *History of West Africa*, 2, ed. A. Ajayi and M. Crowder. New York, 1972.

Cohen, Ronald, and Elman Service, eds. *Origin of the State*. Philadelphia, 1978.

Cohen, William. *The French Encounter with Africans: White Response to Blacks, 1530–1880*. Bloomington, Ind., 1980.

———. "Imperial Mirage: Western Sudan in French Thought and Action," *Journal of the Historical Society of Nigeria*, 7, no. 3 (1974).

———. *Rulers of Empire: The French Colonial Service in Africa*. Stanford, Calif., 1971.

Conrad, David. "Bambara Segou in the Eighteenth and Nineteenth Centuries: Tayiru Banbera's Traditional History." Unpublished ms., n.d.

———. "Slavery in Bambara Society: Segu, 1712–1861," *Slavery and Abolition*, 2, no. 1 (1981).

Cooper, Frederick. "Africa and the World Economy," *African Studies Review*, 24, nos. 2–3 (1981).

———. *From Slaves to Squatters: Labor and Agriculture in Zanzibar and Coastal Kenya, 1890–1925*. New Haven, Conn., 1980.

———. *Plantation Slavery on the East Coast of Africa*. New Haven, Conn., 1977.

———. "The Problem of Slavery in African Studies," *Journal of African History*, 20, no. 1 (1979).

Coquery-Vidrovitch, Catherine, and Alain Forest, eds. *Entreprises et entrepreneurs en Afrique: XIXe et XXe siècles*. Paris, 1983.

Corrigan, Philip, ed. *Capitalism, State Formation, and Marxist Theory*. London, 1980.

Crone, Phyllis. *Slaves on Horses: The Evolution of the Islamic Polity*. Cambridge, Eng., 1980.

Cruise O'Brien, Donald. *Saints and Politicians: Essays in the Organization of a Senegalese Peasant Society*. Cambridge, Eng., 1975.

Crummey, Donald, and C. C. Stewart, eds. *Modes of Production in Africa: The Precolonial Era*. Beverly Hills, Calif., 1981.

Curtin, Philip. "The Abolition of the Slave Trade from Senegambia," in *The Abolition of the Slave Trade: Origin and Effects in Europe, Africa, and the Americas*, ed. David Eltis and James Walvin. Madison, Wisc., 1981.

———. *The Atlantic Slave Trade: A Census*. Madison, Wisc., 1969.

———. *Cross Cultural Trade in World History*. New York, 1984.

———. *Economic Change in Precolonial Africa: Senegambia in the Era of the Slave Trade*. Madison, Wisc., 1975. 2 vols.
———. "Jihad in West Africa: Early Phases and Inter-relationships in Mauretania and Senegal," *Journal of African History*, 13, no. 4 (1972).
———. "Precolonial Trading Networks and Traders: The Diahanke," in *The Development of Indigenous Trade and Markets in West Africa*, ed. Claude Meillassoux. London, 1971.
Daget, S. "La pêche à Diafarabé," *Bulletin d'IFAN*, ser. B, 18 (1956).
Danziger, Raphael. *Abd-el Qadir and the Algerians: Resistance to the French and Internal Consolidation*. New York, 1977.
Davis, David Brion. *The Problem of Slavery in Western Culture*. Ithaca, N.Y., 1966.
Deherme, Georges. *L'Afrique Occidentale française*. Paris, 1908.
De Heusch, Luc. *The Drunken King, or, The Origins of the State*, trans. Roy Wills. Bloomington, Ind., 1982.
Delafosse, Maurice. *Haut Sénégal Niger*. Paris, 1912; repr. 1972. 3 vols.
———. "Monograph historique du cercle de Bamako," *Renseignements coloniaux*, 1910.
Delavignette, Robert. *Freedom and Authority in French West Africa*. London, 1968.
Derman, William. *Serfs, Peasants, and Socialists: A Former Serf Village in the Republic of Guinea*. Berkeley, Calif., 1973.
Douglas, Mary. "Matriliny and Pawnship in Central Africa." *Africa*, 34, no. 4 (1964).
Dubois, Felix. *Notre beau Niger*. Paris, 1911.
———. *Tombouctou, la mystérieuse*. Paris, 1897.
Duby, Georges. *The Early Growth of the European Economy: Warriors and Peasants from the Seventh to the Twelfth Century*, trans. Howard Clarke. Ithaca, N.Y., 1978.
Dumett, Raymond. "Precolonial Gold Mining and the State in the Akan Region: With a Critique of the Terray Hypothesis," *Research in Economic Anthropology*, 2 (1979).
Dumett, Raymond, and Marion Johnson. "The Suppression of Slavery in the Gold Coast and Asante," in *The End of Slavery in Africa*, ed. Suzanne Miers and Richard Roberts. Madison, Wisc., forthcoming.
Dupre, Georges, and Pierre-Phillip Rey. "Reflections on the Pertinence of a Theory and History of Exchange." *Economy and Society*, 2, no. 2 (1974).
Echenberg, Myron. "Paying the Blood Tax: Military Conscription in French West Africa, 1914–1929," *Canadian Journal of African Studies*, 9, no. 2 (1975).
Elwitt, Sanford. *The Making of the Third Republic: Class and Politics in France, 1868–84*. Baton Rouge, La., 1975.

L'équip écologie et anthropologie des sociétés pastorales. *Pastoral Production and Society*. Cambridge, Eng., and Paris, 1979.

Es Sa'di, Abderrahmen ben Abdallah ben Imram ben Amir. *Tarikh es-Soudan*, trans. O. Houdas. Paris, 1900.

Faidherbe, Louis. *Le Soudan français: chemin de fer de Medine au Niger*. Lille, 1883.

Feierman, Steven. *The Shambaa Kingdom: A History*. Madison, Wisc., 1974.

Fisher, Allen G. B., and Humphrey J. Fisher. *Slavery and Muslim Society in Africa*. Garden City, N.Y., 1971.

Freund, Bill. *Labour and Capital in the Nigerian Tin Mines*. London, 1981.

Fried, Morton. *Evolution of Political Society*. New York, 1967.

Friedman, Jonathan, and M. J. Rowlands, eds. *The Evolution of Social Systems*. London, 1978.

Fyfe, Christopher. "Reform in West Africa: The Abolition of the Slave Trade," in *History of West Africa*, ed. A. Ajayi and M. Crowder. New York, 1972.

Fyfe, Christopher, ed. *African Studies Since 1945: A Tribute to Basil Davidson*. London, 1976.

Gallais, Jean. *Le delta intérieur du Niger*. Dakar, 1967. 2 vols.

———. "Signification du groupe ethnique du Mali," *Homme*, 2 (1962).

Gallieni, Joseph Simone. *Deux campagnes au Soudan français, 1886–88*. Paris, 1891.

———. *Mission d'exploration du Haut Niger: voyage au Soudan français: Haut-Niger et pays de Ségou*. Paris, 1885.

Galtier, Gerard. "Correspondances phonétiques et lexicales dans les langues Mande Nord." Paper presented at Conference on Manding Studies, School of Oriental and African Studies, London, 1972.

Geertz, Clifford. *Islam Observed: Religious Development in Morocco and Indonesia*. Chicago, 1968.

Gellner, Ernest. "The Islamic State." Unpublished paper, n.d.

Gemery, Henry, and Jan Hogendorn. "The Atlantic Slave Trade: A Tentative Economic Model," *Journal of African History*, 15, no. 2 (1974).

Genovese, Eugene. *Roll, Jordan, Roll: The World the Slaves Made*. New York, 1974.

Gilbert, Felix, ed. *The Historical Essays of Otto Hintze*. New York, 1975.

Godelier, Maurice. "The Concept of 'Social and Economic Formation': The Inca Example," in *Perspectives in Marxist Anthropology*, trans. Robert Brain. Cambridge, Eng., 1977.

———. "La notion de 'mode de production asiatique' et les schémas marxistes d'évolution des sociétés," in *Sur le "mode de production asiatique."* Paris, 1969.

Golob, Eugene. *Meline Tariff: French Agriculture and National Economic Policy*. New York, 1944.
Goody, Jack, ed. *The Development Cycle of Domestic Groups in Africa*. Cambridge, Eng., 1958.
———. *Technology, Tradition, and the State in Africa*. London, 1971.
Grace, John. *Domestic Slavery in West Africa*. New York, 1975.
Grayzel, John. "The Ecology of Ethnic-Class Identity Among an African Pastoral People: The Doukolomo Fulbe." Ph.D. diss., Univ. of Oregon, 1977.
Green, Kathryn. "The Foundation of Kong: A Study in Dyula and Songui Ethnic Identity." Ph.D. diss., Indiana Univ., 1984.
Guyer, Jane. "Food, Cocoa, and the Division of Labour by Sex in Two West African Societies," *Comparative Studies in Society and History*, 22, no. 3 (1980).
Handloff, Robert. "Trade and Politics in Gyaman." Ph.D. diss., Northwestern Univ., 1982.
Harding, James. *The Astonishing Adventure of General Boulanger*, New York, 1971.
Hardy, Georges. *La mise en valeur du Sénégal de 1817 à 1854*. Paris, 1912.
Hargreaves, John. *Prelude to the Partition of West Africa*. London, 1963.
———. "The Tokolor Empire of Segou and Its Relations with the French," in *Boston University Papers in African History*, vol. 2: *African History*, ed. Jeffrey Butler. Boston, 1966.
Harms, Robert. *River of Wealth, River of Sorrow*. New Haven, Conn., 1981.
———. "The Wars of August: Diagonal Narrative in African History," *American Historical Review*, 88, no. 4 (1983).
Hassan, Farooq. *The Concept of State and Law in Islam*. Washington, D.C., 1981.
Henry, Yves. *Le coton en Afrique Occidentale française*. Paris, 1904.
Hill, Polly. "From Slavery to Freedom: The Case of Farm Slavery in Nigerian Hausaland," *Comparative Studies in Society and History*, 18, no. 1 (1976).
———. "Hidden Trade in Hausaland," *Man*, 4 (1969).
———. "Landlord and Broker: A West African Trading System (with a Note on Kumasi Butchers)," *Cahiers d'études africaines*, 6, no. 3 (1966).
———. *Rural Hausa: A Village and a Setting*. Cambridge, Eng., 1972.
Hiskett, Mervyn. "The Islamic Tradition of Reform in the Western Sudan," *Bulletin of the School of Oriental and African Studies*, 25 (1962).
———. "The Nineteenth Century Jihads of West Africa," in *Cambridge History of Africa*, vol. 5. London, 1976.
———. *The Sword of Truth: The Life and Times of Shehu Usuman dan Fodio*. London, 1973.

Hodgson, Marshall. *The Venture of Islam: Conscience and History in a World Civilization, the Classical Age*. Chicago, 1974.

Holas, B. *Les Senoufo*. Paris, 1966.

Holmes, Levell. "Tieba Traore, Fama of Kenedougou: Two Decades of Political Development, 1873–1893." Ph.D. diss., Univ. of California, Berkeley, 1978.

Hopkins, A. G. "Clio-antics: A Horoscope for African Economic History," in *African Studies Since 1945: A Tribute to Basil Davidson*, ed. Christopher Fyfe. London, 1976.

———. *An Economic History of West Africa*. London, 1973.

Horton, Robin. "African Conversions," *Africa*, 41 (1971).

———. "On the Rationality of Conversion," *Africa*, 45 (1975).

———. "State and Stateless Societies in the History of West Africa," in *History of West Africa*, ed. A. Ajayi and M. Crowder. New York, 1972.

Howard, Allen. "Big Men, Traders, and Chiefs: Power, Commerce, and Spatial Change in the Sierra Leone-Guinea Plain, 1865–1895." Ph.D. diss., Univ. of Wisconsin, 1972.

———. "The Relevance of Spatial Analysis for African Economic History: The Sierra Leone-Guinea System," *Journal of African History*, 18, no. 3 (1976).

Hunwick, J. O. "Religion and the State in the Songhay Empire, 1464–1591," in *Islam in Africa*, ed. I. M. Lewis. London and Bloomington, Ind., 1980.

Hyden, Goran. *Beyond Ujamaa in Tanzania: Underdevelopment and an Uncaptured Peasantry*. Berkeley, Calif., 1980.

Igbafe, Philip. "Slavery and Emancipation in Benin," *Journal of African History*, 16, no. 3 (1975).

Iliffe, John. *A Modern History of Tanganyika*. Cambridge, Eng., 1979.

Inikori, J. E. "The Import of Firearms into West Africa, 1750–1807: A Quantitative Analysis," *Journal of African History*, 18, no. 3 (1977).

Inikori, J. E., ed. *Forced Migration: The Impact of the Export of Slaves on African Societies*. London, 1982.

Irwin, Paul. *Liptako Speaks: History from Oral Tradition in Africa*. Princeton, N.J., 1981.

Izard, Michel. *Introduction à l'histoire de royaumes Mossi*. Paris, 1970. 2 vols.

Jacquemond, Serge. "Les pêcheries de la Boucle du Niger," *Bulletin de la comité des travaux historiques et scientifiques, section géographique*, 77 (1958).

Jah, Omar. "Sufism and Nineteenth Century Jihad Movements in West Africa: A Case Study of al hajj al-Futi's Philosophy of Jihad and Its Sufi Bases." Ph.D. diss., McGill Univ., 1973.

Jaime, Lieutenant. *De Koulikoro à Tombouctou sur la cannonière "le Mage."* Paris, 1894.
Jenkins, R. G. "The Evolution of Religious Brotherhoods in North and Northwest Africa, 1523–1900," in *Studies in West African Islamic History*, ed. J. R. Willis. London, 1979.
Johnson, Marion. "The Atlantic Slave Trade and the Economy of West Africa," in *Liverpool, the Atlantic Slave Trade and Abolition*, ed. Roger Antsey and P. E. H. Hair. Liverpool, 1976.
———. "Cotton Imperialism in West Africa," *African Affairs*, 83, no. 291 (1974).
———. "Cowrie Currencies in West Africa," *Journal of African History*, 11, nos. 1 and 3 (1970).
———. "Economic Foundations of an Islamic Theocracy: The Case of Masina," *Journal of African History*, 18, no. 4 (1976).
Jones, Adam, and Marion Johnson. "Slaves from the Windward Coast," *Journal of African History*, 21, no. 1 (1980).
Jones, William I. "The Food Economy of Ba Dugu Djoliba," in *African Food Production Systems*, ed. Peter McLoughlin. Baltimore, Md., 1970.
Kaba, Lansane. *The Wahhabiyya: Islamic Reform and Politics in French West Africa*. Evanston, Ill., 1974.
Kahn, Joel, and Josep Llobera."Towards a New Marxism, or a New Anthropology?" in *The Anthropology of Pre-Capitalist Societies*, ed. Kahn and Llobera. London, 1981.
Kamara, Cheik Moussa."La vie d'el hadj Omar," *Bulletin d'IFAN*, ser. B, 32 (1970).
Kanya-Forstner, A. S. *The Conquest of the Western Sudan: A Study in French Military Imperialism*. Cambridge, Eng., 1969.
———. "Mali-Tukulor." *West African Resistance: Military Response to Colonial Rule*, ed. Michael Crowder. New York, 1971.
Kati, Mahmoud. *Tarikh el-Fettach*, trans. O. Houdas and Maurice Delafosse. Repr. Paris, 1964.
Kea, Ray. *Settlements, Trade and Politics in the Seventeenth-Century Gold Coast*. Baltimore, Md., 1982.
Kesteloot, Lilyan. "Acteurs et valeurs dans l'épopée bambara de Ségou," *Canadian Journal of African Studies*, 6, no. 1 (1972).
———. *Da Monzon de Ségou: épopée Bambara*. Paris, 1972.
———. "Le mythe et l'histoire dans la formation de l'empire de Ségou," *Bulletin d'IFAN*, ser. B, 40, no. 3 (1978).
Kesteloot, Lilyan, and G. Dumestre. *La geste de Ségou: recontrée par des griots bambara*. Paris, 1979.
Khadduri, Majid. *Islamic Law of Nations: Shaybani's Siyar*. Baltimore, Md., 1966.
———. *War and Peace in the Law of Islam*. Baltimore, Md., 1955.

Klein, A. Norman. "Inequality in Asante: A Study of the Forms and Meanings of Slavery and Social Servitude in Pre- and Early Colonial Akan Asante Society and Culture." Ph.D. diss., Univ. of Michigan, 1981.

———. "Two Asantes: The Ideology of Slavery in Asante," in *The Ideology of Slavery in Africa*, ed. Paul Lovejoy. Beverly Hills, Calif., 1981.

Klein, Martin. "The Demography of Slavery in the Western Soudan in the Late 19th Century," in *African Population and Capitalism: Historical Perspectives*, ed. Dennis Cordell and Joel Gregory. Beverly Hills, Calif., 1986.

———. "The Dyula Revolution Revisited: A Look at the Work of Yves Person." Paper presented at African Studies Association Annual Meeting, 1982.

———. *Islam and Imperialism in Senegal*. Stanford, Calif., 1968.

———. "Slavery, Forced Labor and French Colonial Rule in Colonial Guinea." Paper presented at American Historical Association, San Francisco, 1983.

———. "Slavery and the Conquest of the Western Sudan." Paper presented at African Studies Association Annual Meeting, 1976.

———. "Social and Economic Factors in the Muslim Revolutions in Senegambia," *Journal of African History*, 13, no. 3 (1972).

———. "The Study of Slavery in Africa," *Journal of African History*, 19, no. 4 (1978).

———. "Women in Slavery in the Western Sudan," in *Women and Slavery in Africa*, ed. Claire Robertson and Martin Klein. Madison, Wisc., 1983.

Klein, Martin, ed. *Peasants in Africa*. Beverly Hills, Calif., 1980.

Kodjo, Niakey Georges. "Contribution à l'étude des tribus dites serviles au Songai," *Bulletin d'IFAN*, ser. B, 38, no. 4 (1976).

Kone, Aliou, and Richard Roberts. "La résistance bambara contre les Futanke: histoire et documents." Paper in progress.

Kopytoff, Igor, and Suzanne Miers. "African 'Slavery' as an Institution of Marginality," in *Slavery in Africa*, ed. Miers and Kopytoff. Madison, Wisc., 1977.

Kuisel, Richard. *Capitalism and the State in Modern France*. New York, 1981.

Labouret, Henri. "Le servage, étape entre l'esclavage et la liberté en Afrique Occidentale," in *Afrikanistische Studien*, ed. J. Lukas. Berlin, 1955.

Last, Murray. "Reform in West Africa: The Jihad Movement of the Nineteenth Century," in *History of West Africa*, vol. 1, ed. A. Ajayi and M. Crowder. New York, 1972.

———. *The Sokoto Caliphate*. New York, 1967.

Last, Murray, and M. A. al Hajj. "Attempts at Defining a Muslim in the Nineteenth Century Hausaland and Bornu," *Journal of the Historical Society of Nigeria*, 3, no. 2 (1965).
Latham, A. J. H. *Old Calabar, 1600–1891: The Impact of the International Economy Upon a Traditional Society*. Oxford, 1973.
Law, Robin. *The Horse in African History*. Oxford, 1980.
———. *The Oyo Empire, c 1600–1836: A West African Imperialism in the Era of the Slave Trade*. Oxford, 1977.
Le Barbier, Louis. *Etudes sur les populations Bambaras de la Vallée du Niger*. Paris, 1906.
Lee, Richard. *The !Kung San: Men, Women, and Work in a Foraging Society*. Cambridge, Eng., 1979.
Legassick, Martin. "Firearms, Horses and Samorian Army Organization, 1870–1898," *Journal of African History*, 7, no. 1 (1966).
Lennihan, Louise. "Rights in Men, Rights in Land: Slavery, Wage Labor, and Smallholder Agriculture in Northern Nigeria," *Slavery and Abolition*, 3, no. 2 (1982).
Lenz, Oskar. *Timbuktu, Reise durch Marokko, die Sahara und den Sudan*. Leipzig, 1884. 2 vols.
Le Roy Ladurie, Emmanuel. "Histoire et climat," *Annales ESC*, 14 (1959).
Levillain, Philippe. *Boulanger, fossoyeur de la monarchie*. Paris, 1982.
Lévi-Strauss, Claude. *Myth and Meaning*. New York, 1979.
———. *Structural Anthropology*. New York, 1963.
Levtzion, Neheima. *Ancient Ghana and Mali*. London, 1973.
———. "Early States of the Western Sudan to 1500," in *History of West Africa*, vol. 1, ed. A. Ajayi and M. Crowder. New York, 1972.
———. "Islam and West African Politics: Accomodation and Tension Between the Ulama and the Political Authorities," *Cahiers d'études africaines*, 18, no. 3 (1977).
———. "Northwest Africa: From the Maghrib to the Fringes of the Forest," in *Cambridge History of Africa*, vol. 4, ed. Richard Gray. London, 1975.
———. "A Seventeenth Century Chronicle by Ibn Muktar: A Critical Study of the Tarikh el Fettach," *Bulletin, School of Oriental and African Studies*, 29, no. 3 (1971).
Lewis, I. M. "Introduction," in *Islam in Africa*, ed. I. M. Lewis. London and Bloomington, Ind., 1980.
Lewis, John Van Dusen. "Descendants and Crops: Two Poles of Production in a Malian Peasant Village." Ph.D. diss., Yale Univ., 1979.
Leynaud, Emile. "Fraternités d'âge et société du culture dans la Haute Vallée du Niger," *Cahiers d'études africaines*, 6, no. 1 (1966).
Ligers, Z. *Sorko, maitres du Niger: étude ethnographique*. Paris, 1964. 5 vols.
Lings, Martin. *A Sufi Saint of the Twentieth Century: Shaikh Ahmad al-Alawi*. Berkeley, Calif., 1971.

Lloyd, P. C. "Conflict Theory and Yoruba Communities," in *History and Social Anthropology*, ed. I. M. Lewis. London, 1968.

Long, Ronald. "The Northern Mande Languages: Statistical Pretesting of 22 Idiolects." Paper presented at International Conference on Manding Studies, University of London, 1972.

Lonsdale, John. "States and Social Processes in Africa: A Historiographical Survey," *African Studies Review*, 24, nos. 2–3 (1981).

Lonsdale, John, and Bruce Berman. "Coping with the Contradictions: The Development of the Colonial State in Kenya, 1895–1914," *Journal of African History*, 19, no. 4 (1979).

Lorrain, J. *The Concept of Ideology*. London, 1979.

Lovejoy, Paul. "The Borno Salt Industry," *International Journal of African Studies*, 11, no. 4 (1979).

———. *Caravans of Kola: The Hausa Kola Trade, 1700–1900*. London, 1980.

———. "The Characteristics of Plantations in the Nineteenth Century Sokoto Caliphate (Islamic West Africa)," *American Historical Review*, 84, no. 5 (1979).

———. "Interregional Monetary Flows in the Precolonial Trade of Nigeria," *Journal of African History*, 15, no. 4 (1973).

———. "The Kambarin Beriberi: The Formation of a Specialized Group of Hausa Kola Merchants in the Nineteenth Century," *Journal of African History*, 14, no. 4 (1973).

———. "Kola in the History of West Africa," *Cahiers d'études africaines*, 20, nos. 1–2 (1980–81).

———. "Plantations in the Economy of the Sokoto Caliphate," *Journal of African History*, 19, no. 3 (1978).

———. "Polanyi's 'Ports of Trade': Salaga and Kano in the Nineteenth Century," *Canadian Journal of African Studies*, 16, no. 2 (1982).

———. *Salt of the Desert Sun*. Cambridge, Eng., 1986.

———. "The Salt Industry of the Central Sudan: A Preliminary Survey," in *The Economic History of the Central Savannah of West Africa*, ed. Mahdi Amadu. Zaria, Nigeria, forthcoming.

———. "Slavery in the Sokoto Caliphate," in *The Ideology of Slavery in Africa*, ed. Paul Lovejoy. Beverly Hills, Calif., 1981.

———. *Transformations in Slavery: A History of Slavery in Africa*. Cambridge, Eng., 1983.

———. "The Volume of the Atlantic Slave Trade: A Synthesis," *Journal of African History*, 23, no. 4 (1982).

Lovejoy, Paul, ed. *The Ideology of Slavery in Africa*. Beverly Hills, Calif., 1981.

Lovejoy, Paul, and Steven Baier. "The Desert-Side Economy of the Central Sudan," *International Journal of African Historical Studies*, 8, no. 4 (1975).

Lovejoy, Paul, and Jan Hogendorn. "Slave Marketing in West Africa," in *The Uncommon Market: Essays in the Economic History of the Atlantic Slave Trade*, ed. Henry Gemery and Jan Hogendorn. New York, 1979.
Lovejoy, Paul, and Catherine Coquery-Vidrovitch, eds., *The Workers of African Trade*. Beverly Hills, Calif., 1985.
Low, Victor. *Three Nigerian Emirates*. Evanston, Ill., 1972.
Lubeck, Paul. *Islam and Urban Labor: The Making of a Muslim Working Class*. Cambridge, Eng., forthcoming.
Ly-Tall, Madina. *Contribution à l'histoire de l'empire du Mali (XIIIe–XVIe siècles): limites, principales provinces, institutions politiques*. Dakar and Abidjan, 1977.
———. "The Decline of the Mali Empire," in *General History of Africa*, vol. 4, ed. D. T. Niane. London and Berkeley, Calif., 1984.
MacGaffey, Wyatt. "The Kongo," in *Slavery in Africa*, ed. Suzanne Miers and Igor Kopytoff. Madison, Wisc., 1977.
———. "Lineage Structure, Marriage, and the Family Amongst the Central Bantu," *Journal of African History*, 24, no. 2 (1983).
Mademba, Abd-el Kader. *Au Sénégal et au Soudan français*. Paris, 1931.
Mage, M. E. *Voyage dans le Soudan Occidental*. Paris, 1868.
Mandle, Jay. *The Roots of Black Poverty: The Southern Economy After the Civil War*. Durham, N.C., 1978
Manning, Patrick. "The Contours of Slavery and Social Change in Africa," *American Historical Review*, 88, no. 4 (1983).
———. "The Enslavement of Africans: A Demographic Model," *Canadian Journal of African Studies*, 15, no. 1 (1981).
———. *Slavery, Colonialism, and Economic Growth in Dahomey, 1640–1960*. Cambridge, Eng., 1982.
Markiarius, L. "Observations sur la légende des griots," *Cahiers d'études africaines*, 9, no. 4 (1969).
Marquet, Yves. "Des *Ikhwan al-Safa* à al-hajj ʿUmar b. Saʿid Tall, marabout et conquérant toucouleur," *Arabica*, 15–16 (1968).
Martin, B. G. *Muslim Brotherhoods in 19th Century Africa*. Cambridge, Eng., 1976.
———. "Notes sur l'origine de la Tariqa des Tijaniyya et sur les débuts d'al hagg ʿUmar," *Revue des études islamiques*, 27, no. 2 (1969).
Marty, Paul. *Etudes sur l'Islam et les tribus du Soudan*. Paris, 1920–21. 4 vols.
Marty, Paul, trans. "Chroniques de Oualata et de Nema," *Revue des études islamiques*, 1 (1929).
Marx, Karl. *Capital I*. Moscow, n.d.
———. *Capital III*. Trans. David Fernbach. New York, Vintage, 1981.
———. *The Civil War in France*. Moscow, 1968.

Mason, Michael. *The Foundations of the Bida Kingdom*. Zaria, Nigeria, forthcoming.

Mauny, Raymond. *Tableau géographique de l'Ouest africain au Moyen Age d'après les écrites, la tradition et l'archéologie*. Dakar, 1961.

M'Baye, Gueye. "L'affaire Chantemps (Avril 1904) et la suppression de l'esclavage: le cas du Sénégal," *Bulletin d'IFAN*, 27, nos. 3–4 (1965).

McDougall, Ann. "The 'Desert and the Sown' in Precolonial History: A Case Study of Banamba, Mali." Paper presented at the Centre for African Studies, Dalhousie Univ., 1980.

———. "The Idjil Salt Industry: Its Role in the Pre-Colonial Economy of the Western Sudan." Ph.D. diss., Univ. of Birmingham, 1980.

———. "The View from Awdaghust: War, Trade, and Social Change in Southeastern Sahara, from the Eighth to the Fifteenth Century," *Journal of African History*, 26, no. 1 (1985).

McIntosh, Susan Keetch. "A Reconsideration of Wangara/Palolus, Island of Gold," *Journal of African History*, 22, no. 2 (1981).

McLennan, Gregor. *Marxism and the Methodologies of History*. London, 1981.

McSheffrey, Gerald. "Slavery, Indentured Servitude, Legitimate Trade and Impact of Abolition in the Gold Coast," *Journal of African History*, 24, no. 3 (1983).

Meillassoux, Claude. "Commerce précolonial à Goumbu," in *The Development of Indigenous Trade and Markets in West Africa*, ed., Meillassoux. London, 1971.

———. "Esclavage à Gumbu," in *Esclavage en Afrique précoloniale*, ed. Meillassoux. Paris, 1975.

———. "Essai d'interprétation du phénomène économique dans les sociétés d'autosubsistance," *Cahiers d'études africaines*, 1, no. 4 (1963).

———. "Female Slavery," in *Women and Slavery in Africa*, ed. Claire Robertson and Martin Klein. Madison, Wisc., 1983.

———. *Femmes, greniers et capitaux*. Paris, 1977.

———. "From Production to Reproduction," *Economy and Society*, 1, no. 1 (1972).

———. "Histoire et institutions du *kafo* de Bamako d'après la tradition des Niaré," *Cahiers d'études africaines*, 4, no. 2 (1964).

———. "Plans d'anciennes fortifications (*tata*) en pays Malinké," *Journal de la Société des Africainists*, 6 (1966).

———. "Recherche d'un niveau de détermination dans la société cynegetique," *L'homme et la société*, 6 (1967).

———. "Rôle de l'esclavage dans l'histoire de l'Afrique Occidentale," *Anthropologie et sociétés*, 2, no. 1 (1978).

———. "The Social Organisation of the Peasantry: The Economic Basis of Kinship," *Journal of Peasant Studies*, 7, no. 1 (1972).

Meillassoux, Claude, ed. *The Development of Indigenous Trade and Markets in West Africa*. London, 1971.
———. *Esclavage en Afrique précoloniale*. Paris, 1975.
Meniaud, Jacques, *Haut Sénégal Niger: géographie économique*. Paris, 1912. 2 vols.
———. *Les pionniers du Soudan: avant et après Archinard*. Paris, 1931. 2 vols.
Mercier, Réné. *Le travail obligatoire dans les colonies africaines*. Paris, 1933.
Meyers, Allen. "Class, Ethnicity, and Slavery: The origins of the Moroccan 'Abid.'" *International Journal of African Historical Studies*, 10, no. 3 (1977).
Michel, Marc. *Appel à l'Afrique: contributions et réactions à l'effort de guerre en AOF, 1914–1919*. Paris, 1982.
Miers, Suzanne. *Britain and the Ending of the Slave Trade*. New York, 1975.
Miers, Suzanne, and Igor Kopytoff, eds. *Slavery in Africa*. Madison, Wisc., 1977.
Miers, Suzanne, and Richard Roberts, eds. *The End of Slavery in Africa*. Madison, Wisc., forthcoming.
Miliband, Ralph. *The State in Capitalist Society*. New York, 1969.
Miller, Joseph: "The Imbangala," in *Slavery in Africa*, ed. Suzanne Miers and Igor Kopytoff. Madison, Wisc., 1977.
———. *Kings and Kinsmen: Early States Among the Mbundu of Angola*. Oxford, 1976.
Miller, Joseph, ed. *African Past Speaks: Essays on Oral Tradition and History*. Folkestone, Eng., 1980.
Milward, Alan. *The German Economy at War*. London, 1965.
Mollien, Gaspar Theodore. *Travels in the Interior of Africa to the Sources of the Senegal and Gambia Performed by the Command of the French Government in the Year 1818*. London, repr. 1967.
Monteil, Charles. *Les Bambara du Ségou et du Kaarta: étude historique, ethnologique, et littéraire d'une peuple du Soudan français*. Paris, 1924.
———. *Une cité soudanaise: Djénné, metropole du Delta central du Niger*. Paris, 1932.
Muhammad, Akbar."The Samorian Occupation of Bondouku," *International Journal of African Historical Studies*, 10, no. 2 (1977).
Munson, Patrick. "Archaeology and the Prehistoric Origins of the Ghana Empire," *Journal of African History*, 21, no. 4 (1980).
Nadel, S. F. "Nupe State and Community," in *Comparative Political Society*, ed. Ronald Cohen and John Middleton. Garden City, N.Y., 1967.
N'Diaye, Bokar. *Les castes au Mali*. Bamako, 1970.
———. *Groupes ethniques au Mali*. Bamako, 1970.
Newbury, Colin. "Prices and Profitability in Early Nineteenth Century

West African Trade," in *The Development of Indigenous Trade and Markets in West Africa*, ed. Claude Meillassoux. London, 1971.

Niane, Djibril. *Le Soudan Occidental du temps des grands empires*. Paris, 1975.

Nicholson, Sharon. "The Methodology of Historical Climate Reconstruction and its Application to Africa," *Journal of African History*, 20, no. 1 (1979).

Northrup, David. *Trade Without Rulers: Precolonial Economic Development in South Eastern Nigeria*. Oxford, 1978.

Oloruntimehin, R. Olantunji. "Resistance Movements in the Tukulor Empire." *Cahiers d'études africaines*, 8, no. 1 (1968).

———. *The Segu Tukulor Empire*. New York, 1972.

Oroge, E. Adeniyi. "The Fugitive Slave Question in Anglo-Egbo Relations," *Journal of the Historical Society of Nigeria*, 8, no. 1 (1975).

Pacques, Viviana. *Les Bambara*. Paris, 1954.

Pageard, Robert. *Notes sur l'histoire du Bambara de Ségou*. Clichy, France, 1957.

Park, Mungo. *Mission*, see Park, *Travels*.

Park, Mungo. *Travels in the Interior Districts of Africa. Performed in the Years 1795, 1796, and 1797. With an Account of a Mission to That Country in 1805*. London, 1816. 2 vols. Citations of this work by the short form *Travels* refer to the 1795–97 journey (vol. 1); citations by the short form *Mission* refer to the 1805 journey (vol. 2).

Pasquier, R. "A propos de l'émancipation des esclaves au Sénégal en 1848," *Revue française d'histoire Outre Mer*, 54 (1967).

Pelissier, Paul. *Les paysans du Sénégal: les civilisations agraires du Cayor à la Casamance*. Saint-Yvieux, France, 1966.

Penel, Julien. "Coutumes soudanaises: Les coutumes des Malinkes, Sarakolles ou Soninkes, Khassonkes." Typewritten ms., Bibliothèque Nationale, 4 Li^{33}27, Paris, 1895. 3 vols.

Perignon, A. *Haut-Sénégal et Moyen-Niger: Kita et Ségou*. Paris, 1901.

Perinbam, B. Marie. "The Julas in Western Sudanese History: Long Distance Traders and Developers of Resources," in *West African Dynamics: Archaeological and Historical Perspectives*, ed. B. K. Swartz and R. E. Dumett. The Hague, 1980.

———. "Notes on Dyula Origins and Nomenclature," *Bulletin d'IFAN*, ser. B, 26, no. 4 (1974).

Peroz, Etienne. *Au Soudan français: souvenirs de guerre et de mission*. Paris, 1889.

Perron, Michel. "Pêcheries et sécheries en Europe et en AOF," *Bulletin de l'agriculture générale coloniale*, 22 (1929).

———. "Traditions claniques des groupements Bozos et Somonos du Moyen Niger," *Bulletin d'agriculture générale coloniale*, 23 (1930).

Person, Yves. "Guinea-Samori," in *West African Resistance: Military Response to Colonial Rule*, ed. Michael Crowder. New York, 1971.

———. "Ngolo Jara ou la force de Ségou," in *Les Africaines*, ed. Charles-André Julien, vol. 10. Paris, 1978.

———. *Samori: une révolution Dyula*. Dakar, 1968–73. 3 vols.

"Petite histoire de Nyamina," *Sentiers* (Paris), nos. 22–26 (1968–69).

Pietri, Capitaine Camille. *Les Français au Niger*. Paris, 1885.

Polanyi, Karl. "Ports of Trade in Early Societies," *Journal of Economic History* 23 (1963).

Pollet, Eric, and Grace Winter. *Société soninké (Dyahunu, Mali)*. Brussels, 1972.

Popkin, S. *The Rational Peasant*. Berkeley, Calif., 1979.

Poulantzas, Nicos. *State, Power, Socialism*, trans. Patrick Camiller. London, 1978.

Quellien, Alain. *La politique musulmane dans l'Afrique Occidentale française*. Paris, 1910.

Quinton, Louis. "Etude ethnologique sur le pays entre le Sénégal et le Niger," *Bulletin de la Société de Géographie de Paris*, 2 (1881).

———. "Souvenirs d'un voyage du Sénégal au Niger, 1863–66," *Bulletin de la Société de Géographie de Paris*, 1 (1881).

Raffenel, Anne. "Deuxième voyage," *Revue coloniale*, 1849.

———. *Nouveau voyage au pays de nègres*. Paris, 1856. 2 vols.

Ratcliffe, Barrie. "Cotton Imperialism: Manchester Merchants and Cotton Cultivation in West Africa in the Mid-Nineteenth Century," *African Economic History*, 11 (1982).

Reefe, Thomas Q. *The Rainbow and the Kings: A History of the Luba Empire to 1891*. Berkeley, Calif., 1981.

Renault, François. *L'abolition de l'esclavage en Sénégal: l'attitude d'administration française, 1848–1905*. Paris, 1972.

———. *Liberation d'esclaves et nouvelle servitude: les rachats des captifs africains pour le compte des colonies françaises après l'abolition de l'esclavage*. Dakar and Abidjan, 1976.

Rey, Pierre-Philippe. *Les alliances de classes*. Paris, 1973.

Richter, Delores. "Further Considerations on Caste in West Africa: The Senufo," *Africa*, 50, no. 1 (1980).

Robert, Louis. *La culture du coton en Afrique Occidentale française*. Paris, 1931.

Roberts, Richard. "The Emergence of the Grain Market in Bamako, 1883–1908," *Canadian Journal of African Studies*, 14, no. 1 (1980).

———. "Ideology, Slavery and Social Formation: The Evolution of Slavery in the Middle Niger Valley," in *Ideology of Slavery in Africa*, ed. Paul Lovejoy. Beverly Hills, Calif., 1981.

———. "Linkages and Multiplier Effects in the Ecologically Specialized Trade of Precolonial West Africa," *Cahiers d'études africaines*, 20, nos. 1–2 (1980–81).
———. "Long Distance Trade and Production: Sinsani in the Nineteenth Century," *Journal of African History*, 21, no. 2 (1980).
———. "The Maraka and the Economy of the Middle Niger Valley, 1712–1905." Ph.D. diss., Univ. of Toronto, 1978.
———. "Maraka Historical Texts: Transcripts of Oral Data Collected in the Segu Region of the Republic of Mali, 1976–77." Unpublished texts, compiled 1980.
———. "Maraka Historical Texts, II: Transcripts of Oral Data Collected in the Middle Niger Valley of the Republic of Mali, 1981." Unpublished texts, compiled 1982.
———. "Maraka Historical Texts, III: Transcripts of Oral Data Collected in the Middle Niger Valley of the Republic of Mali, 1984." Unpublished texts, in preparation.
———. "Production and Reproduction of Warrior States: Segu Bambara and Segu Tokolor," *International Journal of African Historical Studies*, 13, no. 4 (1980).
———. "The Rule of Law and Abuse of Power in Early Colonial French West Africa: The Case of Faama Mademba Sy." Paper presented at American Historical Association, New York, 1985.
———. "Women's Work and Women's Property: Household Social Relations in the Maraka Textile Industry of the Nineteenth Century," *Comparative Studies in Society and History*, 26, no. 2 (1984).
Robertson, Claire, and Martin Klein. "Women's Importance in African Slave Systems," in *Women and Slavery in Africa*, ed. Claire Robertson and Martin Klein. Madison, Wisc., 1983.
Robinson, David. *Chiefs and Clerics: Abdul Bokar Kan and the Futa Toro, 1853–1891*. London, 1975.
———. *The Holy War of Umar Tal: The Western Sudan in the Mid-Nineteenth Century*. Oxford, 1985.
Robinson, Ronald, and John Gallagher. "The Imperialism of Free Trade," *Economic History Review*, 2d ser., 6, no. 1 (1953).
Rodinson, Maxime. *Islam and Capitalism*, trans. Brian Pearce. Austin, Tex., 1978.
Ruxton, F. H. *Maliki Law: Being a Summary from French Translations of the Mukhtasar of Sidi Khalil*. London, 1916.
Ryder, Allan. *Benin and the Europeans, 1485–1897*. New York, 1969.
Saad, Elias. *A Social History of Timbuktu*. Cambridge, Eng., 1983.
Saint-Martin, Yves J. "L'artillerie d'El Hadj Omar et d'Ahmadou," *Bulletin d'IFAN*, ser. B, 27 (1965).

———. *L'empire toucouleur, 1848–1897*. Paris, 1970.
———. *L'empire toucouleur et la France: un demi-siècle de relations diplomatiques (1846–93)*. Dakar, 1966.
———. "Un fils d'el hadj Omar: Aguibou, roi de Dinguiray et de Macina," *Cahiers d'études africaines*, 8, no. 1 (1968).
Sako, Lassana. "Traditions de Nyamina." Typewritten ms., 1959. In the possession of Claude Meillassoux, Paris.
Salenc, Jules. "La vie d'Al Hadj ʿOmar: traduction d'un manuscrit arab de la Zaouia tidjania de Fez," *Bulletin du comité d'études historiques et scientifiques d'Afrique Occidentale française*, 1918.
Saulnier, Eugene. *Une compagnie à privilège aux XIXᵉ siècle: la compagnie de Galam du Sénégal*. Paris, 1921.
Schacht, J. *Introduction to Islamic Law*. London, 1964.
Schneider, Harold. *Economic Man*. New York, 1974.
Schoelcher, Victor. *L'esclavage au Sénégal en 1880*. Paris, 1880.
———. *Polémique coloniale*. Paris, 1886. 2 vols.
Scott, James. *The Moral Economy of the Peasantry*. New Haven, Conn., 1976.
Shaban, M. A. *Islamic History: A New Interpretation*. Cambridge, Eng., 1976.
Shea, Philip. "The Development of an Export Oriented Dyed Cloth Industry in the Kano Emirate." Ph.D. diss., Univ. of Wisconsin, 1975.
Shenton, Robert. *Development of Capitalism in Northern Nigeria*. Toronto, forthcoming.
Sidibe, Mamby. "Nouvelles notes sur la chasse au Birgo," *Bulletin du comité d'études historiques et scientifiques d'Afrique Occidentale française*, 13 (1930).
Skocpol, Theda. *States and Social Revolutions: A Comparative Analysis of France, Russia, and China*. New York, 1979.
Smaldone, Joseph. *Warfare in the Sokoto Caliphate: Historical and Sociological Perspectives*. New York, 1977.
Smith, M. G. *Government in Zazzau: A Study in the Hausa Chiefdom of Zaria in Northern Nigeria from 1800–1950*. London, 1960.
Smith, Robert. *Warfare and Diplomacy in Precolonial West Africa*. London, 1976.
Soleillet, Paul. *Voyage à Ségou, 1878–79, redigé d'après les notes et journaux par Gabriel Gravier*. Paris, 1887.
Stewart, Charles C. "Frontier Disputes and Problems of Legitimation: Sokoto-Masina Relations," *Journal of African History*, 17, no. 4 (1976).
Stewart, Charles C., with E. A. Stewart. *Islam and Social Order in Mauretania: A Case Study from the Nineteenth Century*. Oxford, 1973.
Sundiata, I. K. *Black Scandal: America and the Liberian Labor Crisis, 1929–36*. Philadelphia, 1980.

Sundstrom, Lars. *Ecology and Symbiosis: The Niger Waterfolk*. Uppsala, 1972.

Suret-Canale, Jean. *L'Afrique noire occidentale et centrale*. Paris, 1958.

Swindell, Ken. "SeraWollies, Tillibunkas and Strange Farmers: The Development of Migrant Groundnut Farming Along the Gambia River, 1848–95," *Journal of African History*, 21, no. 1 (1980).

Tauxier, Louis. "Chronologie des rois Bambara," *Outre-Mer*, nos. 3–4, 1930.

———. *Histoire des Bambara*. Paris, 1942.

Temperley, Howard. "Capitalism, Slavery, and Ideology," *Past and Present*, 75 (1977).

Terray, Emmanuel. "Contribution à une étude de l'armée asanté," *Cahiers d'études africaines*, 16, nos. 1–2 (1976).

———. "Gold Production, Slave Labor and State Intervention in Precolonial Akan States: A Reply to Raymond Dumett," *Research in Economic Anthropology*, 5 (1983).

———. "Long Distance Exchange and the Formation of the State: The Case of the Abron Kingdom of Gyaman," *Economy and Society*, 3, no. 3 (1974).

Thomas, Robert, and Richard Bean. "Fishers of Men: The Profits of the Slave Trade," *Journal of Economic History*, 34, no. 4 (1974).

Thompson, E. P. "The Moral Economy of the English Crowd in the Eighteenth Century," *Past and Present*, 50 (1970).

———. "Patrician Society, Plebeian Culture," *Journal of Social History*, 7, no. 4 (1974).

———. *The Poverty of Theory*. New York, 1978.

Thornton, John. "Sexual Demography: The Impact of Slave Trade on Family Structure," in *Women and Slavery in Africa*, ed. Claire Robertson and Martin Klein. Madison, Wisc., 1983.

Tilly, Charles, ed. *The Formation of National States in Western Europe*. Princeton, N.J., 1975.

Travele, M. "Notes sur les coutumes des chasseurs Bambara et Malinké du cercle de Bamako," *Revue ethnographique et des traditions populaires*, 1928.

Triaud, Jean-Louis. "La lutte entre la Tidjaniya et la Qadryia dans le Macina," *Annales de l'Université d'Abijan, Ethnosociologie*, ser. F, 1, no.1 (1969).

Triaud, Jean-Louis, and Sidi Mohamed Mahibou, *Voilà ce qui est arrivé: Bayân mâ Waga'a d'al-hâǧǧ 'Umar al-Fûti, plaidoyer pour une guerre sainte en Afrique de l'ouest au XIXe siècle*. Paris, 1983.

Twaddle, Michael. "The Ending of Slavery in Buganda," in *The End of Slavery in Africa*, ed., Suzanne Miers and Richard Roberts. Madison, Wisc., forthcoming.

Tyam, Mamadou Aliou. *La vie d'el hadj Omar: Qacida en Poular*, trans. H. Gaden. Paris, 1935.

Tymowski, Michal. "Les domaines des princes du Songhay: comparaisons avec la grande propriété foncière féodale," *Annales économies, sociétés, civilisations*, 25, no. 6 (1970).

———. "La pêche à l'époque du Moyen Age dans le boucle du Niger," *Africana Bulletin*, 12, 1971.

Vallière, Lieutenant. "Exploration du Lieutenant Vallière," in *Voyage au Soudan français: Haut Niger et pays de Ségou*, by Joseph Simone Gallieni. Paris, 1871.

Vansina, Jan. *The Children of Woot: A History of the Kuba People*. Madison, Wisc., 1978.

Vaughan, James. "Caste Systems in the Western Sudan," in *Social Stratification in Africa*, ed. Arthur Tuden and Leonard Plotnicov. New York, 1970.

Villien-Rossi, M.-L. "Bamako, Capitale du Mali," *Bulletin d'IFAN*, ser. B, 27, nos. 1–2 (1966).

Ward, Jennifer. "The Bambara French Relationship, 1880–1915," Ph.D. diss., UCLA, 1976.

Watts, Michael. *Silent Violence: Food, Famine, and the Peasantry in Northern Nigeria*. Berkeley, Calif., 1983.

Welmers, William. "The Mande Languages," *Georgetown University Monograph Series II*, 1969.

Wilks, Ivor. *Asante in the Nineteenth Century: The Structure and Evolution of a Political Order*. New York, 1975.

———. "Asante Policy Towards Hausa Trade in the Nineteenth Century," in *Development of Indigenous Trade and Markets in West Africa*, ed. Claude Meillassoux. London, 1971.

———. "The Mossi and Akan States, 1500–1800," *History of West Africa*, vol. 1, ed. A. Ajayi and M. Crowder. New York, 1972.

———. *The Northern Factor in Ashanti History*. Legon, 1962.

———. *Political Bipolarity in Nineteenth Century Asante*. Edinburgh, 1970.

Williams, Raymond. *The Sociology of Culture*. New York, 1981.

Willis, John Ralph. "*Jihad fi sabil-Allah*: Its Doctrinal Bases in Islam and Some Aspects of Its Evolution in Nineteenth Century West Africa," *Journal of African History*, 8, no. 3 (1967).

———. "The Torodbe Clerisy: A Social View," *Journal of African History*, 19, no. 2 (1979).

———. "The Western Sudan from the Moroccan Invasion (1581) to the Death of al Muktar al Kunti (1811)," *History of West Africa*, vol. 1, ed. A. Ajayi and M. Crowder. New York, 1972.

———. "The Writings of al-Hajj ʿUmar al Futi and Shaykh Mukhtar b. Wadi ʾal Allah: Literary Themes, Sources, and Influences," in *Studies in West African Islamic History: Cultivators of Islam*, ed. John Ralph Willis. London, 1979.

Willis, Roy. *A State in the Making: Myth, History, and Social Transformation in Precolonial Ufipa*. Bloomington, Ind., 1981.

Wittfogel, Karl. *Oriental Despotism*. New Haven, Conn., 1958.

Wolpe, Harold, ed. *Articulation of Modes of Production: Essays from Economy and Society*. London, 1980.

Wright, D. "Darbo Juula: The Role of a Mandenka Juula Clan in the Long Distance Trade of the Gambia River and Its Hinterland," *African Economic History*, 3 (1977).

Zebadia, Abdel Kader. "The Career and Correspondence of Ahmed al-Bekka'i of Timbuktu." Ph.D. diss., Univ. of London, 1974.

Zeldin, Theodore. *France, 1848–1945*. Oxford, 1972–75. 2 vols.

Zimmerman, Maurice. "L'avenir économique du Soudan nigerien," *Bulletin de la Société Géographique de Lyon*, 19 (1904).

Interviews

"Maraka Historical Texts, I." Unpublished transcription of oral texts collected in 1976–77, transcribed and compiled by R. Roberts, 1980.

Ba, Sidi. 30 Dec. 1976, Markala. Cleric and nephew of El Hadj Bougouni.

Bayoko, Siriba. 20 Jan. 1977, Medina. Village chief.

Bemba, Karim. 14 Feb. 1977, Segu. Merchant.

Danyogo, Sanussi. 1 Feb. 1977, Sinsani. Notable.

Dembele, Cekoro. 12 Dec. 1976, Banankoro. Notable.

Dukure, Bakary. 30 Jan. 1977, Segu. Merchant.

Fane, al hajj Ismaila. 15 Mar. 1977, Tesserela. Cleric.

Haidara, Ba. 8 Mar. 1977, Sinsani. Dyer.

Haidara, Yahaya. 30 Mar. 1977, Sinsani. Merchant.

Jane, Seydu. Session 1, 4 Jan. 1977, Sinsani; session 2, 8 Mar. 1977, Sinsani. Cleric and Imam of the Mosque of the Sofa.

Jare, Massitan. 16 Feb. 1977, Segu. Dyer.

Jare, Massitan and Ny Berete. 18 Feb. 1977, Segu. Dyers.

Jawara, Almamy. 23 Feb. 1977, Segu. Notable.

Kamite, BaSidiki. 20 Dec. 1976, Markaduguba. Cleric.

Kamite, Birama. 17 Dec. 1976, Kokou. Cleric and Imam.

Kane, Karamoko. Session 1, 11 Dec. 1976, Segu; session 2, 6 Jan. 1977, Segu. Somono notable.

Keita, Fama. 18 Jan. 1977, Segu. Notable.

Keita, Koke. 2 Feb. 1977, Sinsani. Notable.

Keita, Musa. Session 1, 12 Dec. 1976, Sinsani; session 2, 30 Dec. 1976, Sinsani. Notable.

Konate, Khalil. 8 Mar. 1977, Sinsani. Griot.

Kone, Mady, and BaIssa Kone. 11 Dec. 1976, Segu. Somono notables.

Kone, Malamine. 7 Feb. 1977, Segu. Notable.

Kone, Sidi Yaya. 1 Feb. 1977, Sinsani. Notable.

Kouyate, Musa. 26 Jan. 1977, Segu. Griot.

Kulubali, Bamakan. 26 Feb. 1977, Segu. Grain merchant.

Kulubali, Cekoro. 26 Feb. 1977, Segu. Notable.
Kulubali, Santa. 21 Mar. 1977, Sinsani. Woloso.
Kuma, Baba. Session 1, 28 Dec. 1976, Segu; session 2, 13 Mar. 1977, Segu. Notable.
Kuma, BaSidiki. 18 Jan. 1977, Segu. Notable and grandson of Koromama Kuma.
Kuma, Binke Baba. Session 1, 19 Dec. 1976, Sinsani; session 2, 21 Mar. 1977, Sinsani. Notable and ex-chief of Sinsani.
Kuma, Tatace. 20 Feb. 1977, Sinsani. Dyer.
Kunta, Bakka'i. 22 Dec. 1976, Markarila. Cleric.
Magane, al hajj Ibrahima. 4 Jan. 1977, Sinsani. Cleric.
Magane, al hajj Moktar. 19 Feb. 1977, Sinsani. Cleric.
Sako, Baba. 9 Jan. 1977, Segu. Notable.
Sako, Suleyman. 4 Jan. 1977, Sinsani. Notable.
Sanago, Amadu. 8 Jan. 1977, Sinsani. Merchant.
Sidibe, Mamby. 25 Nov. 1976, Bamako. Historian.
Sise, Amadu. 1 Feb. 1977, Sinsani. Notable.
Sise, Gaossu. 27 Jan. 1977, N'Denbugu. Notable.
Sise, Malamine. 12 Apr. 1977, Bamako. Historian.
Sise, Mulaye. Session 1, 22 Dec. 1976, Sinsani; session 2, 26 Dec. 1976, Sinsani; session 3, 8 Mar. 1977, Sinsani. Merchant and notable.
Sukule, Binke. 21 Mar. 1977, Sinsani. Cleric and notable.
Sumare, Almamy Mustapha. 11 Feb. 1977, Sibila. Cleric and Imam.
Sumare, Karamoko. 6 Jan. 1977, Segu. Notable.
Suragassi, Demba. 18 Feb. 1977, Segu. Leatherworker.
Sy, Majuma. 10 Mar. 1977, Kirango. Notable and son of Mademba.
Tambara, Sane. 22 Feb. 1977, Segu. Dyer.
Tigana, Tamba. 24 Feb. 1977, Segu. Merchant.
Traore, Babaje. Session 1, 22 Dec. 1976, Sinsani; session 2, 19 Feb. 1977, Sinsani. Woloso.
Traore, Dahou. 11 Feb. 1977, Sibila. Notable.
Traore, Ibrahima. 9 Feb. 1977, Segu. Maraka trader.
Traore, Kuntu. 11 Feb. 1977, Sibila. Notable.
Traore, Mama. 10 Feb. 1977, Niaro. Chief.
Traore, Yakuba. 13 Dec. 1976, Kokou. Notable.
Traore, Yusufu. 13 Dec. 1976, Segukoro. Chief.
Tunkura, Mamadu. 19 Feb. 1977, Sinsani. Notable.
Tunkura, Tata. 3 Jan. 1977, Segu. Dyer.
Ture, Cemoko. 5 Mar. 1977, Segu. Notable.
Yattara, Almamy Malik. 26 Nov. 1976, Bamako. Cleric and employee of Institut de Sciences Humaines, Bamako.
Yattara, Karamoko. 20 Jan. 1977, Medine. Notable.

Yattara, Yusuf. 20 Jan. 1977, Medine. Notable.

"Maraka Historical Texts, II." Unpublished translation of oral texts collected in 1981, transcribed and compiled by R. Roberts, 1982.

Berete, Juma. 3 Aug. 1981, Baraweli. Dyer.
Fane, al hajj Ismaila. 30 July 1981, Tesserela. Marabout.
Fofana, Baye. 20 July 1981, Banamba. Notable.
Fomba, Mamuru, with Ahmadu Traore, Modibo Yerenegore, Alfa Traore, and Sulyman Samake. 21 July 1981, Sinzena. Chief and village elders.
Gaku, Amadu. 3 Aug. 1981, Baraweli. Notable.
Kale, Batene. 31 July 1981, Segu. Dyer.
Kone, Ali. 23 July 1981, Nyamina. Notable.
Kone, Almamy, with Karim Kone, Kassum Kone, Sisi Kone, and Dramane Kone. 23 July 1981, Nyamina. Family elders.
Kuma, al hajj Baba. 3 Aug. 1981, Baraweli. Notable.
Kuma, Binke Baba. 4 Aug. 1981, Sinsani. Notable.
Jane, Seydu. 4 Aug. 1981, Sinsani. Marabout.
Makadji, Kissima. 19 July 1981, Tenimbala. Notable.
Mangane, Demba. 4 Aug. 1981, Sinsani. Trader.
Oulale, Soumama, with Hassana Oulale, Bafusane Oulale, and Badalaye Oulale. 22 July 1981, Nyamina. Family elders.
Sako, Basidiki, with Siriki Sako, Daouda Simpara, Lamu Sako, Marfu Traore, Nunubana Fofana, Bakary Keita, and Maju Kone. 22 July 1981, Nyamina. Family elders.
Simpara, Mustafa, with Baasi Simpara, Bafu Simpara, Danguine Simpara, Fasumara Simpara, Bamaru Simpara, Sadybu Simpara, Mahamy Simpara, Mohktar Simpara, and Sory Konate (griot). 18 July 1981, Banamba. Family elders.
Sylla, Sadya, with Mohamadu Sylla, Yaya Sylla, Brulaye Sylla, and Mohamy Sylla. 20 July 1981, Touba. Family elders.
Sylla, Tijani, with Mambi Sylla. 3 Aug. 1981, Baraweli. Chief and elder.
Traore, Ahmadu. 1 Aug. 1981, Segukoro. Chief.
Ture, Tene. 1 Aug. 1981, Segukoro. Dyer.
Yerenengore, Modibo. 24 July 1981, Sinzena. Notable.

"Maraka Historical Texts, III." Unpublished transcripts of oral texts collected in 1984, in process of transcription and compilation by R. Roberts.

Balo, Fanta. 23 Jan. 1984, Segu. Dyer.
Dembele, Brama. 22 Jan. 1984, Banankoro. Notable.
Kan, Aliou. 23 Jan. 1984, Segu. Assistant Director, COMITEXT.

Jara, Koke, with Amadu Jara and Salama Traore. 29 Jan. 1984, Gouni. Chief and elders.
Jara, Samlaji. 20 Jan. 1984, Marakakungo. Chief.
Keita, BaMusa. 21 Jan. 1984, Sinsani. Notable.
Kontau, hajji Fatmata. 23 Jan. 1984, Segu. Dyer.
Sylla, Tijani. 20 Jan. 1984, Baraweli. Chief.
Togora, Ko. 23 Jan. 1984, M'Peba. Notable.
Traore, Dahou. 21 Jan. 1984, Sibila. Notable.
Tunkara, Fajata. 22 Jan. 1984, Segu. Dyer.

Index

Library of Congress Cataloging-in-Publication Data

Roberts, Richard L., 1949–
Warriors, merchants, and slaves.

Bibliography: p.
Includes index.
1. Mali—Economic conditions. 2. Niger River Valley—Economic conditions. 3. Mali—History.
I. Title.
HC1035.R63 1987 330.966'23 86-23138
ISBN 0-8047-1378-2 (alk. paper)